# Computer Applications for Real Estate

## EDWARD L. CULBERTSON

*MiraCosta College*

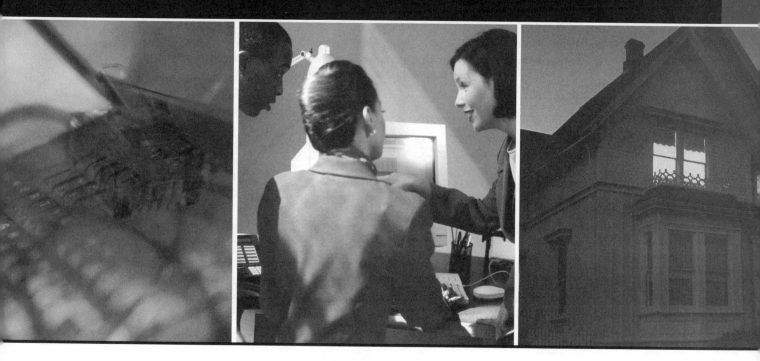

**THOMSON**

**SOUTH-WESTERN**

Australia · Canada · Mexico · Singapore · Spain · United Kingdom · United States

**THOMSON**

**SOUTH-WESTERN**

Computer Applications for Real Estate

Edward L. Culbertson

**VP/Editorial Director:**
Jack W. Calhoun

**VP/Editor-in-Chief:**
Dave Shaut

**Sr. Acquisitions Editor:**
Scott Person

**Developmental Editor:**
Chris Hudson

**Marketing Manager:**
Mark Linton

**Production Editor:**
Margaret M. Bril

**Sr. Technology Project Editor:**
Matthew McKinney

**Manufacturing Coordinator:**
Charlene Taylor

**Production House:**
Electro-Publishing

**Printer:**
Phoenix Color
Hagerstown, Maryland

**Design Project Manager:**
Bethany Casey

**Internal Designer:**
Lisa Albonetti

**Cover Designer:**
Bethany Casey

**Cover Images:**
© Getty Images and © Digital Stock

All Microsoft-related screen shots are reprinted by permission from the Microsoft Corporation®. Microsoft is a registered trademark of Microsoft Corporation in the U.S. and/or other countries.

The name of all products mentioned herein are used for identification purposes only and may be trademarks, or registered trademarks of their respective owners. South-Western disclaims any affiliation, association, connection with, sponsorship, or endorsement by such owners.

# BRIEF TABLE OF CONTENTS

# TABLE OF CONTENTS

# PREFACE

eal estate pundits have for years espoused the wisdom of *location, location, location*. Perhaps the statement can now be replaced with *technology, technology, technology*. No longer is it acceptable to simply embrace technology. It must be mastered! The Internet-savvy consumer demands that real estate professionals have comparable skills in order to conduct business.

This textbook was written for several reasons. Primarily, the book is intended to assist current and future real estate professionals to develop an understanding of technology and learn how to use technology to enhance productivity and profitability. Another reason for the textbook is to help the real estate professional who has not had a chance to learn about technology. Many agents have never had the opportunity to take computer courses simply because they may not have been available or there was little or no time to acquire computer skills. Currently, very little information is available on how computer skills can be used in the practice of real estate.

The purpose of this textbook is to extract computer skills from computer courses such as Microsoft Windows®, Microsoft Word®, Internet Explorer®, Microsoft Outlook®, Microsoft Publisher®, and Microsoft PowerPoint® and demonstrate how the features and functions can be applied to the practice of real estate. In many ways, it is like a one-stop guide on how to use and take advantage of the best of technology. The textbook can be used in its entirety or it could be used to strengthen skills in areas of need. Of special note is the "Reference Guide to Other Operating Systems and Software Packages," located at the back of the book. This lengthy appendix highlights non-Microsoft products and technologies that may be especially useful to the real estate professional.

Most computer or technology books are written in a very technical way. This textbook is written in nontechnical terms by a practicing real estate professional FOR real estate professionals. The textbook considers the role and function of the typical real estate professional and then incorporates only the specific computer skills that are necessary for a successful technology-related practice. Each chapter focuses on the basic skills. It is not intended to comprehensively examine each aspect of the programs covered throughout the book.

The organization of the text was conceived by trying to determine exactly what a real estate professional does and what is needed to be successful. The chapters unfold in a sequence that will build computer skills to reach a point of computer mastery in a wide range of skills. The text follows a format like learning a foreign language or learning how to do complicated mathematics. Once these computer skills have been mastered, they can automatically be used to perform whatever tasks and activities are required to accomplish an objective or goal.

This textbook can be used for a Computer Applications for Real Estate course or it can be used by any aspiring real estate professional who desires to learn the art and science of technology. It can be used for computer training since it has chapters on different aspects of computers and could easily be geared to offer several modules on whatever skills are needed.

The major intent of the textbook is to help each and every real estate professional reach a level of computer mastery that will allow him or her to compete and to relate to the new breed of technologically savvy consumers.

# PROLOGUE

In 1995, the author felt the need for some type of real estate computer class to assist agents in developing computer skills to improve productivity. As a Professor of Real State and practicing licensed Real Estate Broker, the author created and launched a college-level course called *Computer Applications in Real Estate*.

Little if any resources were available for teaching such a course. Drawing from numerous computer courses, a trail was blazed to incorporate various aspects of different computer courses into a single course that was tailored to the practice of real estate. Since no comprehensive textbook was available, the need for such a book was evident.

Once the course was established, the students and agents asked if it could be used for licensing credit through the California Department of Real Estate. The answer was no. All courses on the "list" had to have the approval of the California legislature. To accomplish this task, a new law had to be initiated. With the assistance of California Senator Bill Morrow, Senate Bill 329 was introduced to have such a course be on the approval list for credit. After consideration from the California Association of REALTORS® and the Department of Real Estate and acceptance from both the Senate and the Assembly, the bill became law upon the signature of the governor. The Department of Real Estate embraced the law and set up guidelines that needed to be used for courses to meet state requirements.

The approach of this textbook is to present an overview of technology and then demonstrate how computer concepts can be applied to real estate. The learning stratagem is comprised of the following steps:

1. What is it? (What is the program or concept?)

2. How does it work? (How does one work with the features and functions of a program?)

3. Try it. (Complete the activities related to a program.)

4. Describe how it can be applied to the practice of real estate. (Demonstrate how it can be used.)

Using the above learning approach, it is anticipated that the reader will not only embrace technology but also master it!

It is hoped that this textbook will meet the needs of practicing real estate professionals. The intent is to provide a "one-stop" reference guide. With more than 2.4 million licensed real estate agents and brokers in the United States, it is hoped that this book will play a major role in improving not only computer literacy but also productivity.

Please enjoy this book and try to keep it as a reference tool. And remember, this is a field that is always changing and growing.

Edward L. Culbertson, Ph.D.

# ABOUT THE AUTHOR

**E**dward L. Culbertson, Ph.D. was instrumental in developing one of the first Computer Applications in Real Estate courses in California. In addition to being a licensed Educational Psychologist, he has been a licensed Real Estate Broker since 1980 and holds an advanced degree in Management and a Ph.D. in Human Behavior. Dr. Culbertson is Professor of Real Estate at MiraCosta College in Oceanside, California.

# DEDICATION

This textbook is dedicated to all the Computer Applications in Real Estate students at MiraCosta College, Oceanside, California. They were the original influence that helped shape the content and scope of the textbook. Without their patience and input, this book would not have been possible. I salute all the students who have taken this course over the past years.

Additionally, I would like to honor my wife and family for their patience while I was engaged in the writing of the book.

# CHAPTER 1
## TECHNOLOGY AND THE REAL ESTATE INDUSTRY

## PREVIEW

Chapter One provides a foundation for understanding the development and current state of the electronic era and how it has impacted the real estate industry. Specifically, the chapter highlights the role and function of the "e" (electronic) players in the real estate buying and selling process. The chapter also introduces a new term to describe the real estate professional who utilizes modern computer techniques: the *cyber professional*.

When you finish this chapter, you will be able to:

1. State the impact of the electronic era on society and on real estate in particular.

2. Identify and describe the various "e" entities involved in the real estate process.

3. Recognize key figures and organizations shaping the cyber real estate world.

4. List and describe the characteristics of the cyber professional.

## KEY TERMS

*cyber professional (C-P)*

*e-agent*

*e-buyer*

*e-commerce*

*e-consumer*

*e-PRO*

*e-real estate*

*e-seller*

*Internet Empowered Consumer (IEC)*

*New Real Estate Professional (NREP)*

*Real Estate Cyber Specialist (RECS)*

# 1.1 The E-World

The advent of the World Wide Web set the stage for business on the Internet. It was the perfect combination for commerce without bricks and mortar, or traditional offices in buildings. The dot-com craze resulted in an explosion in the marketing and selling of products, tangible and intangible, over the Internet. Today **e-commerce** is a multibillion-dollar operation functioning worldwide. Studies indicate that business on the Internet is still growing dramatically. Now that security is better assured through encryption, more consumers are using e-commerce for personal and business transactions.

# 1.2 Impact of Technology on Real Estate

In the early nineties, the computer came of age for the real estate professional. Computer prices dropped, making them affordable for the average consumer. Computers were perceived to be efficient, fast, and invaluable in conducting tasks related to the selling and buying process. Numerous software programs to assist the real estate professional were also developed.

Soon many real estate professionals realized the potential of the computer in conjunction with the Internet and the World Wide Web. Real estate business could now be conducted not only locally, but also nationally—even internationally! Furthermore, the Internet and World Wide Web would allow maximum exposure through 24/7/365 access (24 hours per day, 7 days per week, 365 days per year). These technologies also helped level the playing field so that smaller companies could compete with larger organizations. Businesses with a web presence multiply daily.

With this new technology, many laborious, time-consuming tasks can now be completed through the use of software programs. The possibilities for the real estate industry are vast. Today, the real estate professional can disseminate information on the Internet, prospect for new clients, and communicate via e-mail.

E-mail communication has become a standard in people's business and personal lives. Studies indicate that over a trillion e-mail messages are delivered each year, which means that over a billion messages are being exchanged on a daily basis. E-mail is big business.

### *PUTTING IT TOGETHER*

The Internet has changed the world of commerce, which continues to grow exponentially. With the influx of technology, the stage is set for massive changes in real estate services. Technology has affected all aspects of the real estate industry, with innovations introduced on a daily basis.

## *Real Estate Finance*

Technology assists the real estate finance world in numerous ways. Many financial institutions and organizations rely heavily on the Internet for conducting business. Consumers, too, utilize the Internet to obtain financial information. Information acquired on the Internet is often free and can be used by anyone who has an Internet connection. A consumer can, through popular web sites, obtain the following information:

- Amount he or she can afford

- Payment calculations

- Rent versus buy analysis

- Tax benefits of buying

- Types of loans available

- Loan comparisons

- Current interest rates

- Credit reports

- Online loan applications

- Loan processing

Numerous software programs are available to the **e-agent,** or the agent who uses computer technology. These programs can help the agent qualify a buyer, determine payments, check current interest rates, compare loans, and provide insight into the best possible scenario for the client. Some of these programs are discussed later in the book.

## *Property Management*

Property management has become a very complex and sophisticated profession. Gone are the days of using file cards, a Rolodex(R), and manila folders. Professional property management demands an effective and efficient system to record important and relevant information about the properties. Software systems such as the YARDI program have been developed by software engineers to meet the needs of this profession. (YARDI is a sophisticated property management software program that takes into account the major considerations for managing rental property.) Typical software programs assist with tasks such as calculating vacancies, deposits, work orders, and cash on hand. Given this information, profit and loss statements can be formulated and pro forma and relevant tax information can be prepared.

## *Appraisal*

The consumer and the professional appraiser can obtain information on the value of properties via the Internet. Consumers can access the Internet for free and obtain estimates of property values. Appraisers access databases via the Internet to help appraise homes for mortgage lenders. Software programs are also available to assist in the complex appraisal process. Digital cameras that allow the appraiser to download pictures to appraisal reports have become cheaper and more efficient. Programs for the input of appraisal data have also been developed.

Another use of advanced technology is the transfer of appraisal data to lending institutions over the Internet, via a process called Electronic Data Interchange (EDI).

## *Real Estate Practice*

Real estate professionals can use numerous software programs to enhance productivity and profitability. Contact and time management systems are widely used by the e-agent. Practitioners have found that prospecting utilizing the power of e-mail and e-newsletters is very worthwhile. Having an individual domain name and a professional web site has become essential in conducting business worldwide.

# 1.3 The E-Consumer

The combined power of the computer, the Internet, and the World Wide Web has paved the way for a new player in the real estate industry. A new breed of consumer has evolved, called the **e-consumer.** This group is well versed in technology and uses the Internet and the World Wide Web to the fullest extent in meeting real estate goals.

## *The 2002 Internet Versus Traditional Buyer Study*

The California Association of REALTORS® conducted a study to determine the buying patterns of traditional buyers and Internet buyers. *The 2002 Internet Versus Traditional Buyer Study*, released in February 2002, revealed some interesting information. Findings from a survey of 600 buyers throughout California included the following:

- 79 percent of Web buyers found their real estate agent online.

- 63 percent of traditional buyers found their agent through farming materials and referrals.

- 90 percent of Internet buyers were very satisfied with their real estate agent .

- 32 percent of traditional buyers were satisfied with their real estate agent .

- Internet buyers were contacted primarily via e-mail.

- Traditional buyers were contacted by phone or in person.

- 97 percent of Internet buyers indicated they would use their real estate agent again.

- 81 percent of traditional buyers indicated a preference for their real estate agent in the future.

- 66 percent of Internet buyers made $150,000 or more per year.

- 39 percent of traditional buyers made $150,000 or more.

- 12 percent of Internet buyers had a postgraduate degree.

- 3 percent of traditional buyers had a postgraduate degree.

- The median age of the Internet buyer was 37.

- The median age of the traditional buyer was 43.

- Internet buyers saw 7.5 homes before buying.

- Traditional buyers saw 15.2 homes before making a purchase.

In summary, the study found that the Internet buyer was more satisfied, made more money, was more educated, was younger, and took less time to purchase a home than the traditional buyer.

In a follow-up study released in January 2003, the California Association of Realtors again found some interesting details. They included the following:

- 45 percent of homebuyers used the Internet in the home-buying process, compared to 37 percent in 2001.

- Internet buyers were contacted every 4.3 days as opposed to the traditional buyers, who were contacted every 6.5 days.

- Traditional homebuyers were found to look at twice as many homes as Internet buyers.

By and large, the new study was consistent with the earlier findings from 2002. Both studies have strong implications for the cyber professional in terms of how to address the needs of this new type of electronic-savvy client.

---

### *PUTTING IT TOGETHER*

When compared with traditional buyers, Internet buyers:
- Had higher incomes.
- Had more advanced degrees.
- Were younger.
- Viewed fewer homes before purchasing.
- Were more satisfied with the agent.
- Were most likely to use the agent again.

## *The Internet Empowered Consumer*

According to Michael Russer, "Mr. Internet," the real estate industry will experience more changes in the next few years than took place over the past 100 years. This paradigm change is the direct result of the impact of the Internet and the World Wide Web. Mr. Russer has identified a new type of consumer, which he labels the **Internet Empowered Consumer (IEC).** One distinct characteristic about this group of consumers is that they like to be in control. According to Mr. Russer, this group has the following advantages:

- A shield of anonymity and a buffer from personal contact. This allows them to research real estate information without being interrogated by a sales person. No commitment is forced.

- Access to unlimited real estate information, from properties to mortgages.

This situation removes from the equation the classic person-to-person interaction used by the traditional real estate professional. The old interpersonal relationship skills are no longer applicable in dealing with the IEC. Therefore, a new set of relationship skills must be mastered.

Mr. Russer points out four new principles that a real estate professional must understand when working with the Internet client. They are:

- Principle #1: The IEC is in control.

- Principle #2: The IEC expects his or her online privacy to be sacred.

- Principle #3: The IEC values his or her time, saving money, and having choices.

- Principle #4: The IEC will *not* do business with you until he or she trusts you, believes you have his or her best interests at heart, and knows you have the expertise to help him or her.

"Mr. Internet" also suggests four rules of engagement when dealing with the IEC:

- Don't push the IEC to move faster or reveal himself or herself sooner than he or she is ready; otherwise you may never hear from the IEC again.

- Build trust by reassuring the IEC that you respect his or her privacy.

- Be flexible and ready to tailor your services and fees to meet the needs of the IEC rather than force him or her into a "one-model-fits-all" situation.

- Build relationships by giving the IEC what he or she wants in terms of information and advice.

In order to do business with the e-consumer, real estate professionals must apply new and different methods.  As times change, needs of clients change as well. What is true about something today may change tomorrow.

---

### PUTTING IT TOGETHER

Characteristics of the IEC include the following:
- Values anonymity and privacy
- Values time and saving money
- Wants to be in control
- Needs to trust before making a commitment

## The Typical E-Buyer

The **e-buyer** is very sophisticated in applying technology to the housing-hunting process. A typical step-by-step system may include the following activities:

1. Access a preferred search engine.

2. Input search parameters for a desired area.

3. Specify the desired characteristics for a home.

4. Locate information regarding the following:
   - Neighborhoods
   - Schools
   - Crime
   - Cultural events and activities

5. Take a virtual tour of a property.

6. Acquire a map for directions.

7. Contact the agent or owner of the property.

8. Obtain financial information such as current rates and type of loans.

9. Apply for a loan online.

10. Complete as many tasks as possible via the Internet and e-mail.

## The Typical E-Seller

The **e-seller** is equally knowledgeable about how to maximize the value of the Internet. Typical steps for the selling process may include the following:

1. Access a preferred search engine.

2. Research the value of the "subject home" to be sold.

3. Contact potential e-real estate agents to market the home.

4. Request the e-agent to use advanced technology in promoting and selling the home.

5. Utilize e-mail communication.

6. Complete as many tasks as possible to consummate the transaction via the Internet and e-mail.

If the e-seller chooses not to use the services of a real estate agent, he or she might prefer to market the home as a "For Sale By Owner" (FSBO). In this case, a new set of steps may include the following:

1. Locate a For Sale by Owner organization on the Internet.

2. Submit digital pictures of the property and other appropriate materials.

3. Communicate with interested parties via e-mail.

# 1.4 E-Real Estate

In late 1995, the real estate industry was forced, willingly or unwillingly, to catch the wave of technology and ride it. This movement created a paradigm shift in the real estate profession. No longer was the typical real estate agent a "gatekeeper" of vital real estate information regarding the selling and buying process. Information related to real estate became readily available on the Internet. Consumers could now conduct their own searches for many aspects of the real estate transaction process.

The concept of **e-real estate** encompasses the ways in which computer technology can be applied to the real estate profession. A bricks-and-mortar approach, or the traditional way, is no longer viable in the electronic world. To compete in the e-world and in e-business, real estate needs to be involved in e-commerce. The text discusses this topic in subsequent chapters.

## *The E-Agent*

An e-agent is one who understands the value and significance of technology and realizes that technology is the key to competing in the business world. He or she also acknowledges that a new consumer has emerged, one who has the knowledge and skill to make wise use of technology. Many consumers grew up with computers and are as comfortable with them as they are with a phone or fax. They use the computer for business and pleasure. They naturally utilize the computer in the buying and selling process. The e-agent has taken the time and effort to acquire computer skills to meet the needs of the e-consumer.

Special designations have emerged to describe the technology-savvy agents.

## The e-PRO

**e-PRO** is a well-recognized designation sanctioned by the National Association of REALTORS® (NAR) and operated by the Internet Crusade (an Internet company that promotes technology for real estate professionals). To qualify for this prestigious designation, a candidate must meet certain requirements. He or she must be a member of NAR, pay a fee, and complete certain technology skills. The program can be completed online, and there is no test. Once a person has completed the program, he or she can incorporate the e-PRO trademark on all business materials. This designation sends a message that the agent acknowledges the importance of computers in the real estate practice and that he or she can fulfill the needs of the consumer, who has similar goals and skills, to complete the buying or selling process.

## The New Real Estate Professional (NREP)

Saul Klein, the president of Internet Crusade, created the term **New Real Estate Professional (NREP)**. He states that a new type of real estate professional has evolved to address the needs of a computer-savvy real estate consumer. To connect with this type of consumer, the agent must have an equal level of computer expertise. Mr. Klein has identified ten different traits the NREP must have to serve the modern computer-savvy consumer. Without these skills, the implication is that an agent may not want or need a client's business. The characteristics include the following:

1. Is an information commander

2. Is a web surfer

3. Is an e-mail user

4. Has a web site to brag about

5. Works from a mobile office

6. Is a master networker

7. Is always growing

8. Sees technology as a tool of the trade

9. Participates in an online business network

10. Uses real estate assistants

## The Real Estate Cyber Specialist (RECS)

**Real Estate Cyber Specialist (RECS)** is a special designation offered through the Real Estate Cyber Society. To earn this honor, a recipient must become a member of the Real Estate Cyber Society and complete a computer technology course designed to increase awareness of the advantages of working with technology as it relates to the development of skills in conducting a real estate practice. Attending seminars or viewing videotapes on topics related to real estate and technology can qualify a person for this designation. There is no test requirement for this recognition. Once an agent has joined the organization and has completed the course, he or she can attach the Real Estate Cyber Specialist (RECS) trademark on all business-related materials, such as a web site, business cards, flyers, and personal brochures. The society offers a web site for members and gives them the opportunity to participate in e-newsletter campaigns. Other benefits include regular technology tips and information from top professionals in the electronic world. Jack Peckham founded and operates the organization.

## The Emerging E-agent

Much has been said about the e-agent—an agent who has acquired the necessary skills to compete in the electronic arena. What if an agent has not had the time or opportunity to achieve this level of knowledge? Does this mean that the agent is doomed to fail and will not be able to conduct any type of e-business? The primary intent of this book is to address the issue of the agent who wants to become a cyber professional. The agent who embraces the information presented and takes the necessary steps to learn computer skills will be on the road to becoming an *emerged e-agent*.

## The Tech and Touch Professional

This term is adopted from John Neisbett's book entitled *High Tech, High Touch,* written in the eighties. Mr. Neisbett points out that the ultimate professional utilizes the best of the technology world and combines this with a personal touch when conducting business. As in any profession, the tech and touch aspects are important in the real estate business. Conceptually, this term can be broken into four different categories.

***The High Tech, High Touch Professional.*** This category represents one who utilizes all that technology has to offer as it relates to real estate and engages in proven strategies and methods for dealing at the human contact level. Theoretically, this category is the goal of the real estate practitioner today.

***The High Tech, Low Touch Professional.*** Implied in this description is one who has mastered technology and uses it as the focus of practicing real estate. Less regard is given to the human element in conducting business.

***The Low Tech, High Touch Professional.*** In this case, one emphasizes human factors and uses only the necessities of technology for practicing real estate.

***The Low Tech, Low Touch Professional.*** At the opposite extreme is one who does not utilize technology other than what is necessary *and* one who does not use proven human relationship skills.

## THE TECH AND TOUCH PROFESSIONAL

| **High Tech, High Touch** *(Well Balanced)* | **High Tech, Low Touch** *(Out of Balance)* |
|---|---|
| **High Tech:** Uses latest technological tools in the practice of real estate.<br><br>**High Touch:** Uses proven human relationship techniques in the practice of real estate. | **High Tech:** Uses latest technological tools in the practice of real estate.<br><br>**Low Touch:** Does not emphasize human relationship principles. |
| **Low Tech, High Touch** *(Out of Balance)* | **Low Tech, Low Touch** *(Not Balanced)* |
| **Low Tech:** Does not emphasize the use of technological tools in the practice of real estate.<br><br>**High Touch:** Emphasizes modern human relationship techniques in the practice of real estate. | **Low Tech:** Does not use technology in the practice of real estate.<br><br>**Low Touch:** Does not employ human relations factors in the practice of real estate. |

## *The Typical E-agent*

The e-agent today has not only embraced but mastered technology. This agent has a domain name, an e-mail address, and a professional web site. He or she also takes full advantage of modern software programs to become more productive. Typically, e-agent activities include:

- Connecting to the Internet.

- Checking local, state, and national real estate news.

- Checking e-mail and following up with prospects and clients.

- Prospecting for clients via the Internet.

- Checking listings through a Multiple Listing Service (MLS).

- Finding current interest rates.

## *Connecting All the e's*

How does all of this come together, and what are the implications? It has been previously stated that the e-world evolved in late 1995. Since that time, technology has touched almost every aspect of life. This electronic movement has impacted the way business is conducted. A 24/7/365 world is available for accomplishing business and commerce. This new "giant" has no boundaries and is impervious to time barriers. It seems as though nothing but a lack of creativity can stop it.

The real estate industry is fortunate in that it is compatible with this new electronic movement. It has provided the perfect business arrangement. Instead of being a localized operation with a limited base, the real estate industry has risen like the classic phoenix. Real estate has been launched like satellites all over the world.

# 1.5 Real Estate Cyber Gurus

Many individuals, whether real estate practitioners or Internet-savvy professionals, have made monumental contributions to the current status of technology in the real estate profession. This section discusses a few people who have been directly connected to real estate.

# Digital Innovators

Digital innovators are individuals who understand the world of technology and see how this technology can be connected and applied to the realm of real estate. They are people who have a vision of how real estate can take advantage of all the Internet has to offer. This group of innovators is constantly seeking new ways to improve upon the use of technology concepts and tools.

*Mike Russer.* In most circles, Mike Russer is known as "Mr. Internet." "Mr. Internet" recognized early on the power of computers and the Internet as they relate to the e-world. In addition, he understood how the technology could best be utilized for the real estate profession. He has his own web site with an e-newsletter and regularly reports on innovative applications for real estate. One major contribution "Mr. Internet" has made is the development and promotion of what he identifies as the Virtual Assistant, or VA. The VA is an individual who possesses computer hardware and software knowledge and is willing to work with real estate professionals to take best advantage of computer information. The VA works with a real estate practitioner who knows little about computers or who does not have time to acquire a level of expertise. There is even an organization of VAs who are in the business of helping real estate professionals.

One of "Mr. Internet's" major contributions to the real estate world is his research on the e-consumer that he has labeled the Internet Empowered Consumer (IEC). This research has been instrumental in helping the real estate professional better understand the mind-set of the electronically savvy consumer in the real estate market. The information gleaned from this study has been a boon to the real estate professional who wants to understand and communicate with this type of consumer.

*Stefan Swanepoel.* Mr. Swanepoel is another example of an early thinker who saw how real estate could benefit from the power of the computer and the Internet. He has written numerous publications and books on how real estate and computer technology are related. Some of his work has addressed the concept of the e-buyer and the e-seller. Besides offering publications on these topics, he conducts seminars to assist emerging real estate professionals who want to better understand this type of nontraditional consumer.

***Bradley Inman.*** Mr. Inman is known internationally in the real estate profession for his innovative methods of applying technology tools to maximize productivity. He has his own web site and produces a timely e-newsletter related to all aspects of the real estate industry. One of his key contributions is his web site, where e-consumers can connect with e-agents who will assist in promoting and selling a "subject" property. Each year Mr. Inman sponsors a major conference in which he invites top real estate gurus to share and discuss the latest technological advances as well as the issues and trends related to the real estate industry.

## Digital Leaders

This group is characterized not only by their vast knowledge of real estate, but also by their expertise in the technology realm. Digital leaders take the concepts originated by the digital innovators and put them into action. They understand that technology can assist in productivity and profitability. With this background and wisdom, they have taken real estate to a higher level of operation by incorporating computer hardware and software in the real estate business.

***Jack Peckham.*** Mr. Peckham is well known in the circle of commercial real estate. He is the founder of the Real Estate Cyber Society, which is comprised of emerging and emerged e-agents. Each year the society sponsors a National Online Real Estate convention attended *online* by tens of thousands of participants all over the world. This group offers a professional designation known as Real Estate Cyber Specialist (RECS). Its web site offers a wealth of information related to how technology can best be applied to the practice of real estate. The Real Estate Cyber Society has an e-newsletter and sponsors a newscast with the top real estate and technology movers and shakers.

***Saul Klein.*** As the president of the Internet Crusade, Mr. Klein is one of the major figures in the promotion and advancement of applying technology to the realm of real estate. The goal of the organization is to help real estate professionals not only gain an appreciation of technology, but also to embrace it. This organization manages the administration of the e-Pro designation authorized by the Nation Association of Realtors. Mr. Klein was instrumental in introducing the term *New Real Estate Professional*.

***Pat Zaby.*** With a background in real estate, Mr. Zaby has designed a software program called *The Marketing Library* that applies computer applications to real estate. The program is designed to help the e-agent become more efficient and productive. Mr. Zaby also has an e-newsletter devoted to the promotion of technology for real estate professionals. He conducts seminars and has been a keynote speaker for numerous organizations worldwide.

---

### PUTTING IT TOGETHER

Top gurus in the industry include:
- Michael Russer at http://www.russer.com
- Bradley Inman at http://www.inman.com
- Pat Zaby at http://www.patzaby.com

## Digital Practitioners

Members of this group not only have technology expertise and knowledge, but also utilize these tools in the practice of real estate. These high-powered agents use computer hardware and software to enhance and increase profitability in their businesses. They take full advantage of the Internet and communicate via e-mail.

***Stephan Canale.*** Mr. Canale is a noted trainer, speaker, and author, as well as a practicing real estate agent. He publishes an e-newsletter and has his own web site. His newsletter offers the latest information regarding technology for real estate.

***Terri Murphy.*** Ms. Murphy has a successful track record for being a multimillion-dollar real estate producer who actively applies traditional methods as well as technological tools in her real estate practice. She is an author and a speaker on topics related to applying technology to the practice of real estate.

## Digital Brokerages

These institutions apply technological tools to the total operation of a real estate business. These brokerages take full advantage of computer hardware and software. They conduct most of their business over the Internet and utilize e-mail as the major form of communication.

***Zip Realty.*** This web-based operation conducts real estate business on the Internet, much like eBay does in selling merchandise. Its teams of agents are well versed in successful technology methods, and they apply these techniques to operate a successful online real estate business.

***E-loans.*** This online business provides real estate loans via the Internet and by e-mail. Potential buyers of real estate or individuals who want to refinance can use the Internet to apply for loans.

# 1.6 The Cyber Professional (C-P)

This term describes an agent who attempts to go beyond the e-agent. The **cyber professional (C-P)** is one who is striving to find out more about technology and how to apply it to the profession of real estate. He or she has an open mind and is eager to experiment and try out new ideas and concepts. New information and new approaches become a challenge to see whether they can be applied to real estate. A C-P takes traditional real estate's successful methods and the best technological tools to improve on efficiency, effectiveness, and productivity in a real estate practice. The C-P also has the following attributes:

- Owns a state-of-the-art hardware computer system
- Uses state-of-the-art software programs
- Owns a personal domain name
- Has a personalized e-mail account and numerous aliases
- Communicates with prospects and clients via an e-newsletter
- Has a digital camera
- Holds a professional designation in technology
- Regularly attends seminars related to technology
- Subscribes to technology journals and publications
- Is successful in the real estate profession

---

## PUTTING IT TOGETHER

Characteristics of the C-P include the following:
- Has a state-of-the-art computer system
- Has a personal domain name and an e-mail account
- Corresponds via e-mail and e-newsletters
- Stays abreast of and experiments with technology

## THE DIGITAL INVENTORY

Check the choice(s) that best fits your situation:

| | 1 Point | 2 Points | 3 Points | 4 Points |
|---|---|---|---|---|
| 1. I currently use: | ☐ I do not have a computer. | ☐ A desktop | ☐ A laptop | ☐ Both |
| 2. I currently use: | ☐ I do not use software. | ☐ Basic software | ☐ Intermediate software | ☐ Advanced software |
| 3. I am connected to the Internet by: | ☐ I am not connected. | ☐ A modem | ☐ DSL or cable | ☐ Wireless |
| 4. I have a: | ☐ I do not have a domain name. | ☐ Company domain name | ☐ Free domain name | ☐ Personal domain name |
| 5. I have a: | ☐ I do not have e-mail. | ☐ Free e-mail account | ☐ Company e-mail account | ☐ Personal e-mail account |
| 6. I have a: | ☐ I do not have a web site. | ☐ Free web site | ☐ Company web site | ☐ Personal web site |
| 7. I have a: | ☐ I do not have an e-newsletter. | ☐ Company e-newsletter | ☐ Personal e-newsletter | ☐ Both |
| 8. I have a(n): | ☐ I do not have a professional technology designation. | ☐ e-PRO designation | ☐ Real Estate Cyber Specialist designation | ☐ Both |
| 9. I attend seminars: | ☐ I do not attend technology seminars. | ☐ Seldom | ☐ Often | ☐ Consistently |
| 10. My interest in technology is: | ☐ I do not use technology. | ☐ Casual | ☐ Moderate | ☐ Extreme |
| **Total Points** | | | | |
| **CATEGORIES** | **Nondigital** | **Slightly Digital** | **Moderately Digital** | **Very Digital** |
| **POINTS** | **0–10** | **11–19** | **20–29** | **Over 30** |

# RESOURCES FOR FURTHER STUDY

Dooley, Tom. *Real Estate Confronts Reality*. Real Estate Educators Association, 1998.

Segner, Jack. *Sams Teach Yourself Today E-Real Estate*. Sams Publishing, 2000.

Swanepoel, Stefan. *Real Estate Confronts the e-Consumer*. RealSure, Inc., 2000.

Swanepoel, Stefan. *Real Estate Confronts the Future*. South-Western, 2004.

| | |
|---|---|
| http://www.inman.com | Bradley Inman—digital innovator |
| http://www.canale.com | Stephan Canale—digital practitioner |
| http://www.realsure.com | Stephan Swanepoel—digital innovator |
| http://www.patzaby.com | Pat Zaby—digital leader |
| http://www.russer.com | Mike Russer—digital innovator |
| http://www.recyber.com | Jack Peckham—digital leader and Real Estate Cyber Specialist |
| http://www.internetcrusade.com/Saul.asp | Saul Klein—digital leader |
| http://www.ziprealty.com | digital brokerage |
| http://www.eloan.com | digital brokerage |
| http://www.terrimurphy.com | digital practitioner |
| http://www.edesignations.com/epro | e-PRO designation site |

# SELF-ASSESSMENT

To determine the extent of knowledge you acquired in this chapter, choose the correct answer for each of the following.

1. E-commerce:
   a. Is a multibillion-dollar operation
   b. Has dramatically changed the world of business
   c. Has an excellent future for growth
   d. All of the above

2. When did the e-world emerge?
   a. In the early 1990s
   b. In late 1995
   c. In the early 2000s
   d. It has not emerged yet.

3. Who introduced the term *Internet Empowered Consumer?*
   a. Mike Russer
   b. Stephan Swanepoel
   c. Bradley Inman
   d. Saul Klein

4. Which of the following is a professional designation sponsored by the National Association of REALTORS®?
   a. New Real Estate Professional
   b. e-PRO
   c. Real Estate Cyber Specialist
   d. Cyber professional

5. All of the following are characteristic of the Internet Empowered Consumer except:
   a. Spends less time with an agent in locating a property to purchase
   b. Likes having control and anonymity
   c. Prefers the use of electronic means for communicating
   d. Earns less money than the traditional buyer

6. Which one of the following is *not* a characteristic of the traditional buyer?
   a. Has less education than Internet buyer
   b. Earns more money than Internet buyer
   c. Spends more time in the buying process
   d. Pays less money on a purchase

7. What is a typical software program used in the property management profession?
   a. The Marketing Library
   b. Rolodex®
   c. EDI
   d. YARDI

8. The typical e-buyer utilizes which method when searching for a home?
   a. Search engine
   b. Virtual tour
   c. E-mail
   d. All of the above

9. Characteristics of the New Real Estate Professional include all of the following except:
   a. Utilizes e-mail and has a web site
   b. Has an individual domain name
   c. Uses mobile devices such as a laptop and cell phone
   d. Uses only a cell phone and fax

10. The typical e-agent uses all of the following equipment except:
    a. Digital camera
    b. Desktop or laptop computer
    c. Real estate software
    d. Could use all of the above

11. The wired C-P is capable of conducting business:
    a. Between 8 a.m. and 5 p.m.
    b. 24/7/365
    c. Anytime, anywhere
    d. Both b and c

12. Examples of digital innovators are:
    a. Russer and Inman
    b. Canale and Murphy
    c. Peckham and Klein
    d. None of the above

13. To become an e-PRO, one must:
    a. Complete a specific course of study
    b. Be a member of NAR
    c. Pay a fee
    d. All of the above

14. Characteristics of the cyber professional include which of the following?
    a. Utilizes traditional real estate techniques
    b. Utilizes contemporary computer tools
    c. Continuously learns new approaches in the practice of real estate
    d. All of the above

15. The emerging e-agent is best described as an agent who:
    a. Is open to learning technology
    b. Has not had the time to learn about technology
    c. Did not get the opportunity to learn about technology
    d. All of the above

# CHAPTER 2
## THE COMPUTER

## PREVIEW

The first part of this chapter explores the background and history of the computer. The second part identifies and explains the basic features and functions of a modern computer, as well as essential peripherals. Different types of real estate programs are also discussed.

When you finish this chapter, you will be able to:

1. Trace the background and history of the modern computer.

2. Identify and describe the major components of a computer.

3. Describe basic features and functions of computer peripherals.

4. List several software programs used in the real estate business.

5. Develop a working technology vocabulary.

## KEY TERMS

| | |
|---|---|
| *byte* | *hertz* |
| *cache* | *ink jet* |
| *carpal tunnel syndrome* | *laser jet* |
| *CD-ROM* | *LCD* |
| *clock speed* | *memory* |
| *CRT* | *modem* |
| *DVD-ROM* | *QWERTY* |
| *ergonomics* | *RAM* |
| *floppy disk* | *ROM* |

# 2.1 Historical Background of the Computer

The abacus, a calculating device, was invented in Babylonia about 5,000 years ago. As the beginning stepping stone, this simple tool laid the foundation for today's technology. The next significant milestone was the invention of the numerical calculating machine by Blaise Pascal in 1642. With the discovery of electricity by Benjamin Franklin in 1780, the stage was set for the first recognized computer, built by Charles Babbage in 1833. Alexander Graham Bell added his contribution by inventing the telephone in 1911.

These events paved the way for the first major computer company, which came to be called International Business Machines (IBM), with Thomas J. Watson as president. World War II created a surge in computers to help with strategic warfare. Other significant events (1945–1956) included the establishment of the Electronic Numerical Integrator and Computer (ENIAC) and the Universal Automatic Computer (UNIVAC I). The ENIAC had 18,000 vacuum tubes and 70,000 transistors, weighed 80 tons, and occupied a room 8 x 100 feet! It could perform 5,000 additions and 360 multiplications per second. This was the first generation of computers.

In the second generation, (1956–1963), a quantum leap was made when the vacuum tube was replaced with the transistor, which was smaller and used less power. Programming language was also introduced, which led to the development of software. Programming languages included Common Business-Oriented Language (COBOL) and Formula Translation (FORTRAN).

The third generation (1961–1971) began when the integrated circuit was invented by Jack Kilby of Texas Instruments.

## Modern Times

IBM introduced the fourth generation mainframe computer (a large, fast computer) in 1971. Intel developed the microprocessor that same year. The speed of these early models was about .1 MHz. (Today's computer run at over 3.06 GHz.) In 1971, the first personal computer, called the Kenbak I, was invented by John Blankenbaker. Only 40 were sold. Companies such as Commodore, Radio Shack, Microsoft, and Apple were also established in the seventies. A major breakthrough came in 1981 when IBM started selling a personal computer (PC) for home and office use.

## Current Status

Some experts believe this is now into the fifth (and perhaps sixth) generation of computers. More speed, more efficiency, and smaller systems are being emphasized. Major breakthroughs for this period are artificial intelligence, wireless connections, and voice and handwriting recognition software.

### PUTTING IT TOGETHER

The major events in the evolution of technology include the following:
- Abacus
- Electricity
- Telecommunications
- Integrated circuitry
- Transistor
- Programming language

# 2.2 Computer Hardware Components

This section examines the basic components of the modern computer—the three main parts of the computer and the peripherals connected to the computer. This section discusses the "Big Three" components, the "Big Two" input devices, and the "Big Two" output devices.

## *The "Big Three" Components*

The "Big Three" are the processor, **memory,** and storage.

***The Processor.*** The processor is the most important component of a computer. It is the "brain" of the computer. The processor is known as the central processing unit (CPU), which is part of the motherboard (the main circuit board). The CPU interprets programming instructions and data for complicated tasks and controls what the computer does.

Several processor manufacturers are in business today. The two dominant companies are Intel and Advanced Micro Devices (AMD). Each company offers different models of processors. Intel has the Pentium® series and the Celeron®. Advanced Micro Devices has the Athlon™, the Duron™, and the Opteron™. These processors differt in performance and cost.

A significant factor for a processor is speed, that is, how fast the processor executes the tasks requested. Processor speed is measured in terms of **hertz** (Hz). Hertz is a unit of frequency, or how many times something repeats per second. Higher hertz levels result in faster performance. Speed and efficiency of processors has evolved over the years. Early processor speed was measured in megahertz. One megahertz (MHz) means 1 million clock cycles per second. Modern computers, including desktops and laptops, are now in the 1.0 gigahertz (GHz) to over 3.06 GHz speed range. One GHz is equal to one thousand million hertz.

## MEASUREMENTS OF PROCESSOR SPEED

| Category | Definition | Equivalency |
|---|---|---|
| Hertz (Hz) | A unit of frequency, equal to one cycle per second | 0.00000000125 |
| Kilohertz (KHz) | Measure of frequency | 1 thousand hertz |
| Megahertz (MHz) | Measure of frequency | 1 million hertz |
| Gigahertz (GHz) | Measure of frequency | 1 thousand million hertz |
| Teraflop | Measure of frequency | 1 trillion hertz |

Another feature of a processor is **cache.** The purpose of cache is to have often-used data readily available for the processor in order to speed up the execution of tasks. Memory speed for cache is measured in bytes. Higher byte levels produce faster operations. Most experts today do not recommend anything below 265 megabytes (MBs).

*Memory.* Another major feature of a computer is the amount of memory it has to retrieve and hold information. This memory is found in memory chips, which are part of the motherboard. Memory is needed to store computer programs and data that is being processed. Higher memory capacity allows the computer to operate and perform faster.

There are two types of memory: random-access memory (**RAM**) and read-only memory (**ROM**). Each system serves a specific purpose in the overall performance of a computer. Both are important for the computer to run efficiently.

RAM is the main working memory of a computer. Its role is to make the operating system, software programs, and current data available when requested by the processor. RAM is standing guard and ready to take action when called upon. This type of memory is much like short-term memory and is only temporary. If data is not saved or the power source is compromised, the data will vanish. More RAM means the computer can handle more functions simultaneously.

The function of ROM is to permanently store the instructions used by the computer. This memory, unlike the volatile memory of RAM, does not go away, nor can it be changed once it has been established.

One unit of memory is called a **byte,** which has a capacity of 8 bits. A bit represents a binary value of either zero or one. Programming instructions are based on zeros and ones. Complicated computer program languages require more capacity for the writing and storing of code.

Computer memory systems are measured in terms of bytes. A kilobyte represents 1,024 bytes; a megabyte, 1,048,576 bytes; and a gigabyte, just over 1 billion bytes. Many computers, including laptops, have surpassed the 512 MB range and are now measured in terms of gigabytes (GB). If memory starts at 2MB, the next level is 4MB, then 8MB, and so on until it reaches a gigabyte.

### MEASUREMENTS OF RAM

| Category | Definition | Equivalency |
|---|---|---|
| Bit | A single unit of information | One unit |
| Byte | Measure of data capacity | 8 bits |
| Kilobyte (KB) | Measure of data capacity | 1,024 bytes |
| Megabyte (MB) | Measure of data capacity | 1,048,576 bytes |
| Gigabyte (GB) | Measure of data capacity | 1,073,741,824 bytes |
| Terabyte (TB) | Measure of data capacity | 1,099,511,627,776 bytes |

### PUTTING IT TOGETHER

Hertz is used to measure computer **clock speed,** and bytes are used to measure memory capacity.

Like the cache of the processor, there is cache memory for the fast and efficient processing of information and instructions. The computer is programmed to know the types of tasks that are often performed by the user so it can have this data ready. If not for this function, the computer would have to laboriously search the instructions required, thereby slowing down performance.

Most computer manufacturers construct computers so that additional memory can be added. With time, economy of scale, and high levels of competition, the cost of memory has declined significantly. Adding memory capacity can be done by an IT professional or by the user.

Types of memory include double data rate random-access memory (DDR-RAM) and single data rate random-access memory (SDR-RAM). Each type varies in terms of performance and cost.

---

### PUTTING IT TOGETHER

Very high on the list for getting maximum performance from a computer is the capacity of the memory system. A computer has two main memory systems: ROM and RAM. The third system is cache memory. Memory capacity, which has increased greatly in recent years, is measured in terms of bytes.

*Storage.* Several different types of storage systems are available on most computers. The most common, known as the hard drive, is built into the computer. The hard drive holds information and data that can be retrieved upon demand. Most computers, including laptops, have at least 40 MBs of hard drive storage; some have reached the GB level.

Another way to hold data is to save it on a **floppy disk.** The floppy disk started out at 5.25 inches and is now 3.5 inches. It gets its name from being very thin and flexible—thus, "floppy." The disk is available in two types, each with different capacities. A double-density disk has 720 MBs of storage space; a high-density disk has 1.44 MBs. Advantages of a floppy disk include being inexpensive, lightweight, and easy to use and the ability to share them with others. Primary disadvantages are the limited amount of storage capacity and the possibility of the disk being destroyed. Due to these inadequacies, some computer manufacturers no longer include floppy disk drives in computers. An alternative to the floppy disk is the Zip® drive. This type of storage is usually an external device with capacities from 100 to 250 MBs. With advances in technology, a higher-capacity medium, the **CD-ROM,** has replaced floppy disks.

A CD-ROM (compact disc read-only memory) looks just like a music CD. With the use of optical discs and laser technology, CD-ROMs offer more storage capacity. A CD-ROM can store up to 650 MBs of data, which is equal to 20 floppy disks. CDs are lightweight and inexpensive, and they can be shared. The CD-ROM is more durable than a floppy disk, and it lasts longer.

For most desktop computers, CD-ROM drives are standard features built into the computer. Less-expensive computers may not have built-in drives, but they can be purchased as an external device. More expensive models allow the user to copy, or burn, files from an original. CD-ROMs are rated *R* or *RW*. The *R*, for "recordable," means that the CD can be used just once for storing music and/or data. The *RW*, for "rewritable," means that the CD can be reused. CD-ROM devices are also measured in terms of how fast they can write or copy. The higher the X speed, the faster they run. Speeds range from 24X up to 52X.

The next advancement in technology was the development of the **DVD-ROM** (digital versatile disc read-only memory). This medium is the same size as a CD and is capable of holding about 5GBs of data. A definite advantage is that CD-ROMs and DVD-ROMs can be used interchangeably in most devices. The DVD also has R and RW capabilities. A DVD drive is becoming standard on most computers.

---

### *PUTTING IT TOGETHER*

The major types of storage devices include the following:
- Floppy disk
- CD-ROM
- DVD-ROM
- Hard drive
- Zip drive

The "Big Three" components of a basic computer are as follows:
- Processor
- Memory
- Storage

## The "Big Two" Input Devices

The next section discusses peripheral devices that enhance overall functionality. These devices are used to input and manipulate data.

***The Keyboard.*** Anyone who has taken a typing or keyboarding course is familiar with operating a keyboard. A typical computer keyboard has 104 basic keys arranged in a systematic order. The most common order of arrangement is called **QWERTY.** This refers to the first six letters on the upper alphabet row of the keyboard. The QWERTY arrangement was developed to reduce the jamming of frequently used keys in early typewriters. Keyboards are usually included in the purchase of a desktop computer. In the case of laptops, the keyboard is built in. Many users upgrade the keyboard to fit their particular needs.

Keyboards come in many different forms depending on who the manufacturer is and whether the keyboard is used with a desktop or laptop. Beyond the typically used keys, some keyboards have what are called "hot buttons" that can be programmed to access often-used software programs. Some buttons allow the user go directly to the Internet or to e-mail or instant messaging (IM).

Most keyboards have a wire attached to the central processing unit through a port or Universal Serial Bus (USB). An alternative to this system is the wireless keyboard that operates via an infrared wave.

Keyboards have been designed to reduce repetitive stress injury (RSI). **Ergonomics,** the science of designing machines so people can use them safely and efficiently, has made advances in keyboard design to alleviate symptoms of **carpal tunnel syndrome.** This condition is caused by compression of a nerve where it passes through the wrist into the hand. Symptoms include weakness; pain; and burning, tingling, or itching numbness in the hand and fingers.

***The Mouse.*** Another important input device is the mouse. This device was a milestone in the development of the computer. With a mouse, the user can maneuver around the computer screen to complete his or her tasks without using the keyboard.

When a user moves the mouse, a cursor moves on the screen. The user points at what he or she wants and then clicks to make something happen. The term *point and click* denotes the role of the mouse. Mice have two buttons. A single click or a double click of the mouse button is used to execute actions. These functions are commonly programmed for right-handed users, but they can be reprogrammed for left-handed users as well.

Mice come in many types. A common one is the ball mouse. It rolls on a ball positioned under the mouse structure. Other types of mice include a trackball, rollerball, and optical ball. Each has advantages and varies in cost. A major asset of the rollerball mouse is that the user can operate it using his or her thumb or finger without moving the wrist. This can drastically reduce the number of wrist movements, which may help avoid repetitive stress injury. The wireless mouse is a recent innovation. It uses infrared waves much like a wireless keyboard, instead of being connected to the computer by a cable.

Laptops have different types of mice. Most of the mice are built into the laptop in the form of a touch pad or eraser head. A regular separate mouse can also be attached to a laptop.

A mouse can be adjusted to suit the user. Through the computer, the sensitivity of the mouse cursor to hand movement can be adjusted. The style and size of the mouse pointer can also be changed. Accessibility factors can be customized for users with special needs.

### *PUTTING IT TOGETHER*

The two major input devices on a computer are the mouse and the keyboard. Learning how to use these input devices efficiently takes practice. The key is to get the right equipment to enhance productivity.

*Advanced Topics.* In addition to a keyboard and mouse, voice recognition has become another option. Advanced technology, higher memory capacities, and better software have resulted in efficient systems that allow the user to use a microphone to keyboard and to execute mouse tasks. Another trend is handwriting recognition, which converts handwritten prose to printed text.

## The "Big Two" Output Devices

Two output devices are commonly used to deliver documents and products created on a computer. These end products represent the efforts of the user.

*Monitor.* The monitor is the device that displays what a user is inputting into a computer. Modern monitors display exactly what will be printed; this is known as "what you see is what you get" (WYSIWYG). The term *display* is sometimes used interchangeably with *monitor*.

Monitors, like the rest of technology, have evolved over the years. The early models used a cathode-ray tube (**CRT**), which is like the vacuum tube used in televisions to produce images with an electron beam. CRT technology remained at the forefront for many years until the development of the liquid crystal display (**LCD**). This advanced technology is starting to dominate display options for consumers. Most laptops have a thin film transistor (TFT) screen, a type of LCD flat-panel display screen.

The size of the screen display has increased over the years. The screen size for desktops has been 15 to 21-plus inches. Even laptops have increased to the 17-inch range. Related to the size of the screen is the amount of display that is viewable. A 21-inch monitor may have only 19 inches that are viewable. The newer flat screens are easier to view than traditional contoured screens.

Special considerations with regard to monitors include pixels, resolution, and dot pitch. Pixels are individual points of color represented on the horizontal axis and vertical axis of a monitor. Resolution is based on the number of pixels present. A higher number of pixels results in sharper images on the screen. Dot pitch refers to the physical dot size of the pixel. All of these factors are related to how well the monitor graphically displays whatever is input into the computer. Higher quality of these factors implies higher computer costs.

*Printer.* The printer delivers tangible output on paper, called hard copy. Early computer printers could print only in black or monochrome. Color printers were expensive. A common printer for many years was the classic dot matrix style. This type is seldom seen today.

Printers are available in two main types. The most common printer used today is the **ink jet.** When higher quality and speed are needed, the **laser jet** is the printer of choice.

Numerous printer manufacturers in the marketplace offer varying degrees of quality, speed, and cost. Most manufacturers now offer color printers as well. The cost of printers has dropped dramatically over the last few years.

A printer is connected to a computer through cables, or it is connected wirelessly with the aid of infrared waves. Connections in older models are through a serial port, which tend to be slower and less efficient. New models that connect through a USB are faster and more efficient. Portable printers are available for laptops, but they tend to be less efficient and rather costly.

Another factor in the efficiency of a printer is how many pages it can print per minute—often referred to as pages per minute (ppm).

Speed differs when printing in black and white as opposed to color. In most cases, ppm for color is much slower.

Another option when purchasing a printer is an all-in-one device that not only includes the printer, but also a fax modem and scanner.

---

### PUTTING IT TOGETHER

The two major output devices are the monitor and the printer.

## *Other Computer Hardware Peripherals*

Speakers and modems, discussed below, are other hardware peripherals to consider in the purchase of a computer.

***Speakers.*** Most computers come with a built-in speaker system. Speaker systems can be standard types, or they can be rather elaborate. Users can have two or four speakers or surround sound with subwoofers, which are designed to reproduce low audio frequencies. The main factors are cost and user preference.

***Modems.*** A **modem** is a device that allows a computer to connect with the Internet over telephone lines. Users can contract with an Internet service provider (ISP) such as America Online (AOL), Microsoft Service Network (MSN), or Earthlink for a monthly fee and connect to the Internet through a phone line. Modems are usually internal and come installed in most computers. One consideration about a modem connection is the speed of output and input. Speed has improved over the years, with 56 kilobytes per second now the industry standard. Other alternatives for connecting to the Internet are through cable, dedicated service lines (DSL), or a wireless connection.

# 2.3 Computer Software Programs

The first part of this chapter discussed the hardware of a computer. This section discusses software, the programs a computer uses to make things happen.

Without software, a computer would be just a blank machine. The software "tells" the computer to do required tasks. Software analysts try to determine what the user needs; then, using programming language, software engineers develop instructions for the computer to decipher.

## Operating System

The most important software program is the operating system. This system controls the computer and manages all of the other programs. The data it holds allows users to enter information and run programs.

The operating system is preinstalled in new computers and comes in one of two major formats. With PCs, the operating system is usually Microsoft® Windows®. For Apple computers, the system is a version of Mac OS. Operating systems are covered in more detail in Chapter 4.

## Word Processor

A word processor is a program that allows a user to create documents that can be stored, printed, or shared. The word processor serves some of the same purposes as a typewriter, but it is more powerful and efficient.

Most computers come with some type of word processor pre-installed. The major word processors are Microsoft Word and Word-Perfect®. When users buy a computer, they can add different word processors to meet their needs. Microsoft Windows has built-in processors called WordPad and Notepad.  Word processors are discussed further in Chapter 5.

## Browser

A browser allows a computer user to access the Internet and be part of the World Wide Web. There are two well-known browsers in the marketplace: Internet Explorer and Netscape. Choosing which one to use is an individual choice that depends on the needs and wants of the user. Each browser has its strengths and weaknesses. Some users use both. Chapter 6 covers this topic in more detail.

## Real Estate Software

Specialized software programs have been developed specifically for use in the real estate profession. Several examples are discussed below.

***TOP PRODUCER***®. TOP PRODUCER is considered the top-of-the-line real estate software. It addresses the needs of top-producing agents. It is a suite of programs that includes TOP PRODUCER, Hot Marketer™, TOP PRESENTER™, and TOP CONNECTOR™.

The program helps agents create a contact management system, time management system, marketing brochures, and flyers, in addition to completing numerous other tasks commonly performed by highly digital professionals. More information can be found on the TOP PRODUCER web site at http://www.topproducer.com.

***Agent Office***™. Another popular program for the real estate business is Agent Office. This suite has software for real estate contact management, transaction point services, web design, listings, virtual tours, databases, domain registrations, hosting, training, and technical support. Additional information can be found at http://www.realestatepro.fnis.com/products/on-line-agent.htm.

***The Marketing Library***. Pat Zaby, one of the digital innovators, created this software. The Marketing Library contains programs connected to presentations, postcards, marketing pieces, financial calculations, and multimedia. More information can be found at http://www.patzaby.com.

Numerous other software programs have been written and are being used in the real estate business. The software business is always changing to meet the demands of the real estate industry. This text examines some of these throughout the chapters that follow.

## PUTTING IT TOGETHER

Computer hardware and software go hand in hand; one is useless without the other. Both are necessary to operating a computer.

# RESOURCES FOR FURTHER STUDY

http://www.computerhope.com

http://whatis.techtarget.com

http://www.tomshardware.com

http://www.hardwarecentral.com/hardwarecentral

http://www.refdesk.com/comphard.html

http://www.cnet.com

http://www.ontheweb.com/s/microsoft-window-training.html

# SELF-ASSESSMENT

To determine the extent of knowledge you acquired in this chapter, choose the correct answer for each of the following.

1. A common brand name for a CPU is:
   a. Celeron
   b. Athlon
   c. Pentium
   d. All of the above

2. The clock speed for a computer would most likely be related to:
   a. Gigahertz
   b. Megabytes
   c. Nanosecond
   d. Mbps

3. Which storage device holds the most information?
   a. Floppy disk
   b. CD-ROM
   c. Zip drive
   d. DVD

4. All of the following are different types of printers except:
   a. Dot matrix
   b. Modem
   c. Ink jet
   d. Laser jet

5. Cache refers to:
   a. Keyboard
   b. Mouse
   c. Memory
   d. Software

6. A mouse can be any of the following types except:
   a. Trackball
   b. Rollerball
   c. Eraser head
   d. Zip

7. RAM would most likely be measured in:
   a. Hertz
   b. Ppm
   c. Bytes
   d. Kps

8. Pixels are related to:
   a. Sharper images
   b. ROM
   c. RAM
   d. Keyboards

9. Input is to keyboard as output is to:
   a. Mouse
   b. Printer
   c. Monitor
   d. Both b and c

10. Companies that manufacture processors include:
    a. Intel and AMD
    b. Dell and Gateway
    c. Apple and Microsoft
    d. Toshiba and Sony

11. In the development of the computer, which event occurred first?
    a. Supercomputer
    b. Microcomputer
    c. Telephone
    d. Abacus

12. Which term is used in connection with a monitor?
    a. Output device
    b. CRT/LCD
    c. TFT
    d. All of the above

13. Use of which of the following may result in repetitive stress injury?
    a. Keyboard/Mouse
    b. Printer/Monitor
    c. CD-ROM/DVD-ROM
    d. RAM/ROM

14. What is the most important component of a computer?
    a. Monitor
    b. Keyboard
    c. Processor
    d. Mouse

15. Examples of real estate computer software include:
    a.  TOP PRODUCER
    b.  Agent Office
    c.  The Marketing Library
    d.  All of the above

# CHAPTER 3
## CHOOSING A COMPUTER PACKAGE

## PREVIEW

The primary goal of this chapter is to help the cyber professional decide what type of computer package to purchase. Chapter 2 presented basic information about computer hardware and software. This chapter examines the dilemmas and specifications related to the purchase of a computer package.

When you finish this chapter, you will be able to:

1.  Decipher and understand a commercial computer advertisement.

2.  Critically analyze computer dilemmas and make informed decisions regarding each topic.

3.  Conduct a computer walk-through on key features of a computer package.

4.  Critically evaluate various computer manufacturers' products.

5.  Complete a plan of action to purchase a computer package.

## KEY TERMS

*bundled*                          *stand-alone*

*desktop*                          *tech support*

*laptop*                           *virus protection*

*PC*                               *warranty*

*protection plan*

# 3.1 Computer Choices

The cyber professional has many decisions to make when purchasing a computer system. This can be a confusing and frustrating process. The marketplace has many choices and many computer specialists ready to offer advice. This section attempts to clarify the process.

### TYPICAL COMMERCIAL COMPUTER ADVERTISEMENT

**PC Computer Systems Starting at $799.99**

**All Laptops and Desktops on Sale Now!**

When faced with a decision about what type of computer package to purchase, the cyber professional must consider several factors. By analyzing each choice, he or she is better able to make informed decisions.

## PC or Mac

The decision of whether to buy a Mac or a **PC** is often based on early influences as opposed to rational reasons. Each system has special characteristics that best serve the needs of the user. The user should research the specifics of each type of computer before making a decision on which one to buy. PCs generally have more software choices than Macs. But special software is available that lets Mac users take advantage of most of the software available to PC users. Macs have a reputation for performing well with graphics.

## Desktop or Laptop

Only a few years ago, the question of whether to buy a desktop or a laptop was not an issue due to the high price and limited capability of the **laptop**. Now the laptop rivals the **desktop,** and in many cases, it has identical specifications. Each has advantages and disadvantages. Choosing between the two depends on how the cyber professional decides to conduct business.

**The Desktop.** Advantages generally include lower price and higher capabilities than the laptop. The monitor is usually larger, ranging up to 21-plus inches; it may also be a flat screen with superior dot pitch. The desktop can usually handle more peripherals than the laptop, such as a printer or scanner.

Disadvantages of the desktop include size and lack of portability. Monitors often take up a large portion of the user's desk. Surrounding the CRT and CPU are other peripherals, which result in a great deal of clutter, leaving little room to work.

### PUTTING IT TOGETHER

Advantages of the desktop include these:
- Lower price
- Larger monitor
- Larger keyboard

**The Laptop.** Benefits include size and portability. The newer laptops have as much capability as most desktops. Screen size is up to 17 inches, with viewing available from all angles. Modern laptops are beginning to do what most desktops can do.

The major downsides of the laptop are affordability and limited connectivity. (Due to intense competition, however, the prices of laptops have dropped dramatically.) Also, laptops are often stolen, lost, or damaged. Due to limited size of the screen and keyboard, they can be more difficult to work with. Peripherals are often limited and may be expensive.

The cyber professional must consider all of those factors when deciding what computer will meet his or her needs. One way to solve this dilemma is to purchase both a desktop and a laptop! The cyber professional can divide his or her budget between the two computers in terms of what works best for the tasks/activities required.

---

### PUTTING IT TOGETHER

Advantages of the laptop include these:
• Portability
• Smaller size
• Capacities similar to a desktop

## Purchase or Lease

Is it better for cyber professionals to buy or lease a computer? It depends. When they own a computer, they have their own device to use as they wish. In addition, they won't have to transfer all of their files and documents to a new computer, as they do when a lease is up.

The buyer needs to decide whether to pay cash or to finance the purchase. He or she should carefully examine the interest rate and terms for a finance package. Often manufacturers and computer outlet stores offer no-money-down and delayed interest programs. With a lease, the user can have a new computer every few years and wont' be stuck with an outdated system. When a new model comes out and the price of technology goes down, the lessee can stay on the cutting edge of technology by trading in the older model for a new one. The buyer should compare the lease package with the financing package to determine the cost for each. Often a monthly lease fee is lower than a purchase fee. In many cases, the computer can be purchased at the end of the lease period. One major issue with a leased computer is transferring files and data from one model to the next. However, software is available for competing this task.

## Stand-Alone or Bundled

When purchasing a computer, a buyer can choose between individual components piece by piece or a **bundled** package. A bundled package includes all components, including software, from the same vendor. This is often less expensive than buying the pieces separately. In the case of a **stand-alone** purchase, the CPU may be purchased from one vendor and the peripherals from another.

## New or Refurbished

The advantage of buying a new computer is that all of the current warranties and return policies come with the purchase. The buyer has choices regarding the components.

Refurbished means that the computer was returned with some type of problem or defect or that the buyer changed his or her mind. Refurbished models are available for a lower price. Major companies often carry refurbished models . For example, Dell sells refurbished computers from its web site.

The novice who has a limited budget and wants to experiment with technology may find buying a refurbished computer to be a viable alternative. It is a gamble, though, on how well and how long the equipment will continue to work. However, warranties are often in effect on these products.

### PUTTING IT TOGETHER

Many factors are involved when choosing a computer. Decisions include whether to:
- Purchase or lease.
- Buy new or refurbished.
- Buy Stand-alone or bundled.

## Customized or Standard Package or Build Your Own

The buyer has other options with regard to purchasing a computer. These are discussed below.

*Customized.* Many computer companies offer purchasers the option to customize their computer. The buyer chooses the specifications he or she wants, and the computer is constructed as directed. With this method, the buyer does not buy unneeded hardware or software.

***Standard Package.*** This option is preselected by the computer company and is often based on common preferences of the general population. It may not be what a cyber professional needs to conduct real estate business. With a standard package, he or she may waste money in purchasing unnecessary equipment.

***Build Your Own.*** The build-your-own option is for the technologically savvy computer user. This option requires advanced skills and may be a time-consuming task. In many cases, building your own computer costs as much as a purchased model.

## *Brand Name or Clone*

Brand name refers to computers from well-known computer companies such as Dell, Hewlett-Packard, and Gateway. These companies' reputations are well established, and they are likely to be around for a long time.

A clone, on the other hand, often has the same specifications as a brand-name computer and, in many cases, is better. But it is built by a lesser-known manufacturer who may not have an established track record or who may not be around to provide technical support after the purchase is made.

# 3.2 Computer Manufacturers

With so many companies and brand names in the marketplace, choosing the right computer may seem like a difficult task. Consumer reports, consumer research, and reviews about computers are readily available for inspection. The computer user should carefully examine this information before making a purchase.

Factors about brand that a buyer should consider before making a decision include the following:

- Performance

- Reputation

- Reliability

- **Warranty**

- **Protection plan**

- Service

- Technical support

- Price

- Standard features

- Options available

Often the decision to buy one computer over another is based on input from a friend who has had a good or bad experience with a particular brand. The buyer needs to make sure he or she understands the friend's experiences, making a decision based on facts.. In the end, the computer user is the person who must pay for the system and take responsibility for his or her actions.

## Computer Manufacturer Comparison Chart

With information garnered from the Internet and consumer reports, look at each of the main computer manufacturers and vendors and rate the basic features available on a scale of 1 to 4 by circling the applicable number (1 = superior; 2 = good; 3 = fair; 4 = poor).

| FEATURES | DELL | HEWLETT-PACKARD / COMPAQ | APPLE | SONY | IBM | TOSHIBA | OTHER |
|---|---|---|---|---|---|---|---|
| Reputation | 1 2 3 4 | 1 2 3 4 | 1 2 3 4 | 1 2 3 4 | 1 2 3 4 | 1 2 3 4 | 1 2 3 4 |
| Service | 1 2 3 4 | 1 2 3 4 | 1 2 3 4 | 1 2 3 4 | 1 2 3 4 | 1 2 3 4 | 1 2 3 4 |
| Warranty | 1 2 3 4 | 1 2 3 4 | 1 2 3 4 | 1 2 3 4 | 1 2 3 4 | 1 2 3 4 | 1 2 3 4 |
| Protection Plan | 1 2 3 4 | 1 2 3 4 | 1 2 3 4 | 1 2 3 4 | 1 2 3 4 | 1 2 3 4 | 1 2 3 4 |
| Tech Support | 1 2 3 4 | 1 2 3 4 | 1 2 3 4 | 1 2 3 4 | 1 2 3 4 | 1 2 3 4 | 1 2 3 4 |
| Purchase/Lease Plan | 1 2 3 4 | 1 2 3 4 | 1 2 3 4 | 1 2 3 4 | 1 2 3 4 | 1 2 3 4 | 1 2 3 4 |
| Specials/Discounts | 1 2 3 4 | 1 2 3 4 | 1 2 3 4 | 1 2 3 4 | 1 2 3 4 | 1 2 3 4 | 1 2 3 4 |
| Add-Ons | 1 2 3 4 | 1 2 3 4 | 1 2 3 4 | 1 2 3 4 | 1 2 3 4 | 1 2 3 4 | 1 2 3 4 |
| Upgradable | 1 2 3 4 | 1 2 3 4 | 1 2 3 4 | 1 2 3 4 | 1 2 3 4 | 1 2 3 4 | 1 2 3 4 |
| Customizable | 1 2 3 4 | 1 2 3 4 | 1 2 3 4 | 1 2 3 4 | 1 2 3 4 | 1 2 3 4 | 1 2 3 4 |
| Basic Software included | 1 2 3 4 | 1 2 3 4 | 1 2 3 4 | 1 2 3 4 | 1 2 3 4 | 1 2 3 4 | 1 2 3 4 |
| Advanced Software included | 1 2 3 4 | 1 2 3 4 | 1 2 3 4 | 1 2 3 4 | 1 2 3 4 | 1 2 3 4 | 1 2 3 4 |
| State-of-the-Art Technology | 1 2 3 4 | 1 2 3 4 | 1 2 3 4 | 1 2 3 4 | 1 2 3 4 | 1 2 3 4 | 1 2 3 4 |
| Cost | 1 2 3 4 | 1 2 3 4 | 1 2 3 4 | 1 2 3 4 | 1 2 3 4 | 1 2 3 4 | 1 2 3 4 |

Once the research is completed, rank the computer companies in terms of quality, to help make an informed decision on which brand to choose.

The following computer manufacturers' web sites can assist in the analysis of each of the manufacturers and its computers:

- http://www.dell.com
- http://www.apple.com
- http://www.compaq.com
- http://www.toshiba.com
- http://www.hewlettpackard.com
- http://www.sony.com
- http://www.gateway.com
- http://www.ibm.com

## Computer Walk-Through

Circle the category that represents your decisions about the following components and peripherals:

| COMPUTER CATEGORIES | LEVEL I (Novice) | LEVEL II (Seasoned) | LEVEL III (Expert) |
|---|---|---|---|
| Processor Speed | Up to 1 GHz | 1–2.4 GHz | Faster than 2.4 GHz |
| Keyboard | Standard 104 keys (QWERTY) | Ergonomically designed | Wireless |
| Mouse | Ball Touch ball | Optical Trackball Rollerball | Wireless Optical |
| Monitor | CRT | CRT/Flat Screen | LCD/Flat Screen |
| Monitor Size | Up to 15 inches | 15–19 inches | Larger than 19 inches |
| Connectivity | Modem | DSL/Cable | WiFi 801.1 lb/g |
| Speakers | 2 standard speakers | 4 standard speakers | Surround subwoofer |
| Printer | Monochrome/ Color dot matrix | Color ink jet | Color laser jet |
| Printer Speed | Up to 5 ppm black Up to 3 ppm color | 5–12 ppm Black 3–10 ppm Color | Above 12 ppm black Above 10 ppm color |
| Peripheral Storage | Floppy disk Zip drive (50 MB) | Floppy disk Zip drive (250 MB) CD-ROM | Floppy disk CD-ROM DVD-ROM |
| Cost | Up to $1,500 | $1,500–$2,500 | More than $2,500 |

# *Plan of Action*

Place an X in the box that represents your decision regarding each of the following statements:

1. I will purchase a: ☐ PC  ☐ Mac.

2. I will purchase a: ☐ desktop  ☐ laptop  ☐ both.

3. I will purchase a: ☐ new  ☐ refurbished  ☐ lease.

4. I will purchase a: ☐ stand-alone  ☐ bundled  ☐ build own ☐ computer package.

5. Operating system I will purchase: ☐ Windows  ☐ Mac OS X.

6. Word processor I will use: ☐ Microsoft Word  ☐ WordPerfect ☐ other.

7. Browser I will use: ☐ Internet Explorer  ☐ Netscape  ☐ both ☐ other.

8. Manufacturer I will use: ☐ Dell  ☐ Hewlett-Packard  ☐ Apple ☐ Sony  ☐ Toshiba  ☐ IBM  ☐ other.

9. Processor I will use: ☐ Pentium  ☐ Celeron  ☐ Athlon  ☐ Duron ☐ Opteron  ☐ other.

10. I want to have: ☐ **virus protection**  ☐ manufacturer's warranty ☐ security  ☐ protection plan  ☐ **tech support**  ☐ all of these.

11. My mouse will be a(n): ☐ ball  ☐ optical  ☐ wireless ☐ trackball  ☐ touch ball  ☐ rollerball.

12. My printer will be: ☐ monochrome  ☐ color, using ☐ dot matrix  ☐ ink jet  ☐ laser jet technology, and will print at least _____ ppm for black and at least _____ ppm for color.

13. My monitor will be: ☐ CRT  ☐ LCD with at least ☐ 15 inch, ☐ 19 inch,  ☐ +19 inch display size.

## PUTTING IT TOGETHER

With a comprehensive understanding of basic computer hardware and software and an analysis of basic specification considerations, the cyber professional is ready to purchase his or her computer package.

## *Where to Shop for a Computer Package*

After the decision-making process is complete, the cyber professional is ready to buy. One source for a computer is a big-name store that specializes in computers. Another source is a smaller independent company that builds clones for consumers. Shopping on the Internet is also a possibility, as is going directly to a computer manufacturer.

---

### *PUTTING IT TOGETHER*

When deciding to purchase a computer package, the buyer should consider the following:

- Performance
- Reputation
- Price
- Tech support
- Warranty

---

# RESOURCES FOR FURTHER STUDY

http://shopper.cnet.com

http://www.savvyshopping.net/guides/pc.php

http://www.staples.com/content/article/a-b/buyingram.asp

http://www.geek.com/htbc/glanbuy.htm

http://www.pcbargainhunter.com

http://www.helpwithpcs.com/buying/buying.htm

# SELF-ASSESSMENT

To determine the extent of knowledge you acquired in this chapter, choose the correct answer for each of the following.

1. An example of a computer manufacturer includes:
   a. Dell
   b. IBM
   c. Hewlett-Packard
   d. All of the above

2. What is the major advantage of a laptop over a desktop?
   a. Portability
   b. Large size
   c. Large keyboard
   d. More hard drive capacity

3. The decision to buy a Mac over a PC may be related to:
   a. Durability
   b. Users' needs
   c. Emotional needs
   d. Cost

4. Which of the following is an operating system?
   a. WordPerfect
   b. Windows
   c. DVD
   d. All of the above

5. A refurbished computer would most likely:
   a. Cost more
   b. Cost less
   c. Not have an extended warranty
   d. Be easy to find and purchase

6. What is the criterion for choosing a computer manufacturer?
   a. Performance
   b. Repetition
   c. Reliability
   d. All of the above

7. A customized computer would:
   a. Be made to order
   b. Cost less
   c. Have unnecessary hardware
   d. Have unnecessary software

8. What is a major consideration when buying a computer package?
   a. Technical support
   b. Warranty
   c. Service
   d. All of the above

9. The term *bundled* refers to:
   a. A single computer by itself
   b. A total computer package
   c. A computer missing major parts
   d. A computer without any software

10. What is the device that is used to connect to the Internet?
    a. Modem
    b. DSL
    c. Cable
    d. All of the above

11. A typical word processor is:
    a. Windows
    b. OS X
    c. QWERTY
    d. Microsoft Word

12. What is a common type of software for the cyber professional?
    a. TOP PRODUCER
    b. Agent Office
    c. The Marketing Library
    d. All of the above

13. Which of the following is a commonly used Internet browser?
    a. Netscape
    b. MSN
    c. AOL
    d. Earthlink

14. What is an advantage of building your own computer?
    a. No need for technical skill
    b. Ease of assembly
    c. Speed of assembly
    d. None of these

15. A major decision when selecting a computer includes:
    a. PC or Mac
    b. Desktop or laptop
    c. Manufacturer
    d. All of the above

# CHAPTER 4
## THE COMPUTER OPERATING SYSTEM: MICROSOFT WINDOWS

## PREVIEW

The text has discussed how technology developed, how the computer works, and how to choose a computer package. This chapter discusses how to use a computer. The material also describes the system that makes the computer useful to users. The Microsoft Windows operating system is featured.

When you finish this chapter, you will be able to:

1. Understand the role and importance of an operating system.

2. Identify the key features and functions of an operating system.

3. Master a series of competencies for working with Windows.

## KEY TERMS

*Control Panel*

*graphical user interface (GUI)*

*Help and Support*

*icons*

*My Computer*

*My Documents*

*operating system (OS)*

*Recycle Bin*

*Start button*

*Taskbar*

# 4.1 Background

The first section covers the basic concepts of operating systems and includes the history of how operating systems evolved. This section includes a discussion of peripheral devices used to interface, or communicate, with the operating system.

## The Operating System

The **operating system (OS)** is the preinstalled software that allows the computer to function. If the CPU is the brain of the computer and storage is the body, then the OS is the oxygen of the computer. Without such a system, the hardware and software cannot work together to deliver what the user expects. It is a method by which the user interfaces with the computer to achieve desired results.

### PUTTING IT TOGETHER

The operating system (OS) enables the computer to perform the tasks and actions requested by the user.

Early OSs allowed the user to communicate with the computer by entering commands with the keyboard. This system, called the disk operating system (DOS), was complicated. An improvement in operating systems occurred with the invention of graphics, or small pictures that resemble the task required. These graphics are also called **icons.** The user controls the operating system by clicking on the icons with the mouse. This approach is called **graphical user interface (GUI).** The introduction of GUI ("gooey") was a breakthrough that opened doors to computer use for many nontechnical users.

### *PUTTING IT TOGETHER*

Graphical user interface (GUI) allows the user to interact with the computer using graphics rather than commands. This innovation opened the door for a user-friendly computer world.

Several types of OSs came on the market. The major players were Apple and Microsoft, with minor roles for Red Hat and Linspire (formerly Lindows). Apple Computer developed Mac OS; several companies developed distributions based on Linux, creating products such as Red Hat Linux and Lindows; and Microsoft created Windows. Microsoft Windows continues to dominate the OS market. The battle over which OS is best continues to be an issue. Since Microsoft Windows is so prevalent, the remainder of this chapter focuses on the key features and functions of Windows. It should be noted, however, that Linux systems are growing in popularity. In fact, Dell is already offering Linux as an option on some of their computers

### *PUTTING IT TOGETHER*

The main types of operating systems are Windows, Mac OS, and Linux.

## *User Interface Tools*

With GUI, a user is able to communicate with the computer via the mouse and keyboard. Each of these devices has special features and functions that allow the user to perform various tasks. A newer alternative is voice recognition, the ability to issue commands to a computer by speaking to it.

***Mouse.*** As mentioned in Chapter 2, several types of mice are available for computer users, but they all have similar functions. The mouse has two buttons: a primary button on the left and a secondary button on the right. The buttons are activated by clicking. When the mouse is right-clicked (i.e., the secondary button is pressed), a menu of actions is activated. The primary button has a different set of functions. Its role is to execute actions such as selecting, pointing, and dragging.

The mouse responds to both single- and double-clicking. Each action causes different results. The mouse also controls where the pointer (it looks like an I-beam) goes on the screen. The mouse has special properties that the user can change depending on how he or she prefers to work. For example, the user can reverse the functions of the primary and secondary buttons. The user can also change the appearance of the pointer and the speed at which it moves across the screen. These changes are made through **Control Panel** in Microsoft Windows.

*Keyboard.* On a typical keyboard, numerous functions can be executed with the keys. These are considered shortcuts, which can be used instead of clicking the mouse. To execute a shortcut, the user holds down the Control (CTRL) key and another key at the same time. Some common executions include, but are not limited to, the following:

- Redo: CTRL + Y

- Underline: CTRL + U

- Italic: CTRL + I

- Open: CTRL + O

- Print: CTRL + P

- Select All: CTRL + A

- Save: CTRL + S

- Find: CTRL + F

- Undo: CTRL + Z

- Cut: CTRL + X

- Copy: CTRL + C

- Paste: CTRL + V

- Bold: CTRL + B

- New: CTRL + N

The keyboard can also be programmed to meet individual needs in terms of slow, fast, repeat, and delay. These adjustments are found in Control Panel of Microsoft Windows.

*Voice Recognition.* Voice recognition software has been garnering attention in computer circles. Due to advances in software and increased memory, voice recognition has become an alternative to the mouse and keyboard.

Using a headset that includes a microphone, the user talks to the computer. His or her voice is converted to text on the screen. To reach a high level of efficiency, the computer must learn a user's voice and speaking style.

Voice recognition can help reduce the chance of repetitive stress injury and carpal tunnel syndrome. The cost of the software varies depending on the brand. Common software brands include ViaVoice™ and Dragon NaturallySpeaking™. A speech recognition program is also available in Windows XP and can be found in Control Panel.

# 4.2 Getting Acquainted with Microsoft Windows

This section illustrates the basic properties of Microsoft Windows. Understanding these key elements will aid the reader in becoming a skilled cyber professional.

## *Background on Windows*

Microsoft has had several versions of Windows over the years and continues to improve and upgrade the system as technology evolves. Earlier versions include Windows 3.1, 95, 98, Me, and 2000. The latest version is Windows XP. Within the XP series are several editions, including Home Edition, Office Small Business Edition, Professional, Tablet PC Edition, and Media Center Edition.

## *The Windows XP Advantage*

The XP series, mentioned above, has many special features. These include a more user-friendly screen; simplified menus; built-in security; special digital media functions; and a system for setting up a network whereby users on different computers can share Internet files, photos, music, and a printer.

## *Microsoft Windows Desktop*

A computer may be used by only one person or by several people. If only one person uses the computer, as is assumed here, it needs only one configuration, or user account. When only one user account has been set up, Windows XP automatically logs on using that account when the computer is started. When a computer is turned on, Windows XP may open with a screen similar to the following:

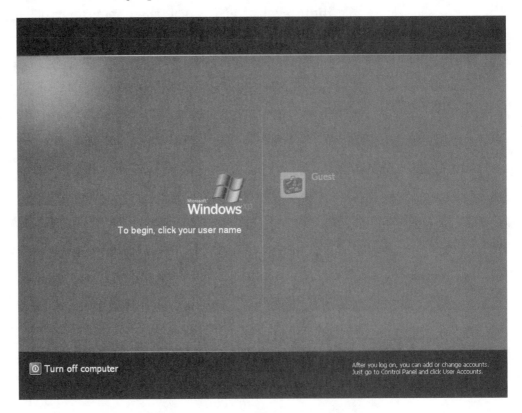

After logging on, the user will see a Windows XP desktop similar to the following:

***Icons.*** On the desktop are several graphic symbols known as icons. Each icon represents a task to be executed. Although each desktop may be different, several standard icons are found on most computers. Note that icons can be added to the desktop using a function called Create Shortcut. A typical icon found on the desktop is the **Recycle Bin,** which serves the same purpose as a wastebasket. Deleted files are placed in the Recycle Bin. This clears the computer of unnecessary materials that take up space on the hard disk. Items that have been deleted from the screen remain in the Recycle Bin until the user empties it. The user can recover deleted files from the Recycle Bin or empty the Recycle Bin and permanently delete the files.

***Taskbar.*** This navigational tool is found on the bottom of the Windows screen. It contains the **Start button** at the left end, the notification area and clock at the right end, and the Quick launch toolbar and taskbar in between for showing open programs.

***Start Button.*** When the user clicks the Start button, the following screen appears:

Typically seen at the top left side of the Start menu are links to the following pinned programs:

• Internet. This icon represgents an Internet connection. Clicking this icon launches the Internet browser.

- E-mail. The user can program Outlook Express to be the default e-mail program.

- Microsoft Word. The user can pin a link to Word to make the program easy to find and start.

A variety of other programs may appear below the pinned programs.

Typically seen at the top right side of the Start menu are links to the locations where the user is most likely to store files, a link to a directory of other computers on the user's network, and links to tools the user may use while running the computer. Some of these links are as follows:

- **My Documents.** This folder contains all saved documents.

- My Recent Documents. This folder contains the documents that were most recently saved.

- My Pictures. This folder contains digital pictures that have been downloaded and saved for future use.

- My Music. This folder holds all music files that have been stored in the computer.

- **My Computer.** When this link is clicked, the right pane displays the drives and folders contained in My Computer. The left pane displays a list of tasks and places that are relevant to My Computer. The My Computer screen is shown below.

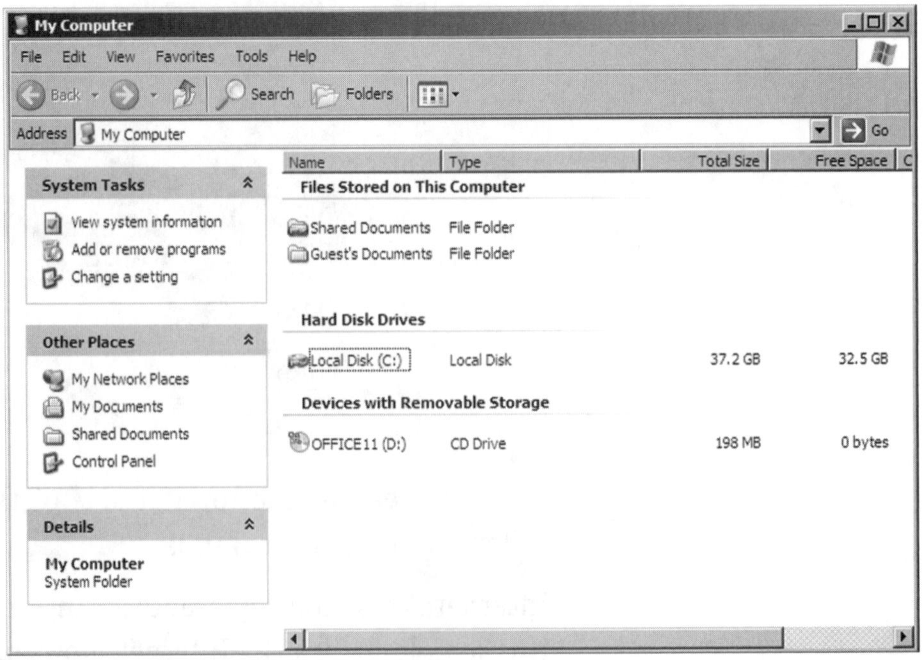

Below My Computer are the following:

- Control Panel. Control Panel allows the user to change a variety of different Windows and system settings. These settings are grouped according to category. Clicking the icon of a category displays a window with specific options or starts a wizard that leads the user through the steps of making changes. See the illustration below.

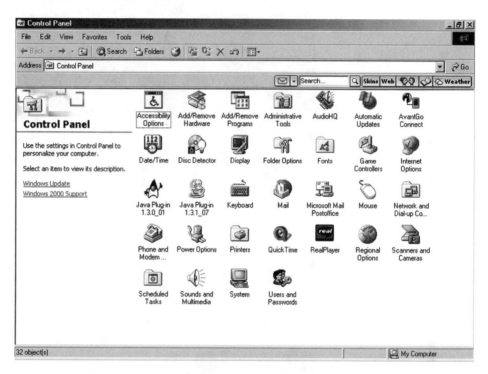

- **Help and Support.** The Help and Support Center combines certain features (for example, Search, Index, and Favorites) with current online content. It includes help from other Windows XP users and from online support personnel. An illustration of Help and Support follows.

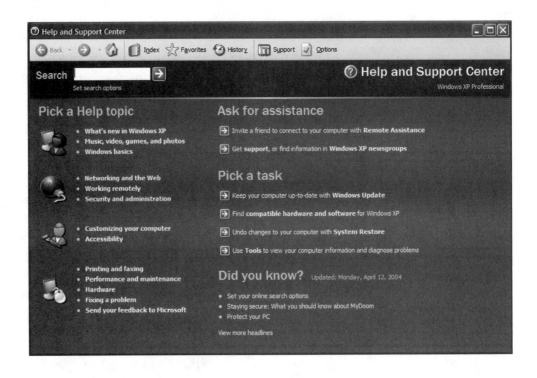

- Search. This feature allows the user to search for files, printers, and computers. See the illustration below.

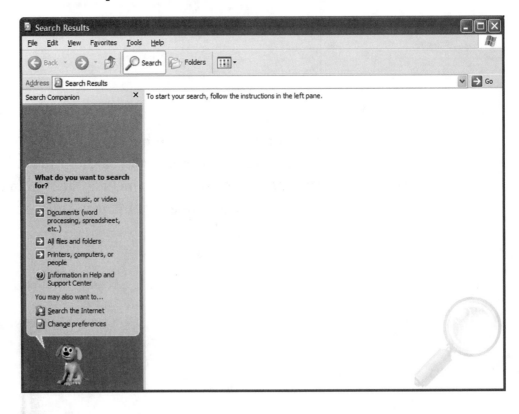

- All Programs. By clicking All Programs, the user can see all software programs installed on the computer. See the illustration below.

- Turn Off Computer. When the user clicks this feature, a dialog box appears. Three options are shown: (1) Hibernate saves the session and turns off the computer. The next time the computer is started, the session is restored to the place where the user left off. (2) Turn Off ends the Windows session and turns off the computer. (3) Restart ends the session, shuts down Windows, and then starts Windows again without turning off the computer. See the illustration below.

# RESOURCES FOR FURTHER STUDY

http://www.microsoft.com/windows/default.mspx

The home page for Microsoft Windows provides a detailed account of the different types of Windows operating systems.

http://www.microsoft.com/windowsxp/pro/default.asp

This site gives specifics about Windows XP.

http://www.microsoft.com/windowsxp/tabletpc/default.asp

This site covers the special Windows program for PC Tablet.

http://www.microsoft.com/windowsxp/pro/using/default.asp

This sites gives suggestions on how to take full advantage of Windows XP Professional.

http://v4.windowsupdate.microsoft.com/en/default.asp

Windows updates are available on this site.

http://www.computerhope.com/os.htm

This site includes information on various operating systems.

# SELF-ASSESSMENT

To determine the extent of knowledge you acquired in this chapter, choose the correct answer for each of the following.

1.  The turning point for efficient computer operation was the development of:
    a.  GUI
    b.  DOS commands
    c.  Browser
    d.  Internet

2.  Key devices used to work with an operating system are:
    a.  Modem/Cable
    b.  Mouse/Keyboard
    c.  Monitor/Printer
    d.  Internet Explorer/Netscape

3.  A pointer:
    a.  Looks like an I-beam
    b.  Is controlled by the mouse
    c.  Can be controlled to move around the screen
    d.  All of the above

4.  The keyboard command to print is:
    a.  CTRL + V
    b.  CTRL + B
    c.  CTRL + P
    d.  CTRL + I

5.  The Windows desktop taskbar is found where?
    a.  Right side of the screen
    b.  Left side of the screen
    c.  Top of the screen
    d.  Bottom of the screen

6.  All of the following can be found on the Start button except:
    a.  GUI
    b.  My Documents
    c.  My Computer
    d.  Programs

7. Settings that can be changed for the mouse include:
   a. Speed
   b. Pointer
   c. Single/double click
   d. All of the above

8. The taskbar contains:
   a. Start button
   b. Notification area
   c. Open programs
   d. All of the above

9. Which of the following is referred to as "gooey"?
   a. Disk operating system
   b. Graphical user interface
   c. Control keys
   d. Voice recognition software

10. Which Windows version came first?
    a. Windows XP
    b. Windows 95
    c. Windows Me
    d. Windows 3.1

11. Which of the following is an operating system?
    a. Linux
    b. Windows
    c. Mac OS
    d. All of the above

12. What is a special key features of Windows XP?
    a. More user-friendly
    b. Enhanced digital features
    c. Ability to establish a home network
    d. All of the above

13. To place an icon on the Windows desktop, you use which command?
    a. Create Shortcut
    b. Taskbar
    c. Control Panel
    d. Start button

14. What does the term *interface* mean?
    a. To log on
    b. To delete
    c. To communicate
    d. To save to My Documents

15. One way to avoid repetitive stress injury is to use:
    a. The mouse only
    b. The keyboard only
    c. Voice recognition software
    d. Handwriting recognition software

# CHAPTER 5
## THE WORD PROCESSOR: MICROSOFT WORD

## PREVIEW

Now that you have acquired an understanding of an operating system, you are ready to develop your word processing skills. These skills are the underpinning of computer efficiency. A word processor is basically a complex and sophisticated typewriter. Learning how to use a word processor is essential for applying computer applications to real estate. The intent of this chapter is to familiarize the cyber professional with the key features and functions of word processing. The chapter emphasizes Microsoft Word.

When you finish this chapter, you will be able to:

1.  Understand what a word processor is and what it can do for the cyber professional.

2.  Identify the features and functions of Microsoft Word.

3.  Demonstrate mastery in the key functions of Microsoft Word.

## KEY TERMS

| | |
|---|---|
| *Bold* | *Open* |
| *Close* | *Paste* |
| *Copy* | *Restore* |
| *Cut* | *Save* |
| *F key* | *Save As* |
| *File* | *Select All* |
| *Italic* | *title bar* |
| *Maximize* | *toolbars* |
| *menu bar* | *Underline* |
| *Minimize* | |

# 5.1 The Word Processor

Knowing how to use a word processor is a necessary to ensure success in real estate. With this skill, the cyber professional can:

1. Create documents that can be saved, retrieved, and printed.

2. Create flyers, brochures, and related marketing materials.

3. Create letters, memos, faxes, and e-mails.

This section covers what a word processor is and what it can do. It also discusses different types of word processors and provides some related background.

Essentially, the word processor plays the role of a typewriter (and for the most part has replaced the typewriter). With all of their options, word processors allow the user to work more efficiently. With a word processor, the user can create, edit, save, and print documents.

The most popular word processors are WordPerfect and Microsoft Word. Two basic word processing tools, Notepad and WordPad, are found in Microsoft Windows. The word processing program Word is found in Microsoft Works Suite.

---

### *PUTTING IT TOGETHER*

---

Typical word processors include Microsoft Word and WordPerfect.

---

Microsoft has a suite of software programs that includes not only Word but also several other programs. Users have a choice of using Microsoft Home Edition or the Professional series, depending on the purpose and level desired. Microsoft has another program called OneNote, which lets users organize and save notes.

Determining which program to use depends on the user's purpose and past experience. Most word processor systems have similar features and functions that help in the creation of professional-looking documents. In most cases, a word processing system is preinstalled on the computer. Which one is included depends on the computer brand.

This chapter is not intended to be a thorough course in how to use word processing software. Instead, it focuses on features and functions the cyber professional must know to use word processing in their profession.

# 5.2 Getting Acquainted with Microsoft Word

This part of the chapter identifies the features and functions of Microsoft Word. Assistance in understanding Word can be found by clicking the Help button and keying a question for the program to answer. Another built-in feature is the Office Assistant that assists in the creation of documents by giving suggestions on spelling, grammar, formatting, and other tasks.

---

### *PUTTING IT TOGETHER*

---

The Office Assistant provides help with spelling, grammar, formatting, and other tasks.

## Microsoft Word

Microsoft Word is preinstalled in many computers, but it can be purchased separately and installed on any computer that meets minimum RAM requirements. Once Word is installed, it can be accessed through the Start menu. After the computer is booted up, or started, the Windows desktop appears. Click the Start button at the bottom of the Windows screen. Select All Programs and then Microsoft Word. When you click on Word, a document window appears. You can also open Word by creating a shortcut on the Windows desktop.

Once Word has been launched, it looks like this:

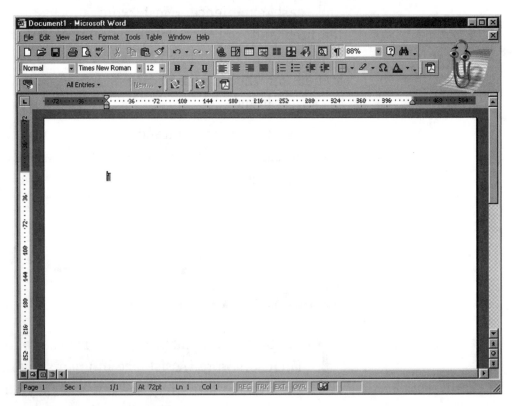

## Microsoft Word Features

In this section, the individual parts of Word are identified along with what they do. Not all features are covered in this basic introduction.

***Title Bar.*** The **title bar** is located at the top of the screen and shows the name of the application and the name of the active document. Also, in the same line to the right are the **Minimize, Maximize, Restore,** and **Close** buttons. The title bar is shown below.

*Menu Bar.* The **menu bar** gives the user the choice of commands used to instruct Word to perform specific functions. The menu bar includes the following menus:

- File

- Edit

- View

- Insert

- Format

- Tools

- Table

- Window

- Help

The menu bar is shown below.

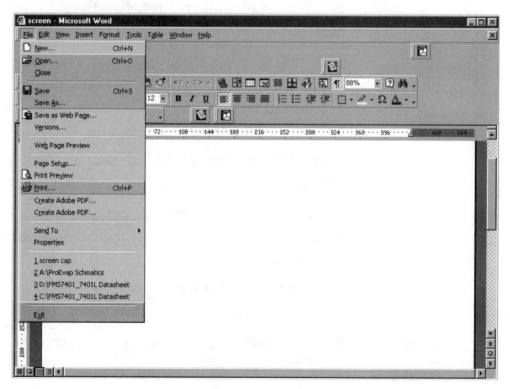

*File Menu.* This menu gives the user the ability to open a new blank document, open an existing file, close a file, save the information, save as a special document, do a print preview, or print. The File menu is shown below.

***Edit Menu.*** Different editing tasks can be found in this menu. Several options include **Cut, Copy, Paste,** and **Select All.**

***View Menu.*** This menu gives the user choices of how to view the document: normal, web layout, print layout, or outline. Also found here is a list of **toolbars,** including the Standard and Formatting toolbars.

***Insert Menu.*** This menu gives the user the capability of inserting information into a document. Options include adding page numbers, date and time, pictures from existing files, and hyperlinks that go directly to the Internet.

***Format Menu.*** Located in this menu are options to change font style and font size and to include bullets and numbering.

***Tools Menu.*** Options in this menu include a spelling and grammar check and a mail merge used to create addresses for letters, labels, and envelopes.

***Table Menu.*** In this menu, the user can draw or create a table with a set number of rows and columns.

***Window Menu.*** This menu allows the user to create another window or to split the window into two parts.

***Help Menu.*** Here a user can ask questions about how to do a task. This is where the Office Assistant is displayed.

***Using the Mouse and Keyboard with Word.*** As with Windows, the two main devices for working with Word are the mouse and the keyboard. The mouse can be used to select commands on the Word menu, or it can be used independently to launch actions by right- and left-clicking. Another important function of the mouse is to move the pointer for the insertion of text and graphics. The keyboard can also be used; keyboard shortcuts usually consist of pressing a function key, **F key,** or pressing ALT or CTRL plus another key.

---

### PUTTING IT TOGETHER

F keys are used as shortcuts to accomplish tasks on a word processor. Typical F keys include these:

F1 = Help
F2 = Move text or graphics
F4 = Repeat the last action
Keyboard Shortcuts:
CTRL + A = Select All
CTRL + X = Cut
CTRL + C = Copy
CTRL + V = Paste

## Top Five Tasks for Word

Only the important functions of Word are explained here. The tasks most often used include the following:

1. Opening a new document

2. Creating a document

3. Saving a document

4. Formatting a document

5. Printing a document

***Opening a New Document.*** To key a document, you must have a blank screen open. You do this by launching Word and clicking a Word icon found on the Windows desktop or clicking the Start button (then clicking All Programs and Microsoft Word). A new document appears when Word is opened.

***Creating a Document.*** With a blank screen, you are ready to create a document. Different actions you can take include, but are not limited, to the following:

- Selecting a font style

- Selecting a font size

- Adding **bold,** *italic,* or <u>underline</u> to a word, sentence, or paragraph

- Aligning text in one of four ways: right, left, center, or justify

- Adding bullets or numbering

- Increasing or decreasing paragraph indents

- Inserting page numbers

- Inserting the date and time

- Conducting a spell check

- Drawing a table

- Inserting items into a document

- Adding a header or footer

- Copying, cutting, and pasting information to another document

- Deleting items in a document

***Saving a Document.*** Once you have keyed a document , you can save it and then retrieve it whenever necessary . To save a document, go to **File** on the menu bar and click **Save As.** In the dialog box, give the document a file name. Next, decide if the document is to be saved in the My Documents folder, on the Desktop, or on a floppy disk or another storage device. Click **Save** and the document will be saved as directed. The saved document can be retrieved whenever it is needed.

***Organizing Files and Folders.*** To organize your documents, you should create folders to hold similar documents. To create a folder, go to My Documents and double-click. Click File, New, and then Folder. Name the folder. Now you can use it for saving related documents. You can place documents into the folder by dragging and dropping (clicking and holding the primary mouse button while moving the file to the folder and then releasing the mouse button).

***Printing a Document.*** To print a document, open the document, click the File menu and click Print. Before actually printing the document, however, you may want to preview the document to make sure it is formatted correctly. You do this by selecting File, then Print Preview. Click once to enlarge the preview of the document; click again to decrease the preview. Then click Close on the Print Preview toolbar to exit the Preview window.

## Basic Word Processing Skills

When using the mouse or keyboard, you can perform numerous commands. Often-used commands include the following:

- **Open,** close
- Minimize, restore, and maximize
- Highlight
- Drag and drop
- Scroll
- Single- or double-click the mouse buttons
- Right- or left-click the mouse
- Press the Enter key
- Use the Space Bar
- Use the Control (CTRL) key
- Scroll down
- Select
- Point and click
- Move right, left, up, and down with the keyboard or mouse

# 5.3 Working with Microsoft Word

In this section, you demonstrate your skill in executing tasks and commands in Microsoft Word.

**Skill Mastery
Exercise**

Formatting a document. The following sample document illustrates common formatting features. After examining the document, refer to the instructions that follow to rekey the document.

---

9/26/2003      **1—Insert date**

Dear Mr. and Mrs. Seller:    **2—Align left**

**3—Color**

You may be interested in selling your home located at

5415 State Street    **4—Align center**

Middletown, CA    **5—Font style and size**

**6—Bold**             **7—Italic**                        **8—Underline**

**Our** office has many *buyers* willing to buy a home just like <u>yours</u>. Each of our buyers has been:

1. Prequalified
2. Preapproved    **9—Numbering**

In addition, they also:

• Have 20 percent to put down
• Need to close in 30 days    **10—Bullets**

Information about your neighborhood reflects the following:

**11–Insert table**

| Address | 6211 State Street | 6433 State Street | 6667 State Street |
|---|---|---|---|
| Selling Price | $275,000 | $285,500 | $289,900 |

We look forward to hearing from you soon. Please call us at 877-555-0156.

Mr. and Mrs. Real Estate Agent
**12–Align Right**

Locate items 1–12 in the document above and refer to the following instructions to learn how to perform each task.

1—Insert date
    a. Click Insert on the menu bar.
    b. Click Date and Time.
    c. Choose a date format. Click OK.
    d. The date will be inserted.

2—Align left
    a. Highlight/Select the text to be aligned by double-clicking or clicking and dragging.
    b. Click Align Left located on the Formatting toolbar.
    c. The text will align left.

3—Color
    a. Highlight/Select the text.
    b. Click the down arrow next to the Font Color button on the Formatting toolbar.
    c. Choose a color from the palette.
    d. The text will appear in the color selected.

4—Align center
    a. Highlight/Select the text to be centered.
    b. Click Center located on the Formatting toolbar.
    c. The text will align at the horizontal center of the page.

5—Font style and size

    To change font style:
    a. Highlight/Select the text.
    b. Click the Font style box found on the Formatting toolbar.
    c. Scroll down and find the font desired.
    d. Click the font name.
    e. The text will reflect the font selected.

    To change font size:
    a. Highlight/Select the text.
    b. Click the down arrow next to the Font Size box on the Formatting toolbar.
    c. Find the font size desired and click it.
    d. The text will reflect the font size selected.

6—Bold
    a. Highlight/Select the text.
    b. Click Bold located on the Formatting toolbar.
    c. The text will appear bold.

7—**Italic**
   a.  Highlight/Select the text.
   b.  Click Italic found on the Formatting toolbar.
   c.  The text will appear in italic.

8—**Underline**
   a.  Highlight/Select the text.
   b.  Click Underline on the Formatting toolbar.
   c.  The text will appear underlined.

9—Numbering
   a.  Press the Enter key twice to begin a new paragraph.
   b.  Click Numbering on the Formatting toolbar.
   c.  The number 1 will appear. Key the information next to number 1. Press Enter. The number 2 will appear.

10—Bullets
   a.  Press the Enter key twice to begin a new paragraph.
   b.  Click on Bullets on the Formatting toolbar.
   c.  A bullet will appear. Key the text for the first bullet. When you press Enter, another bullet will appear.

11—Insert table
   a.  Click the Table menu on the Formatting toolbar.
   b.  Click Insert.
   c.  Click Table.
   d.  A dialog box will appear.
   e.  Select how many columns and rows are required and click OK. The table will be inserted into the document.
   f.  Fill in the information desired in each cell of the table.

12—Align right
   a.  Highlight/Select the text.
   b.  Click Align Right on the Formatting toolbar.
   c.  The text will be aligned at the right.

## Advanced Topics

More advanced users can learn to use Mail Merge. Using this feature, you can create personalized letters for clients. It involves a two-step process that merges a generic letter with the names and addresses in a contact list. Labels and envelops can also be created.

## *Additional Features of Microsoft Word*

| FEATURE | WHAT IT IS | WHERE IT IS | USE |
|---|---|---|---|
| Help | Gives information on how to do something | Located at top of screen in the menu bar | Use to answer questions about Word |
| Office Assistant | Provides quick suggestions and help | Located at right of screen | Click it and key a question to get advice and tips |
| Mail Merge | Process to merge names, addresses, and other information into letters | Located in the Tools menu | Quick way to address letters from contact list |
| Envelopes and Labels | Places names and addresses on envelopes and letters | Located in the Tools menu | Quick way to address envelopes and make labels |
| AutoCorrect | Corrects commonly misspelled words automatically | Located in the Tools menu | Corrects spelling errors and saves time |
| WordArt | Adds special effects to text | Located in Insert, Picture and on the Drawing toolbar | Adds variety to a document |
| AutoShapes | Adds shapes to a document | Located in Insert, Picture and on the Drawing toolbar | Adds different shapes to a document |
| Spelling and Grammar | Helps to identify spelling and grammar errors | Located in the Tools menu | Helps prevent errors and saves time |
| Hyperlinks | Links to web pages via the Internet | Located in the Insert menu | Inserts links to web pages |

# RESOURCES FOR FURTHER STUDY

One of the best ways to learn about Word is to use the built-in Help feature. If you have a question about buttons on a toolbar, a menu command, or other areas of the document window, you can click on the What's This? option in the Help menu. When you move the question mark over an item and click, a description appears. More information on how to work with Microsoft Word can be found on the following web sites:

- http://www.baycongroup.com/wlesson0.htm
- http://www.electricteacher.com/tutorials.htm
- http://www.nailitnow.com.au/word

# SELF-ASSESSMENT

To determine the extent of knowledge you acquired in this chapter, choose the correct answer for each of the following.

1. A word processor available in the marketplace is:
   a. Apple
   b. Linux
   c. Microsoft Word
   d. All of the above

2. A word processing program can be found in:
   a. Internet Explorer
   b. Netscape
   c. Microsoft Windows
   d. My Documents

3. A word processor can be used for which of the following activities?
   a. Prospecting
   b. Marketing
   c. Communicating
   d. All of the above

4. A Word document can be saved in:
   a. Control Panel
   b. Accessories
   c. My Documents
   d. Title bar

5. To execute a command in Microsoft Word, the cyber professional:
   a. Uses the mouse
   b. Uses the keyboard
   c. Uses voice recognition
   d. All of the above

6. All of the following are fonts except:
   a. Times New Roman
   b. New American
   c. Tahoma
   d. Verdana

7. What feature should the cyber professional use when he or she has a question about how to work with Microsoft Word?
   a. Search
   b. Find
   c. Help
   d. None of these

8. To make sure a business letter or memo looks professional, the cyber professional can:
   a. Call tech support
   b. Run a virus check
   c. Run a spell check
   d. Add the date and time to the document

9. What should the cyber professional do if My Documents becomes too cluttered with necessary documents?
   a. Delete the documents
   b. Send the documents to the Recycle Bin
   c. Create a folder in My Documents
   d. Do nothing

10. Some of the commands that can be used in Microsoft Word include:
    a. Cut, Copy, Paste
    b. Bold, Italic, Underline
    c. Align right, left, center
    d. All of the above

11. All of the following can be found on the menu bar except:
    a. File
    b. Help
    c. Control Panel
    d. Tools

12. The first step in changing how text looks is to:
    a. Print it
    b. Select/Highlight it
    c. Delete it
    d. Copy it

13. The Minimize button:
    a. Appears on the File menu
    b. Appears on Control Panel
    c. Appears with the Maximize, Restore, and Close buttons
    d. Opens a document

14. What does a software suite imply?
    a. Several programs bundled in one package
    b. Only one feature in the package
    c. Available only to businesses
    d. Available only to cyber professionals

15. The menu bar contains all of the following except:
    a. View
    b. Format
    c. Windows
    d. WordArt

# CHAPTER 6
## THE INTERNET AND THE WORLD WIDE WEB

## PREVIEW

The aim of this chapter is to help the cyber professional acquire a basic understanding of the Internet and the World Wide Web. It provides a brief historical overview of the Internet and the World Wide Web and explains the role of Internet service providers. Included is a discussion about different types of providers and what to look for when choosing one. Also included are mastery skill exercises for connecting to the Internet and using a search engine.

When you finish this chapter, you will be able to:

1. Describe the benefit of the Internet and the World Wide Web to the cyber professional.

2. Trace the background and history of the Internet and World Wide Web.

3. Describe the role and function of Internet service providers.

4. Demonstrate how to connect to the Internet.

5. Conduct meaningful searches utilizing a search engine.

## KEY TERMS

*crawlers*

*directory*

*Internet*

*Internet service providers (ISPs)*

*search engine*

*spiders*

*Uniform Resource Locator (URL)*

*vortal*

*World Wide Web*

# 6.1 How the Internet and the World Wide Web Can Benefit the Cyber Professional

The cyber professional needs to understand how the Internet and the World Wide Web work in order to take advantage of the technology. This knowledge will enable the cyber professional to:

1.  Obtain relevant real estate information from the Internet.

2.  Download and copy important real estate data from the Internet.

3.  Locate essential web sites critical to the selling and buying process.

4.  Communicate via e-mail.

5.  Establish an Internet presence by having a personal web site.

# 6.2 Historical Background

Think about life without the Internet. Today it is as commonplace as the cell phone and the fax machine. People of all ages use the Internet.

## The Internet

The **Internet** is a global network of millions of computers. Imagine a "Galactic Network" connecting people for the exchange of data and information all over the world. J. C. R. Licklider conceived such a concept in 1962. This idea is considered to be the "cradle of the Internet."

The launching of Sputnik by the USSR in 1957 was the beginning point for the concept of the Internet. The United States wanted to establish itself as a world leader in technology. Under President Eisenhower, an organization within the Department of Defense, the Advanced Research Projects Agency (ARPA), was established. A system was needed to decentralize power hubs. The thinking was that if a network of "power centers" could be established throughout the United States, the power could be shifted in the event of an attack on the heart of defense.

## PUTTING IT TOGETHER

National defense was the motive behind the Internet. The launching of Sputnik in 1957 by the USSR was the impetus for creating a "Power Hub" system that could be connected in the event of a disruption of power.

Long before this event, however, numerous other inventions had to be developed. The telegraph, invented in 1836, allowed people to communicate quickly over long distances for the first time. The next stepping stone was the invention of the transatlantic cable in 1858, which established the use of cables for long, direct, and instantaneous communications. The telephone, too, was instrumental as a way to connect computers. Another crucial development was the introduction of packet switching as a way to transfer data. This event was important because it allowed data to take different routes without being interrupted.

The next step was to devise a method that would allow computers to "talk," or network, with each other. This happened in 1965 when a computer in Massachusetts, through a dial-up telephone, was connected to a telephone in California. At UCLA in 1969, the first host computer became operational.

The next milestone occurred in 1972—the launching of e-mail by Ray Tomlinson. Another key element in the advancement of the Internet took place in 1982 with the development of Transmission Control Protocol (TCP)/Internet Protocol (IP), called TCP/IP. This system provided a method for computers to communicate in the same language. In the eighties, this concept was greatly expanded and became more prevalent. Now it is the basic communication language of the Internet. The nineties demonstrated the commercial value of the Internet, particularly in the real estate industry.

---

### PUTTING IT TOGETHER

Ray Tomlinson invented e-mail in 1972.

---

The next chain of events was the introduction of the concept of the World Wide Web.

## The World Wide Web

The computer, the Internet, and the World Wide Web are inextricably connected but the Internet and the World Wide Web are not the same. They serve different purposes and need each other to operate. The Internet is a massive network of networks. The **World Wide Web** is a way of accessing information and communicating over the Internet.

As with many events in history, the World Wide Web was an offshoot of another endeavor involving scientific research. Tim Berners-Lee, a scientist for an organization called CERN, a research laboratory in Europe, invented the World Wide Web in 1989.

---

### PUTTING IT TOGETHER

The World Wide Web was invented in 1989 by Tim Berners-Lee.

---

For the World Wide Web to be able to organize and retrieve information, a device called a browser had to be created. The first widely used browser was used at the University of Illinois in 1993; it was called Mosaic. A browser is capable of locating different pages on the Internet by using bots (short for "robots") that utilize **spiders** or **crawlers** to index Web sites. Once located, the information is retrieved for the user. So computers connected to the Internet could communicate with one another, a common language or special set of rules was established, known as Transmission Control Protocol/Internet Protocol (TCP/IP), discussed earlier.

---

**PUTTING IT TOGETHER**

---

The first browser was called Mosaic.

# 6.3 Internet Service Providers (ISPs)

his section of the chapter discusses ISPs, selection of an ISP, and methods of connecting to the Internet.

**Internet service providers (ISPs)** are companies that provide access to the Internet, thereby allowing the user to take advantage of the World Wide Web. The only way to connect to the Internet is through an ISP. Today there are over 12,000 different ISPs; some are free, while others charge a monthly fee. Common ISPs include Earth-Link (http://www.earthlink.com), Microsoft Network (MSN) (http://www.msn.com), and America Online (AOL) (http://www.aol.com).

---

**PUTTING IT TOGETHER**

---

Popular ISPs include EarthLink, Microsoft Network, and America Online.

## *Criteria for Choosing an ISP*

Deciding which ISP to choose requires the user to analyze his or her needs and the costs involved. When choosing an ISP, the user should consider the following:

- Business and personal needs. Each user needs to assess his or her requirements for operating a successful real estate business. If the user needs the Internet for basic information such as accessing a Multiple Listing Service, then a basic package may be the best solution. On the other hand, if the user has bigger needs, then a more elaborate system may be in order.

- Cost. The old adage "you get what you pay for" applies to choosing an ISP. The cost for an ISP can be a few dollars a month to more than $100 a month. The cyber professional should consider what is included in the package and whether those services meet his or her professional needs. All ISPs are not created equal. The cyber professional may want to research ISPs to find the best one. Many web sites are available that offer comparisons of ISPs.

- Technical support. Another significant factor is whether help is available when it is needed. The user should be able to contact a Help Desk to solve a problem. Having a toll-free number to call is a plus, as is having technical support provided on a 7/24/365 basis. The user may want to make a trial call or check with other users to learn about the quality of service. Is the service prompt? Do the tech support specialists put users on hold and make them wait? Is there prerecorded telephone support that offers solutions to common problems? Does the ISP provide a Help button or a troubleshooting index to help solve issues? Are the tech support specialists helpful and friendly? These are all important considerations. The user may need to commit time and effort in order to learn which ISP will best serve his or her needs.

- Virus and spam protection. With the increased threat of viruses and worms, having a built-in virus protection program is essential. This protection is invaluable when downloading e-mail messages to prevent the spread of viruses or worms. Many ISPs advertise spam protection programs. (Spam, or unsolicited messages, has now become a government issue with laws being enacted to prevent it and substantial fines being assessed to abusers.) Also available are parental controls to protect children from undesirable materials and e-mails. Often these services are part of a package or may be added for an additional fee. The elimination of pop-up advertisements also may be part of the contract.

- E-mail capability and web space capacity. Most ISPs offer the user an e-mail service as part of the package. User considerations include efficiency of the e-mail service and options or enhancements that make the service efficient and useful. Some ISPs offer numerous e-mail aliases, which may be an advantage for real estate professionals who offer numerous services for clients. Having the option to install a program that automatically responds to e-mail, such as an autoresponder, may be beneficial as well. Many ISPs also allow web space in order for the user to establish a web site. The user should consider how elaborate the web site can be and how much space is provided. Often more capacity can be added for a fee.

- Reputation. This is a major factor in the decision-making process. Information about ISPs can be found in IT journals and magazines as well as in e-newsletters. These sources discuss how well an ISP performs and what it has to offer in terms of services and reliability.

- Accessibility for local use and travel. Being able to access an ISP anywhere in the world is becoming more important. Does the ISP provide this service? Does it provide local dial-up without the need to use a long-distance carrier, which can be expensive?

- Privacy and security. These factors refer to the user's account being free from unwanted access or virus attacks.

- Speed of the connection. This is of major concern to the Internet user and may be the most important consideration for choosing an ISP. More about this topic is discussed next.

## Methods and Speed of Connections

The cyber professional has several choices for how to connect to the Internet. The choices range from slow and inexpensive to fast and expensive. Typical means to connect to the Internet include the following:

**Dial-up.** This method, which is the least expensive and the slowest, is accessed through existing telephone lines and piggybacks with a home or business phone. Usually, only one function can be used at a time—the telephone or the Internet. With this method, agents may miss important business calls. Dial-up services are quickly losing market share due to faster connections being offered by competitors at comparable prices. This method of connection may not be feasible for many real estate professionals.

**Broadband.** This system uses existing phone lines or cable, but with vastly improved connection speeds and data transfer. By paying slightly higher fees, the cyber professional can accomplish a lot more in less time.

**Digital Subscriber Lines (DSL).** DSL is a popular way to connect to the Internet for personal as well as business use. This method also uses telephone lines, but they are dedicated for Internet connections only. This method allows the user to make and receive telephone calls and use the Internet at the same time. DSL is much faster than dial-up, but transfer speed depends on how many users are using the system.

**Cable Modem.** This method is also widely used by business professionals since it has superior speed when compared with a dial-up system. However, connection speed is dependent upon how close the user is to the power source.

**Satellite Dish.** This may be the only alternative for those users who do not have access to DSL or cable. This option is much faster than a dial-up.

**Wireless.** The wireless era has arrived in many areas in the United States. In the past, wireless service was spotty, notoriously slow, and not very cost-effective. It has a gained new ground with improved technology and may be commonplace in the future.

---

### PUTTING IT TOGETHER

Common ways to connect to the Internet include dial-up, cable, and DSL. Wireless is becoming more economical and commonplace.

---

The speed of the connection is of utmost concern. Connection speed is measured in terms of bits per second (bps). Faster speeds—kilobits (Kbps), megabits (Mbps), and gigabits (Gbps)—are more costly. Each type of connection has advantages and disadvantages. Determining which method and speed to choose is based on need and budget. Once the user has made a decision, he or she must get connected. This process can be done by the user or by professionals. It will be covered in the Skill Mastery section of this chapter.

## Internet Browsers

The browser is the mechanism that allows the user to interface with the World Wide Web by looking for information with the use of spiders and crawlers. With the aid of Hypertext Transfer Protocol (HTTP), the browser is able to communicate with web servers on the Internet and locate and retrieve information requested by the user. As was mentioned earlier, the first browser was called Mosaic. It was introduced in 1993.

***Types of Browsers.*** Several different browsers are available. Choosing which one to use will depend on the user's needs and preferences. All browsers perform similar tasks. The browsers used by most Internet users are Netscape Navigator and Internet Explorer. Each has its own special characteristics. Other browsers include Apple's Safari, Opera, and Lynx. New browsers are in the works, while those already on the market are always being upgraded. Since Microsoft's Internet Explorer is so popular, the textbook will illustrate its main features and functions.

---

### PUTTING IT TOGETHER

Netscape and Internet Explorer are two popular browsers.

***Internet Explorer.*** Internet Explorer has gone through several versions over the years. The goal of each upgrade is to make the browser work more efficiently and to offer more options for the user. Usually, a browser is preinstalled on new computers. Should a user want a different browser or want to add an additional one, he or she can do so by downloading the browser program, usually free of charge. Many users take advantage of both Netscape and Internet Explorer.

## Search Engines

A **search engine** is a computer program used to locate and retrieve information from the World Wide Web. To accomplish this task, a search engine uses tools called spiders and crawlers to hunt down specific information on the Web via links. It is estimated that there are over 12,000 different types of engines, divided into two groups. The individual type does a search from its own databases, whereas the metatype searches from other multiple databases. Interestingly, search engines detect only a sampling of the 2 billion-plus web pages! Therefore, several search engines should be used in conducting a search. Determining which one to use creates a challenge for the user. The choice the user makes depends on his or her preferences and experiences.

***Types of Search Engines.*** Common search engines include the following:

- Google (http://www.google.com)

- AltaVista (http://www.altavista.com)

- Dogpile (http://www.dogpile.com)

- Ask Jeeves (http://www.ask.com)

- About (http://www.about.com)

***Search Strategies.*** When searching the Web for information, a search engine retrieves possibilities called "hits." These hits represent information about the topic being searched. To narrow their search and get exactly they need, users should use search strategies that make the activity less time-consuming and more accurate. One popular method for searching is called Boolean logic. This technique attempts to isolate precise information by using special words such as *AND, OR,* and *NOT.* These words are capitalized to assist the search engine in seeking out the desired information. Boolean logic means that the search should include something AND something else, OR to search for either one, or NOT include something. Other suggestions for improving a search include the following:

- Use keywords or phrases.

- Be specific.

- Use correct spelling.

- Use nouns and objects.

- Keep the search simple.

---

### PUTTING IT TOGETHER

The Boolean operators are AND, OR, and NOT.

---

***Directory and Vortal.*** Besides search engines, the user can also use directories. Often these two terms are used interchangeably. Technically, the **directory** is a list of categories or subjects that link to more information on a given topic. It does not utilize keywords for a search, but instead uses a list of possible topics. A **vortal** (Vertical Industry Portal) is a web site that provides information and resources for a particular industry. Vortals typically provide news, research and statistics, discussions, newsletters, online tools, and other services that educate users about a specific industry. An example is http://www.realtor.com, which addresses itself strictly to real estate topics.

---

### *PUTTING IT TOGETHER*

A directory lists numerous categories for a search. A vortal provides information on a specific topic.

## Computer Applications

The next section helps the cyber professional develop skills in setting up an Internet connection, navigating the Web, and using a search engine.

**Skill Mastery Exercise 1**

Setting up an Internet connection. To set up an Internet connection, complete the following steps. (These steps will vary depending on the version of Windows you are using.)

1. From the Start button, select Control Panel. Then from the Network and Internet Connections category, select Create a New Connection.

2. From the Welcome screen, select Next. Then in the New Connection Wizard, select Next.

3. With the help of the Wizard, select Connect to the Internet. Then select Next.

4. With the help of the Wizard, select either Choose from an ISP list or Set-up manually for a dial-up. (To do this, have an account name, password, and the phone number of the ISP ready when prompted by the Wizard.)

5. From the Completing the New Connection screen, select Finish or go online.

In Windows XP, follow these steps:

1. Click the Start button. Then click Control Panel.

2. Choose Network and Internet connections. Then choose Set up or change your Internet connection.

3. The Internet Properties dialog box appears, with the connections tab selected. Click the Setup button.

4. The New Connection Wizard Welcome screen appears. Click Next.

5. The option Connect to the Internet is already selected. Click Next.

6. Select from these options: Choose from a list of Internet service providers (ISPs), Set up my connection manually (for a dial-up connection), or Use the CD I got from an ISP. For the dial-up connection, you need an account name, a password, and the phone number of the ISP. Click Next.

7. Follow the Wizard's instructions. Click Finish when you are done.

After following these directions, you are ready to access the Internet.

The following illustrations show steps in the setup of an Internet connection.

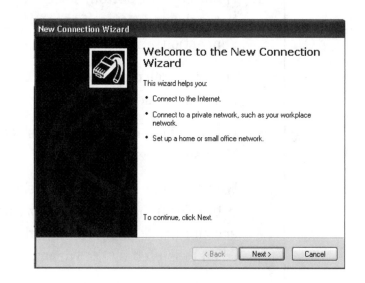

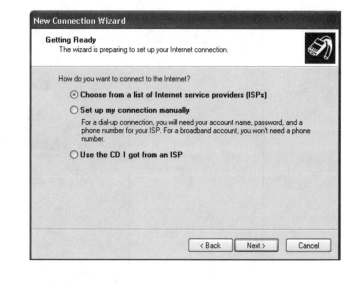

After setting up an Internet connection, when trying to access the Web, you will see a screen like the one shown below.

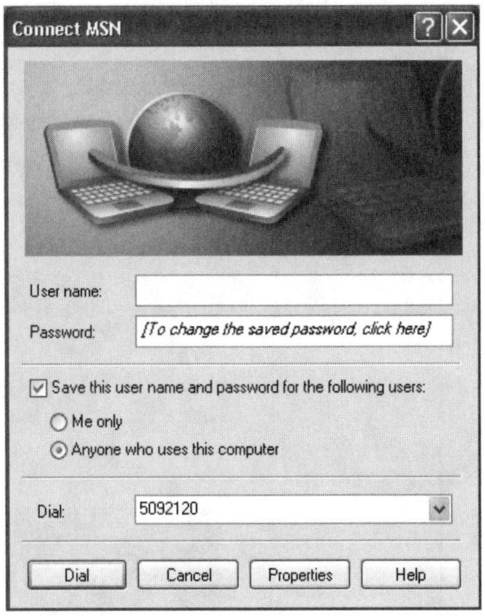

Simply key a user name and password. To make a dial-up connection, select Dial. You are now ready to use the World Wide Web.

---

**Skill Mastery Exercise 2**

Accessing the World Wide Web. To start working on the Web, complete the following steps:

1. In the Address Bar, key the address of the web site you want to access. The address will be a **Uniform Resource Locator (URL).** The address you key in will look similar to this: http://www.realtor.com.

Each web site has a different address. Most browsers today do not require that you include the *http://* in front of *www.*

2. After you key the URL in the Address Bar, press the Enter key on the keyboard or the Go button on the same line as the URL. The web site will appear.

---

**Skill Mastery Exercise 3**

Using a search engine. To locate information using a search engine, complete the following steps:

1. In the Address Bar, key http://www.google.com.

2. In the search box, key the following keywords: Feng Shui.

3.  Click the Search button. Numerous hits, or matches, for information will appear on the screen.  Click on the links to search for the information required.

| | |
|---|---|
| **Skill Mastery Exercise 4** | Using a search engine. Try using a different search engine.<br><br>1.  In the Address Bar, key http://www.altavista.com.<br><br>2.  In the search box, key the following keywords: Feng Shui.<br><br>3.  Click the Find button. Compare this search with that of Google. |
| **Skill Mastery Exercise 5** | Using a directory. A directory represents information related to categories. To locate information from a directory, complete the following steps:<br><br>1.  In the Address Bar, key http://www.yahoo.com.<br><br>2.  Locate a link to an area of interest, such as real estate.<br><br>3.  Click on the topic desired. Compare this system to that of a search engine |
| **Skill Mastery Exercise 6** | Using a vortal. A vortal is a web site that includes information related exclusively to a specific topic, such as real estate. To locate information from a vortal, complete the following steps:<br><br>1.  In the Address Bar, key http://www.ired.com.<br><br>2.  Locate an area of interest, such as Feng Shui.<br><br>3.  Compare the information you found here with that of a search engine and a directory. |

## RESOURCES FOR FURTHER STUDY

Kersnar, Scott. *NetSuccess: How Real Estate Agents Use the Internet.* O'Reilley & Associates, 1996.

Lehnert, Wendy G. *Internet 101:  A Beginner's Guide to the Internet and the World Wide Web.* Addison-Wesley, 1998.

# SELF-ASSESSMENT

To determine the extent of knowledge you acquired in this chapter, choose the correct answer for each of the following.

1. What was the impetus behind the development of the Internet?
   a. The stock market
   b. Consumer needs
   c. E-commerce
   d. National defense

2. When did the World Wide Web become a reality?
   a. 1989
   b. Early 1990s
   c. 2000
   d. 1972

3. Who was the person responsible for the invention of the World Wide Web?
   a. Ray Tomlinson
   b. Tim Berners-Lee
   c. President Eisenhower
   d. J. C. R. Licklider

4. Which of the following is an example of an ISP?
   a. MSN
   b. EarthLink
   c. America Online
   d. All of the above

5. An example of a search engines is:
   a. AltaVista
   b. Ask Jeeves
   c. Google
   d. All of the above

6. Which words are included in a Boolean search?
   a. AND, OR, NOT
   b. And, or, not
   c. ALL, BOTH, NONE
   d. None of these

7. The concept of spiders and crawlers refers to:
   a. Microsoft Windows
   b. Microsoft Word
   c. The Internet
   d. Search engines

8. Methods of connecting to the Internet include:
   a. Cable modem
   b. DSL
   c. Dial-up
   d. All of the above

9. Which of the following suggests a faster speed for an Internet connection?
   a. 10 bps
   b. 10 Kbps
   c. 10 Mbps
   d. 10 Gbps

10. To set up an Internet connection on a computer, the user goes to:
    a. Toolbar
    b. Status bar
    c. Control Panel
    d. Menu bar

11. In terms of an Internet service provider, what does DSL stand for?
    a. Designated Subscriber Lines
    b. Digital Subscriber Lines
    c. Double Speed Lines
    d. None of these

12. Where is a URL entered?
    a. Address Bar
    b. Menu bar
    c. Taskbar
    d. Control bar

13. Which of the following statements about spam is true?
    a. There is no way to prevent it.
    b. It is solicited e-mail.
    c. Many ISPs protect against it.
    d. The government has not become involved in the issue.

14. Examples of browsers include all of the following except:
    a. Netscape
    b. Opera
    c. Internet Explorer
    d. Windows

15. An important consideration for choosing an ISP includes all of the following except?
    a. Cost
    b. Business needs
    c. Brand of computer
    d. Technical support

# CHAPTER 7
## THE BROWSER: INTERNET EXPLORER

## PREVIEW

This chapter discusses the Internet browser program called Internet Explorer and its benefits to the cyber professional. The chapter briefly discusses the benefits to the cyber professional, then continues with a getting-acquainted section on the basic features and functions of Internet Explorer. Next, the chapter covers how to work with Internet Explorer and provides activities to acquire skill in using the browser.

When you finish this chapter, you will be able to:

1. Describe the benefits of Internet Explorer to the cyber professional.

2. Identify and describe the basic features and functions of Internet Explorer.

3. Navigate Internet Explorer effectively to accomplish tasks required of a cyber professional.

4. Demonstrate skill in working with several key functions of Internet Explorer.

## KEY TERMS

| | |
|---|---|
| *Address Bar* | *Internet Explorer* |
| *Back* | *menu bar* |
| *Explorer bar* | *navigation bar* |
| *Favorites* | *Refresh* |
| *Forward* | *scroll bar* |
| *Help* | *Search* |
| *home page* | *Stop* |
| *hyperlink* | *title bar* |

# 7.1 How Internet Explorer Can Benefit the Cyber Professional

Knowing how Internet Explorer works and understanding how to navigate in the program allows the cyber professional to do most of the computer applications work in real estate. This knowledge will enable the cyber professional to:

1. Acquire information from the Internet.

2. Maneuver within Internet Explorer.

3. Utilize special tools available in Internet Explorer to be more efficient.

# 7.2 Historical Background

As explained in Chapter 4, the concept of GUI is critical to being able to navigate with **Internet Explorer.** Internet Explorer, like most programs, has evolved over time with newer and better versions being developed. New versions introduced to the market update former versions and take advantage of advances in technology.

### PUTTING IT TOGETHER

GUI was a major breakthrough in allowing the smooth and effective navigation of the Web.

# 7.3 Getting Acquainted with Internet Explorer

Several methods allow you to access Internet Explorer. Each is listed below.

- Go to the Start menu and click Programs. Then locate and click Internet Explorer.

- Click the Internet Explorer icon found on the Windows desktop.

- Launch Internet Explorer from the shortcut bar.

- Program the computer to automatically launch Internet Explorer when the computer is turned on.

- Click a "hot key" programmed on the keyboard.

---

### *PUTTING IT TOGETHER*

There are several ways to launch Internet Explorer:
- Start menu
- Internet Explorer icon on the desktop
- "Hot key" on the keyboard

## *Title Bar*

The **title bar,** as in Microsoft Word, displays the name of the application and the name of the active document. It is located at the top of the screen. Also found on this line are the Minimize, Maximize, Restore, and Close buttons. An illustration of the title bar follows.

Welcome to MSN.com - Microsoft Internet Explorer

## *Menu Bar*

The **menu bar** is located below the title bar. An illustration is shown below.

File   Edit   View   Favorites   Tools   Help

Not all menus on the menu bar are presented here. Only often-used menus are discussed below.

- File. The File menu contains New, Open, Save, Save As, and Print.
- Edit. The Edit menu contains Cut, Copy, Paste, and Select All.
- View. The View menu contains Toolbars, Status Bar, Stop, and Refresh.
- Favorites. The **Favorites** menu contains Add To Favorites, Organize Favorites, and an established list of favorites
- Tools. This menu contains Mail and News, Synchronize, and Internet Options.
- Help. The **Help** menu contains the Contents and Index of a list of troubleshooting topics. An Online Support option is also available.

Also located on the menu bar is the Microsoft Network icon. It indicates the status of the network connection.

## Navigation Bar

The **navigation bar,** located below the menu bar, is shown in the following illustration.

As you can see, it contains the following buttons:

- **Back.** This button allows the user to go back to the previous web page.
- **Forward.** This button allows the user to go forward from the current web page.
- **Stop.** This button stops the activity just activated by the user.
- **Refresh.** This button updates the currently displayed web page.
- Home. Each browser has a **home page,** the web page that a browser is set to use when it starts up. This home page can be a web site that the user programs. When this button is clicked, the browser goes directly to the home page. (The setup of this

feature is presented in Computer Applications later in the chapter.)

---

### PUTTING IT TOGETHER

Navigation buttons include Back, Forward, Stop, Refresh, and Home.

## Address Bar

The **Address Bar** is below the navigation bar. It has an area where the user can key in a URL. An illustration is shown below.

| Address | ⬀ http://www.msn.com/ | ▼ | ⟳ Go | Links » |

Located next to the address bar are the following:

- A down arrow. ▾ When this button is clicked, a drop-down list of previously visited sites is displayed.

- Go. ⟳Go When this button is clicked, the browser takes the user to the URL shown in the address bar.

## Explorer Bar

The **Explorer bar** is located below the address bar. It is shown below.

| Google ▾ | | ▼ | 🔍 Search Web ▾ | 📑 36 blocked | 🔧 Options |

The Explorer bar contains the following buttons:

- Search. The **Search** button opens a search engine. The user does a search, which returns relevant topics, or "hits."

- Favorites. When clicked, Favorites brings up a list of previously added **hyperlinks,** elements in an electronic document that link to another place in the same document or to an entirely different document. (Organizing Features is presented in Computer Applications later in the chapter.)

- Media. The Media menu contains My Documents, My Videos, More Media, and Radio Guide.

- History. History shows all of the web sites visited for however long the user chooses. (Working with this function is covered in Computer Applications later in the chapter.)

## Status Bar

The status bar is located at the bottom of the screen. It displays information about the transfer of a web document to the browser. An illustration is shown below.

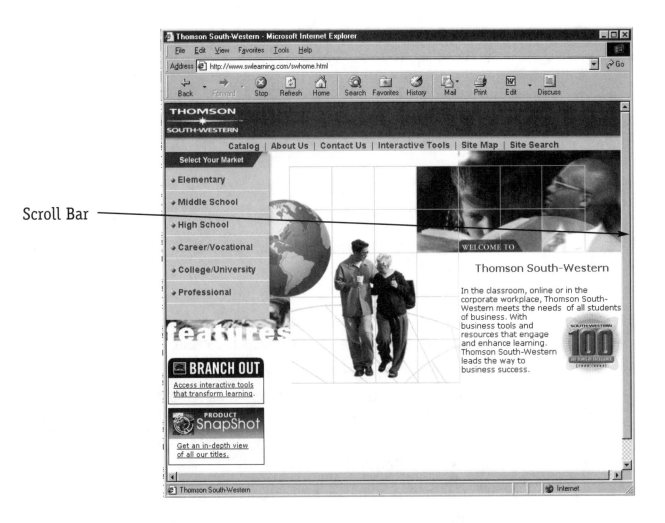

## Scroll Bar

The **scroll bar** is located on the right side of the screen. It is used to move the screen up or down within a web page. An illustration is shown on the next page.

## INTERNET EXPLORER QUICK REFERENCE GUIDE

| ICON | MENU/BUTTON | APPLICATION | WHERE IT IS |
|---|---|---|---|
| File | **File** | Allows the user to get a new file, open an existing file, and save a file | On the menu bar |
| Edit | **Edit** | Allows the user to cut, copy, and paste | On the menu bar |
| View | **View** | Allows the user to change how a web page is viewed or how Internet Explorer looks | On the menu bar |
| Favorites | **Favorites** | Allows the user to save or bookmark selected web sites | On the menu bar |
| Help | **Help** | Allows the user to find information on how to do something in the program | On the menu bar |
| Back | **Back** | Allows the user to go back to the previous web page | On the navigation bar |
| Forward | **Forward** | Allows the user to go to the next web page | On the navigation bar |

## *INTERNET EXPLORER QUICK REFERENCE GUIDE (CONTINUED)*

| ICON | MENU/BUTTON | APPLICATION | WHERE IT IS |
|------|-------------|-------------|-------------|
|  | **Stop** | Allows the user to discontinue an activity | On the navigation bar |
|  | **Refresh** | Allows the user to update the currently displayed web page | On the navigation bar |
|  | **Home** | Allows the user to go directly to the home page | On the navigation bar |
| Address | **Address Bar** | Allows the user to key in a URL | Next to the address window |
| Search | **Search** | Allows the user to look for information on a selected topic | On the menu bar |
| Media | **Media** | Allows the user to go directly to media services | On the menu bar |
|  | **History** | Allows the user to see what web sites have been recently visited | On the menu bar |
|  | **Scroll Bar** | Allows the user to navigate up and down the screen | On the right side of the screen |

# 7.4 Computer Applications

This section demonstrates how to work with some of the features and functions of Internet Explorer.

**SKILL MASTERY EXERCISE 1**

Accessing web sites. To learn how to access web sites using URLs, complete the following steps:

1. Open Internet Explorer.

2. Locate the Address Bar.

3. Key the following URL: http://www.realtor.com.

4. Click Go or press the Enter key.

The home page for REALTOR.com® should appear. It should look like this:

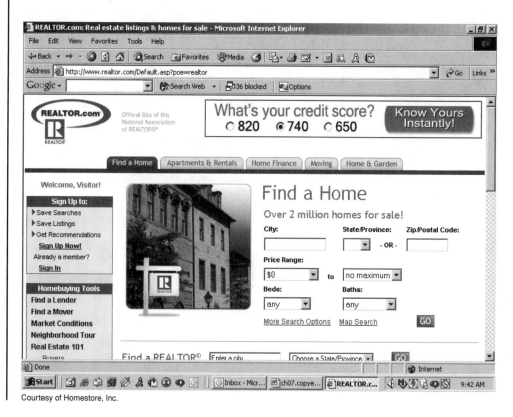

Courtesy of Homestore, Inc.

**SKILL MASTERY
EXERCISE 2**

Accessing web sites. Try accessing another web site.

1.  Key the following URL: http://www.homes.com.

2.  Click Go or press the Enter key.

The Homes.com web site should appear. It should look like this:

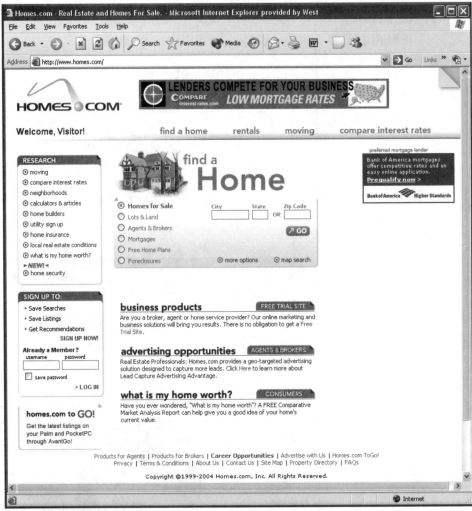

Courtesy of Homes.com

**SKILL MASTERY
EXERCISE 3**

Accessing web sites. Try accessing another web site.

1.  Key the following URL: http://www.internetcrusade.com.

2.  Click Go or press the Enter key.

The home page for RealTown's InternetCrusade should appear. It should look like this:

Courtesy of Real Estate Electronic Publishing Company

Why is being able to access a web site so important? Locating information on the World Wide Web is critical for being a successful agent. It allows the user to access online Multiple Listing Services and information about loans, neighborhoods, and more.

**SKILL MASTERY
EXERCISE 4**

Setting a home page. Learn how to set the home page with a web site that appears whenever Internet Explorer is accessed or when Home is clicked on the menu bar.

1. On the menu bar, click Tools.

2. Select Internet Options.

3. On the General tab, locate Home page.

4. In the text field, key the URL of the web site that is to be used as the home page; in this case, http://www.realtor.com. Click OK.

**SKILL MASTERY
EXERCISE 5**

Setting a home page. Try setting another home page.

1. On the menu bar, click Tools.

2. Select Internet Options.

3. On the General tab, locate Home page.

4. In the text field, key the URL of a web site that you want as your home page. Click OK.

Your home page should appear.

Why is knowing how to set a home page important? The main purpose of setting a home page is to be able to quickly access a site that is used on a regular basis. The user saves time by not having to key the URL each time he or she wants to access the web site.

**SKILL MASTERY
EXERCISE 6**

Setting up a web site list. To create a Favorites list, work through the following steps:

1. In the Address Bar, key http://www.realtor.com.

2. Click Favorites on the menu bar.

3. Click Add. Click OK.

The web site http://www.realtor.com has been added to your Favorites list. Your screen should look like this:

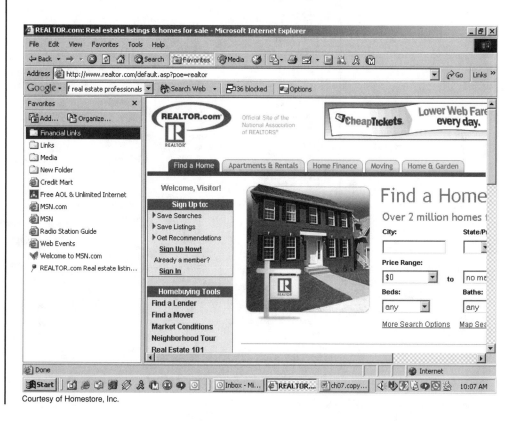

Courtesy of Homestore, Inc.

**SKILL MASTERY EXERCISE 7**

Setting up a web site list. Try using Favorites again.

1. Go to http://www.internetcrusade.com.

2. Click Favorites. Click Add. Click OK.

RealTown's InternetCrusade has been added to your Favorites list.

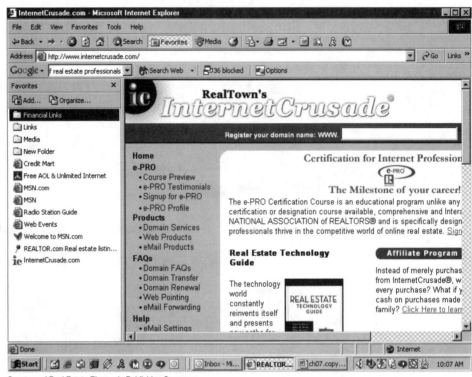

Courtesy of Real Estate Electronic Publishing Company

**SKILL MASTERY EXERCISE 8**

Organizing the Favorites list. Learn how to create a folder for organizing the Favorites list.

1. If not already done, add http://www.homes.com and http://www.internetcrusade.com to Favorites.

2. Select Favorites from the menu bar.

3. Click Organize.

4. Click Create Folder.

5. In New Folder, key *Real Estate Web Sites*.

6. Click Close.

You will see the new folder you just created.

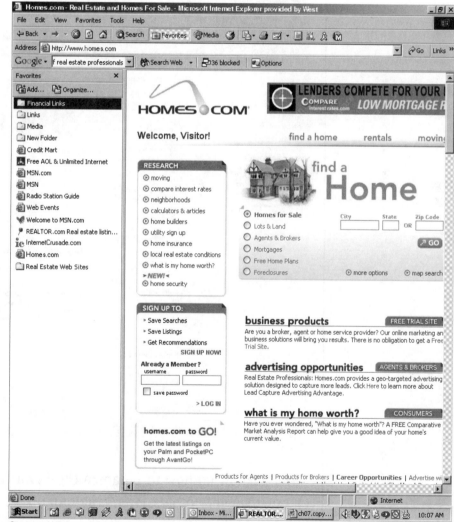

Courtesy of Homes.com

**SKILL MASTERY**
**EXERCISE 9**

Organizing the Favorites list. Now you can place all relevant web sites in the new folder.

1.  Click Favorites.

2.  Click Add to Favorite.

3.  Click on the Real Estate Web Sites folder to open it.

4.  Click and drag each of the three real estate web sites to the folder.

Now all of the web sites related to real estate are organized in one folder.

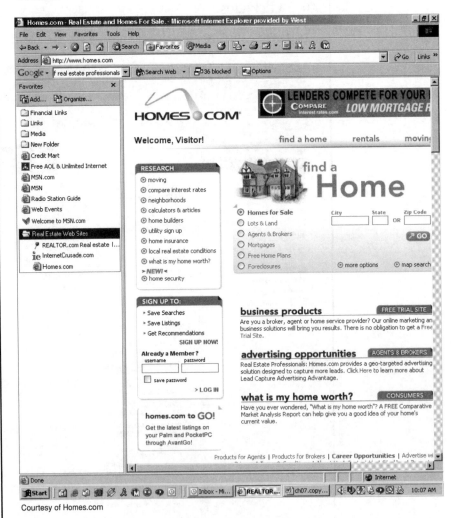

Courtesy of Homes.com

Why is knowing how to organize the Favorites list important? This helps the cyber professional stay organized. He or she is able to access a folder that contains all web site addresses pertaining to a particular topic.

**SKILL MASTERY
EXERCISE 10**

Deleting temporary files. This action deletes unnecessary files that get stored in the hard drive. It's a good idea to delete these temporary files occasionally to free up hard disk space.

1.  Go to Tools on the menu bar.

2.  Click Internet Options.

3.  In Temporary Internet files, click Delete Files. Click OK.

The unnecessary temporary files are erased.

Why is being able to delete temporary files important? A computer can get bogged down with unused files. When files are deleted, more memory becomes available on the hard disk.

**SKILL MASTERY**
**EXERCISE 11**

Clearing links. Learn how to clear folders that contains links to pages you have visited. You can keep the links between 0 and 999 days.

1. Click Tools on the menu bar.

2. Click Internet Options.

3. Under History, change the setting so the computer keeps pages in history or Clear History.

The list of recently visited web site is erased when you click Clear History. An advantage of having a history is being able to access a web site quickly because you did not add it to Favorites or because you forgot its URL.

Why is being able to clear links important? This is another option you can use to free up hard disk space.

# SELF-ASSESSMENT

To determine the extent of knowledge you acquired in this chapter, choose the correct answer for each of the following.

1. One of the most popular browsers for interfacing with the World Wide Web is:
   a. Opera
   b. Safari
   c. Internet Explorer
   d. Internet Windows

2. What type of program is necessary to interact with the World Wide Web?
   a. Windows
   b. Word processor
   c. Browser
   d. Search engine

3. Why would a new version of a browser be introduced?
   a. To take advantage of advances in technology
   b. To correct past problems
   c. To increase the efficiency of the browser
   d. All of the above

4. All of the following can be found on the menu bar except:
   a. View
   b. Edit
   c. File
   d. Search

5. The File menu contains which of the following:
   a. Cut
   b. Paste
   c. Select All
   d. None of these

6. The primary function of Favorites is to:
   a. Access frequently used web sites
   b. List the top ten web sites on the Internet
   c. Use as a search engine
   d. Troubleshoot computer problems

# RESOURCES FOR FURTHER STUDY

Kersnar, Scott. *NetSuccess: How Real Estate Agents Use the In*
O'Reilly & Associates, 1996.

Lehnert, Wendy G. *Internet 101: A Beginner's Guide to the Int*
*and the World Wide Web.* Addison-Wesley, 1998.

Mayo, Don. *Learning the Internet.* DDC Publishing, 1999.

http://www.boutell.com/newfaq/basic

http://www.computerhope.com

http://whatis.techtarget.com

Note: Microsoft has had to respond to the increased activity o
"hackers" on the internet by providing special "patches" and
"updates" to protect the integrity of its Internet Explorer brow
These updates can be found at http://www.microsoft.com und
"Security."

Internet users may wish to explore other avenues for connectir
the Net. Popular alternatives to Internet Explorer include Opera
(http://www.opera.com) and Mozilla (http://www.mozilla.org).
browsers are free.

7. You may see all of the following in the Address Bar except:
   a. Home page web address
   b. E-mail address
   c. Favorites web address
   d. URL

8. The Explorer bar contains which of the following?
   a. Search
   b. History
   c. Media
   d. All of the above

9. Frequently used web sites are found in:
   a. Search
   b. Help
   c. Favorites
   d. View

10. Save As is found in what menu?
    a. File
    b. Edit
    c. View
    d. Favorites

11. When a cyber professional wants to print a document, he or she goes to:
    a. Edit
    b. Status bar
    c. Address Bar
    d. File

12. To change the start page, the cyber professional goes to:
    a. Start
    b. Title bar
    c. Tools
    d. Status bar

13. Which of the following is a navigation tool?
    a. Back
    b. Forward
    c. Stop
    d. All of the above

14. To save an often-used URL, the cyber professional goes to:
    a. Favorites
    b. Search
    c. Help
    d. None of these

15. Why might the cyber professional use Internet Explorer?
    a. To search real estate web sites
    b. To access the Multiple Listing Service
    c. To obtain information about real estate topics
    d. All of the above

# CHAPTER 8
## THE BASICS OF E-MAIL

## PREVIEW

Chapters Eight and Nine provide the basics of e-mail and discuss Microsoft Outlook®. To compete in the electronic era, the cyber professional must understand e-mail and be able to use this popular mode of communication. As stated in Chapter One, the Internet Empowered Consumer not only expects it, but also demands it!

When you finish this chapter, you will be able to:

1. State how e-mail can benefit the cyber professional.

2. Understand the role of e-mail in the real estate industry.

3. Describe the basic elements of e-mail.

4. Set up a free e-mail account.

## KEY TERMS

| | |
|---|---|
| *blind carbon copy (bcc)* | *Hotmail* |
| *body* | *netiquette* |
| *carbon copy* | *spam* |
| *emoticons* | *Subject* |
| *encryption* | *Yahoo* |

# 8.1 How E-mail Can Benefit the Cyber Professional

If the cyber professional expects to compete in the e-real estate arena, having an e-mail account and personal e-mail address is a must. With an e-mail address, the cyber professional can:

1. Conduct business on a 24/7/365 basis.

2. Stop paying for telephone and fax calls.

3. Stop playing telephone tag.

4. Communicate with individuals and groups through a contact list.

5. Create e-newsletters that can be distributed to a contact list.

6. Achieve a higher level of satisfaction with buyers and sellers.

The list of benefits from using e-mail is continually growing. The use of e-mail has become a standard for conducting everyday business. As such, it is useful in the real estate profession.

### PUTTING IT TOGETHER

E-mail is essential for doing business on a 24/7/365 basis.

Since its invention by Ray Tomlinson in 1972, e-mail has become a form of communication used by billions of people. Studies show that most businesses use this form of communication and that e-mail has made a significant impact on productivity, efficiency, and satisfaction.

# 8.2 How E-mail Works

With the assistance of an ISP, e-mail messages are transmitted from sender to recipient. The message to be sent is transferred to a server using a protocol called Simple Mail Transfer Protocol (SMTP). The mail server, in turn, delivers the message out to the Internet. The mail server also stores incoming messages for users. When requested, these messages are retrieved using a protocol called Post Office Protocol 3 (POP3). SMTP and POP3 provide the basis for electronic communication between sender and recipient. To set-up an e-mail account, the cyber professional must be connected to the Internet via an ISP. The next step is to set up an account with an e-mail provider. Knowing the outgoing and incoming mail server names is necessary to establish a connection. With some providers, this function may be done automatically.

For e-mail to work, an e-mail account must be created. Every e-mail account has an associated e-mail address. An example of an e-mail address is as follows: eculbertson@cyberprofessional.com. The first part of the address, the username, identifies the sender. The @ sign (read "at") comes next, followed by the domain name. Several domain names are available. This will be discussed in a later chapter

# 8.3 Basic Features and Functions

The following material explains the different parts of an e-mail message.

## The Anatomy of an E-Mail Message

The format used for e-mail messages may vary slightly depending on the program used. The message window in Outlook Express® looks similar to this:

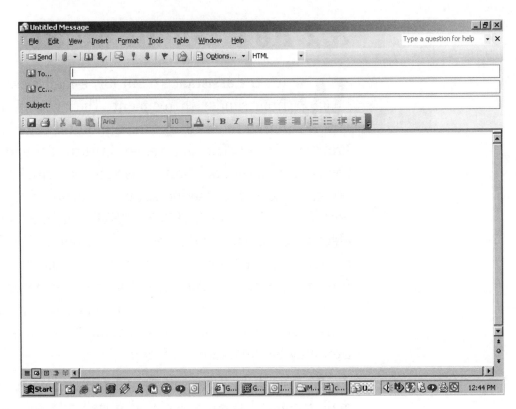

## Headings of an E-Mail Message

- To:  Is the e-mail address of the recipient or recipients

- Cc:  Stands for **carbon copy;** gives the sender the option of sending the same message to other recipients

- Bcc:  Stands for **blind carbon copy;** used to send a copy of the message to  someone without the receiver knowing the other mail recipients

- **Subject:**  States what the message is about; is important to include since many recipients choose to read or delete messages based on the content of the subject line

- Attachments. Used to attach a file to the e-mail message (A mastery skill exercise will show how to send attachments later in the textbook.)

The **body** is the main section of the e-mail message. A set of guidelines, called **netiquette,** dictates the proper way to communicate on the Internet. Netiquette is addressed later in the chapter.

A typical e-mail message looks similar to this:

---

## PUTTING IT TOGETHER

The format of e-mail messages is similar in most e-mail programs.

---

When composing a message, the cyber professional can use the same formatting features that are found in Microsoft Word. Some of these features include the following:

- Font

- Font Size

- Font Style (Bold, Italic, and Underline)

- Align left, center, align right, and justify

- Numbering and bullets

- Font Color

***Title and Menu Bars.*** The title bar shows the subject of the message being composed as well as the minimize, maximize, and close buttons. The menu bar displays the different operations that can be performed, such as:

1. File

2. Edit

3. View

4. Insert

5. Format

6. Tools

7. Table

8. Window

9. Help

***Toolbar.*** This contains different options for the user and may include the following:

1. Send

2. Insert File

3. Address Book

4. Check Names

5. Permission

6. Importance High

7. Importance Low

8. Message Flag

9. Create Rule

10. Options

11. Message Format

# 8.4 Using E-Mail

This section discusses Hotmail and Yahoo, two free web-based e-mail programs. With web-based programs, the user can read or write e-mail wherever he or she has access to the Internet. This section also discusses topics of netiquette, spam, and emoticons, among others.

## *Hotmail*

**Hotmail** is a popular free e-mail service. It is part of the Microsoft Network (MSN) that comes preinstalled on many computers. Hotmail is simple to set up and easy to learn how to use. It offers many services of fee-based programs and is an excellent program for individuals new to e-mail. A downside of Hotmail is that it may be vulnerable to **spam,** which is unsolicited "junk" e-mail sent to large numbers of people to promote products or services. Users often find spam to be offensive. Another disadvantage of Hotmail is its limitations in terms of how much data can be stored and the number of activities that can be conducted in a 24-hour period. Overall, Hotmail serves as a good introduction to web-based e-mail and many of the features that are available with non-web based e-mail clients such as Eudora. Once the cyber professional has mastered Hotmail, he or she may decide to move on to a more advanced system.

---

### *PUTTING IT TOGETHER*

Hotmail is free and is simple to learn and use.

---

***How to Set Up Hotmail.*** Setting up an account takes only a few minutes. Complete the following steps:

1. Launch Internet Explorer.

2. In the Address Bar, key http://www.hotmail.com.

3.  Locate and click the New Account Sign Up tab.

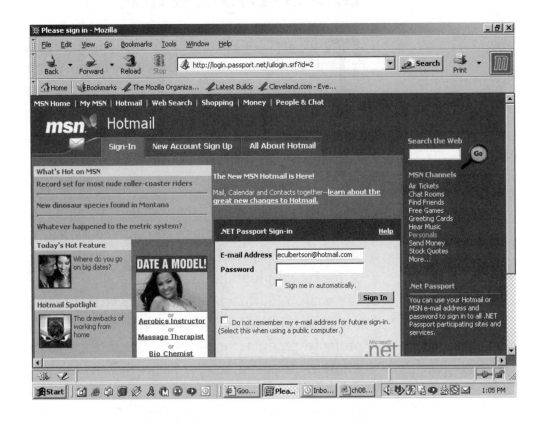

4.  Fill in the profile information requested by the Wizard.

To complete this task, you must choose an e-mail address and a password. Keep the e-mail address simple and remember your password. You may choose to write down your password in case you forget it. Keep in mind that writing down your password is like leaving your keys in the ignition—it's not advised. If you do write down your password, keep it in a secure place. If the e-mail address you select has already been taken, choose an alternative.

5.  Once you have filled out the required information, MSN will ask you to accept or reject its Terms of Use. If you agree, select I Agree and click Continue.

**Get a .NET Passport - Microsoft Internet Explorer**

File   Edit   View   Favorites   Tools   Help

Back · · · | Search | Favorites | Media | | |

Address  https://registernet.passport.net/reg.srf?id=2&lc=   Go    Links »   Norton AntiVirus  ·    SnagIt

**msn  Hotmail**          Sign-In    New Account Sign-Up    All About Hotmail

## Registration

Complete this form to register for a Hotmail account, which is also a Microsoft .NET Passport.

The Hotmail e-mail address and password you create are your .NET Passport credentials. You'll need them to access your Hotmail account and to sign in where you see the .NET Passport sign-in button:  **Sign In** net

**Note** Passport shares your profile information only with MSN sites where you sign in.

What if I want to close my account later?

What does Passport do with my information?

### Profile Information

Help

| | |
|---|---|
| **First Name** | |
| **Last Name** | |
| | Your first and last names will be sent with all outgoing e-mail messages. |
| **Language** | English |
| **Country/Region** | United States |
| **State** | [Choose One] |
| **ZIP Code** | |
| **Time Zone** | Universal Time - GMT |
| **Gender** | ○ Male  ○ Female |
| **Birth Date** | Month   Day    (ex. 1999) |
| **Occupation** | [Select an Occupation] |

### Account Information

| | |
|---|---|
| **E-mail Address** | @hotmail.com |
| **Password** Six-character minimum; no spaces | |
| **Retype Password** | |
| **Secret Question** | Favorite pet's name? |
| **Secret Answer** | |
| **Alternate E-mail Address** (Optional) | |
| | Password-reset instructions are sent to this account. More... |
| **Registration Check** | Type the characters that you see in this picture. Why? |

I can't see this picture.

Characters are not case-sensitive.

Done                                                          Internet

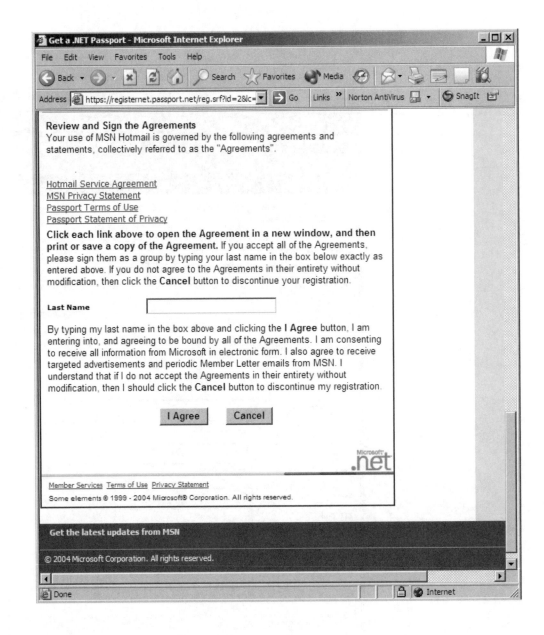

Your new account should look similar to this:

You are ready to begin sending and receiving e-mail messages through Hotmail. Close the program and launch Internet Explorer again. In the Address Bar, key http://www.msn.com. Locate the Sign-In tab and insert your new e-mail address and password. Click Sign In. You're ready to start using your e-mail account.

***Features and Functions of Hotmail.*** Hotmail includes the following links:

- MSN Home. This link takes you back to the MSN home page.

- Mail. Using this tab takes you to your in-box and allows you to send messages.

- Contacts. Using this tab, you can compile an "address book" of contacts.

- Options Using this tab allows you to take advantage of features such as creating a personal signature and protecting against junk e-mail.

- Help. This feature offers help in Hotmail.

More features are available to the user. The best way to learn how to use Hotmail is to experiment with sending and receiving messages.

## *Yahoo*

**Yahoo** is another free web-based e-mail program that has features similar to other programs. Yahoo is easy to set up and easy to operate. To set up a free Yahoo account:

1. Launch Internet Explorer.

2. In the Address Bar, key http://mail.yahoo.com.

3. Follow the directions to set up an e-mail account.

Although Yahoo and Hotmail are similar, the cyber professional should use both of them to see what they offer and which best serves his or her needs. The cyber professional may find that he or she wants to use both programs, but for different purposes.

After using Hotmail and/or Yahoo, the cyber professional may want to use a commercial software program such as Eudora. While Hotmail and Yahoo are web-based, commercial e-mail programs are run on the computer and offer different benefits from web-based e-mail. Eudora has a free version as well as a paid version that includes more options. It can be downloaded and/or purchased at http://www. eudora.com. Another commercial e-mail software program is Microsoft Outlook. This e-mail system will be covered in Chapter Nine.

## *Advanced Topics*

It is not within the scope of this chapter to cover every detail of e-mail. A few related topics are explained here.

***Netiquette.*** Netiquette is an informal set of guidelines that dictates the proper way to communicate on the Internet. The cyber professional should know and adhere to the guidelines. He or she doesn't want to risk inadvertently ending a relationship because of unacceptable behavior. One example of netiquette is not keying messages in all uppercase letters. Another example is not to send spam. More on this topic can be found by going to your favorite search engine and inserting the keyword *netiquette.*

### *PUTTING IT TOGETHER*

The Internet has special rules for conducting business, called netiquette.

**Spam.** Spam is unwanted and unsolicited bulk e-mail that clogs up people's in-boxes. Many e-mail programs and providers have ways to block this type of information. Lawmakers have proposed legislation to make it illegal to send spam.

**Emoticons.** **Emoticons** are a combination of keyboard characters sometimes used in e-mail messages to convey a particular meaning, much like tone of voice is used in spoken communications. An example of an emoticon is the smiley face: :-). More emoticons can be found on the Web.

Acronyms have also made their way into the world of e-mail messages. Frequently used acronyms and their meanings include the following:

- **BTW**    By the way
- **IMHO**   In my humble opinion
- **LOL**    Laughing out loud
- **TIA**    Thanks in advance

**Virus Protection.** Having antivirus software installed on a computer is an absolute must in order to protect against unwanted viruses and worms. Opening e-mail messages that contain contaminated files can cause headaches for the user, as well those people listed in his or her address book, who may become infected as well. E-mail users should avoid opening attachments from untrusted sources.

**Encryption.** **Encryption** is the transformation of data that prevents any unauthorized party from reading or changing data. To encourage computer users to do their banking or to use credit cards online, security programmers have created encryption programs that scramble data and that require special software for interpretation.

**Autoresponder.** An autoresponder is a computer program that automatically responds with a prewritten message to anyone who sends an e-mail message to a particular e-mail address. This lets the sender know that the message has been received. A major criticism of e-agents has been the lack of follow-through in responding to e-mail. Use of an autoresponder can help rectify this source of frustration on the part of the sender.

***Voice E-mail.*** This software program allows the sender to verbally dictate e-mail messages. Another program allows the receiver to hear the messages. The receiver can retrieve these messages from smart phones.

## RESOURCES FOR FURTHER STUDY

http://www.learnthenet.com/english/html/09netiqt.htm

This site provides additional information on netiquette.

http://www.website101.com/email_e-mail

This source provides e-mail news, tutorials, and e-mail basics.

http://www.learnthenet.com/english/section/email.html

This site explains how e-mail works.

# SELF-ASSESSMENT

To determine the extent of knowledge you acquired in this chapter, choose the correct answer for each of the following.

1. Why is encryption software used?
   a. To prevent the intended recipient from reading a sensitive e-mail message
   b. To promote data security in Internet business transactions
   c. To prevent unauthorized parties from reading or changing data.
   d. Both b and c

2. Which two protocols are necessary for e-mail to be processed?
   a. SMTP/POP3
   b. TIA
   c. URL/WWW
   d. None of these

3. What is a common web-based e-mail program?
   a. Yahoo
   b. Hotmail
   c. Eudora
   d. Both a and b

4. If the cyber professional wants to send a message to a group of clients without others knowing about it, he or she uses:
   a. To
   b. From
   c. Cc
   d. Bcc

5. To compose a new message, the cyber professional clicks on which feature?
   a. Reply
   b. Forward
   c. New
   d. In-box

6. To receive and read a message, the cyber professional uses which feature?
   a. In-box
   b. Compose
   c. New
   d. Delete

7. When sending a message, the cyber professional should always include which of the following:
   a. Signature
   b. Subject
   c. Autoresponder
   d. Attachment

8. What is a primary advantage of Hotmail and Yahoo e-mail accounts?
   a. They are free.
   b. They are easy to learn and to use.
   c. They can be used anywhere there is Internet access.
   d. All of the above

9. What is a major disadvantage of a free e-mail account?
   a. It is vulnerable to spam.
   b. It has limits on how much data it can store.
   c. It has limits on how many activities can be conducted in a 24-hour period.
   d. All of the above

10. For the cyber professional to set up an e-mail account, he or she must have:
    a. Encryption software
    b. An autoresponder
    c. A password
    d. Emoticons

11. To get information on how to work with e-mail, the cyber professional goes to:
    a. Search
    b. Help
    c. Find
    d. Compose

12. Junk mail is the same as:
    a. Acronyms
    b. Spam
    c. Netiquette
    d. Emoticons

13. Which of the following is an e-mail address?
    a. http://www.realtor.com
    b. eagent at realtor.com
    c. eagent@realtor.com
    d. None of these

14. What is an example of an acronym that might be used in the body of an e-mail message?
    a. POP3
    b. SMTP
    c. @
    d. LOL

15. The main section of an e-mail message is found where?
    a. To
    b. Subject
    c. Body
    d. Signature

# CHAPTER 9
## ADVANCED E-MAIL:
## MICROSOFT OUTLOOK

## PREVIEW

This second of two chapters on e-mail deals specifically with the features and function of Microsoft Outlook. It also covers how to operate the Outlook e-mail system.

When you finish this chapter, you will be able to:

1. Describe the benefits of Microsoft Outlook to the cyber professional.

2. Understand the features and functions of Outlook.

3. Complete e-mail actions necessary for conducting business.

4. Develop a series of e-mail competency skills.

## KEY TERMS

*attachment*                    *Outlook Today*

*Outlook Express*               *signature*


# 9.1 How Microsoft Outlook Can Benefit the Cyber Professional

Microsoft Outlook meets the needs of most businesses. When using Outlook, the cyber professional can:

1.  Establish a professional presentation for sending e-mail messages.

2.  Establish an Address Book to expedite the sending of e-mail messages.

3.  Create a distribution list for mass e-mail communications.

4.  Create unique stationery and themes for e-mails messages.

5.  Insert a **signature** in each e-mail message.

6.  Include a programmed autoresponder for each e-mail message received.

# 9.2 Introduction

Microsoft Outlook is one of the most commonly used e-mail programs. It comes standard with most versions of Office and can be purchased and installed separately. The program includes most of the features and functions required to conduct a successful real estate practice. This chapter discusses the program and demonstrates how to perform e-mail tasks that will help the cyber professional be successful.

## *Setting Up Microsoft Outlook*

If Outlook is not already installed on a computer, the user must purchase and install the system. Installation is quite simple. All that is required is an Internet service connection with an e-mail account. Once Outlook is installed, the user can access it by creating a shortcut on the Windows desktop or by using the Start button, selecting Programs and then Outlook. Another way the user can access Outlook quickly is to set it up so it opens automatically when the computer is turned on.

---

### *PUTTING IT TOGETHER*

Outlook can be started in several ways.

When Outlook is started, it looks similar to this:

# Outlook Today

**Outlook Today** represents an overview of the entire e-mail system. It allows the user to see the big picture in terms of the Calendar of Events; Tasks to be completed; and the Message Center, which include the Inbox, Drafts, and Outbox. The user can take advantage of many options, some of which are illustrated here.

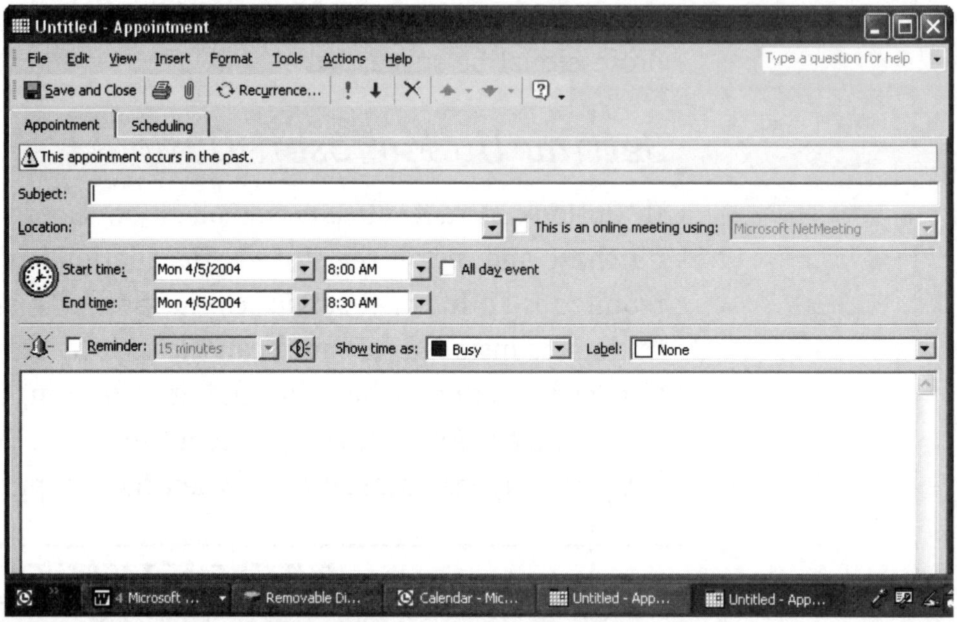

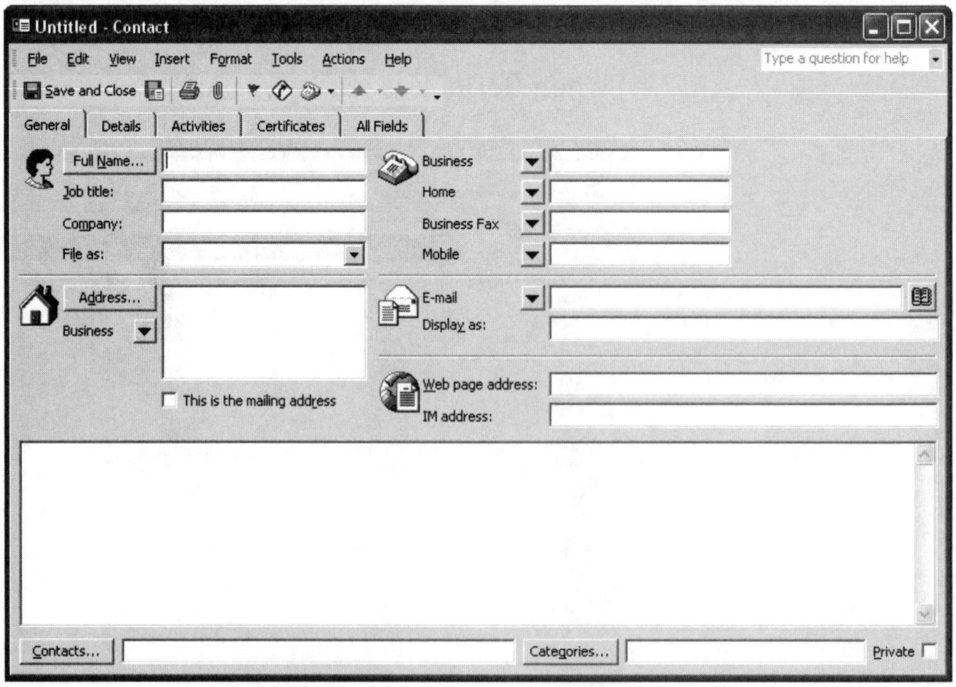

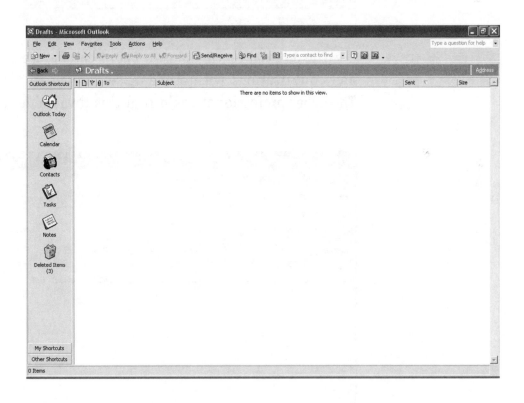

The Journal feature shown below can be used to record all actions and conversations with a client, serving as an electronic paper trail. The cyber professional could find this invaluable in a legal situation.

Notes in Outlook, shown below, are electronic sticky notes. They can be used as handy reminders.

4/5/2004 11:29 AM

***Title Bar.*** As in other Microsoft programs, this bar at the top of the screen displays the name of the application and the name of the active document. Also on this line are the minimize, maximize, restore, and close buttons.

***Menu Bar.*** Included on the menu bar are the following features:

- File. This menu offers options for selecting a new Outlook action, opening an existing folder, printing a document, and exiting the program.

- Edit. This menu offers options for undoing typing, cutting, copying, and pasting.

- View. This menu contains Go To, Outlook Bar, Folder List, and Toolbars.

- Favorites. This menu lists your favorite web pages.

- Tools. This menu contains Address Book, Customize, and Options.

- Actions. This menu offers the option to flag a message for further action.

- Help. This menu contains Outlook Help, Office Assistant, and What's This?

---

### PUTTING IT TOGETHER

Outlook's functions are similar to those of other Microsoft programs.

***Message Window.*** The screen below is what the user sees when he or she is ready to create a new message.

***Outlook Express.*** **Outlook Express** is available as a shortcut for accessing e-mail without having to go through Microsoft Outlook. It can be used to send out or read a quick message. It can be accessed through an icon placed on the Windows desktop. It is used as a convenience or by those who want to use e-mail only, without the other features Outlook offers. The opening screen may look like:

## *PUTTING IT TOGETHER*

Outlook Express is a fast and easy way to get and send e-mail.

# 9.3 Computer Applications

In this section, you complete activities that are essential in operating an e-mail system successfully.

**SKILL MASTERY EXERCISE 1**

Composing and sending an e-mail message. This is the number one tool used by the cyber professional to communicate with prospects, service providers, and clients. Complete the following steps:

1. Start Microsoft Outlook.

2. In the Outlook Today window, click on New. The message window should appear,

3. In the To box, insert your e-mail address.

4. In the Subject box, key *Trial Message.*

5. In the body of the message, key *This is a trial e-mail message. Please let me know if you receive this message. Thank you.*

6. Press the Send button and verify that it was sent.

7. Close Outlook.

Your message should look like this:

| Trial Message - Microsoft Internet Explorer provided by MiraCosta College | | _ □ X |
|---|---|---|
| Reply   Reply to all   Forward   🖨   🗋   X   ▲   ▼ | | Help |
| From:    Culbertson, Edward | | Sent:Mon 4/5/2004 10:16 PM |
| To:       Culbertson, Edward | | |
| Cc: | | |
| Subject:  Trial Message | | |
| Attachments: | | |
| | | View As Web Page |

This is a trial e-mail message.  Please let me know if you received this message.  Thank you.

Your message should have been sent and routed to your inbox. To verify that you did this correctly, try the next skill mastery exercise.

Receiving and responding to an e-mail message. Also important is knowing how to open e-mail and then responding to the message or forwarding the message to someone else. To read and reply to e-mail messages, follow these steps:

1.  Start Microsoft Outlook.

2.  In the Outlook Today window, click on the inbox.

3.  Click on the e-mail message that you sent to yourself.

4.  Click Reply and key the following text in the body: *I did receive your e-mail. Thank you very much.*

5.  Click Send. Your message should have been sent back to the sender (in this case, you).

Using the Reply to All button lets you reply to everyone included in the original e-mail message, not just the sender.

Your message should look like this:

**SKILL MASTERY EXERCISE 3**

Creating a document and attaching it to or inserting it in a message. Once a document is created and saved, it can be sent to others via e-mail. This document may be an article, a marketing plan, or a database, among others. This is how the cyber professional sends clients digital files of photos of homes. Sending a document is a two-step process. To accomplish this task, complete the following steps:

1. Start Microsoft Word or another word processing program.

2. Create a new document. The content of the document should read as follows: *To Whom It May Concern: Please read the article entitled "How to Buy a Home." Thank you.*

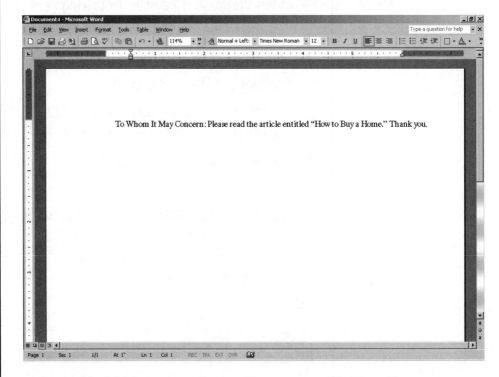

3. Save the document with the file name *A Trial Attachment*. (Outlook uses Insert File.)

4. Save the document in the My Documents folder.

5. Start Microsoft Outlook and click New.

6. Create another e-mail as before but change the subject line to the following: *Trial Attachment*. Key the following as the body: *Please read the attached document. Thank you.*

7. Click the Insert File icon (**Attachment**).

8. In My Documents, locate and click on the document you just created, A Trial Attachment.

9. Click the Insert button. The message should have been inserted into the e-mail message

10. Click Send, then Close.

To verify that this process worked, follow the procedure described in Skill Mastery Exercise 2. In the inbox, click on the Trial Attachment message. Then open the message to see the attachment, the inserted file. The document you created should appear on the screen.

**SKILL MASTERY EXERCISE 4**

Creating a signature for outgoing e-mail messages. As a cyber professional, you will send many e-mail messages. Adding your name, address, and phone numbers each time you create a new message can take a lot of time. As a remedy, Outlook allows you to create a signature that will automatically accompany each new message. To create a signature, follow these steps:

1. In Outlook Today, click Tools.

2. Select Options.

3. Select the Mail Format tab.

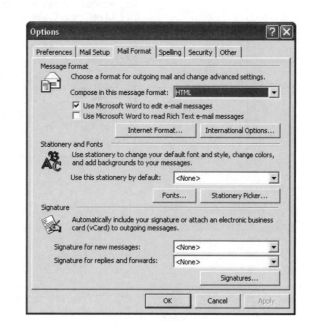

4.  Find Signature. Then click on Signature for new messages.

5.  In the window provided, key how you want your signature to appear in your new e-mail messages.

6.  Click Next, then OK.

Your signature should now be ready to use. You can include it in an e-mail by clicking on the Signature icon the toolbar.

**SKILL MASTERY EXERCISE 5**

Creating a folder for messages. It doesn't take long for e-mail messages to accumulate in the inbox, making it difficult to find a particular message. To solve this problem, a special folder can be created for a particular topic or client. To set up a folder, follow these steps:

1. In the Outlook Today window, select File.

2. Select Folder, then New Folder.

3. In the Create New Folder window, key a name for the folder: *Trial Folder.*

4. The newly created folder will be added to Personal Folders.

Once a folder has been created, an e-mail message can be stored in that folder. Then the user can easily keep track of his or her e-mail messages.

# 9.4 Advanced Topics

Taking advantage of Outlook Express can save time. The cyber professional can quickly access his or her inbox. The cyber professional can use his or her computer together with a personal digital assistant (PDA), a handheld computer that provides a calendar, an organizer for personal information, and e-mail capabilities, among other options. This allows the cyber professional to write and read e-mail messages, enter contact information, and view appointments even while away from his or her computer. The PDA can be synchronized with the computer when convenient.

Another useful tool provided in Outlook is instant messaging. It allows the cyber professional to communicate with clients in real time. He or she must pay a fee for this service, however. Outlook also offers the user the option of making Internet phone calls.

For the cyber professional, an additional advantage of Outlook Today is being able to access the Favorites list, which can hyperlink him or her to a desired web site without having to open Internet Explorer.

# RESOURCES FOR FURTHER STUDY

More information on how to work with Microsoft Outlook can be obtained from the Help functions on the Outlook menu bar, and also from the web site listed on page 168.

Microsoft Outlook Help

**Microsoft Outlook Help**

**What's New**
Learn about the new features in Microsoft Outlook and all Microsoft Office programs.

**Microsoft Office Web Site**
Visit the Microsoft Office Web site to find additional products, services, and assistance.

**Getting Help**
Learn about the different resources available to get help while you work.

**Help Topics**
- Accessibility features
- Keyboard shortcuts
- Add or remove an e-mail account
- About data files
- Color appointments and meetings in your calendar
- About the Microsoft Office Internet Free/Busy Service

**Web Pages**
Click a link to visit the World Wide Web.
- Microsoft Press
- Microsoft Product Support Services

Microsoft Outlook Help

▲ Home

**What's New**

▼ Show All

**Key new features in Microsoft Outlook**
- Color appointments
- Multiple reminders in a single dialog box with **Dismiss All** button
- Automatically complete e-mail addresses as you type

**More new features in Outlook**
- E-mail accounts, profiles, messaging, and contacts
- Storing, organizing, and backing up data
- Working offline
- **Calendar** and scheduling
- Unlocking data
- Security
- Multilingual features
- Accessibility

**New Microsoft Office features**
- Everyday tasks
- Error prevention and recovery
- Language-specific features

```
Microsoft Outlook Help                                                      _ ☐ ✕
☐ ◁▯ ⇦ ⇨ 🖨 🗗▾
                                                                        ▾ Show All ▲

About getting help while you work
If you need help while you work, you can use the following resources:
  ▶ Ask a Question box
  ▶ The Office Assistant
  ▶ Help
  ▶ ScreenTips
  ▶ Help on the World Wide Web




                                                                                ▾
```

http://officeupdate.microsoft.com

This site offers information about new features of the program. (It gives up-to-date information about all Office products as well, not just Outlook.)

# SELF-ASSESSMENT

To determine the extent of knowledge you acquired in this chapter, choose the correct answer for each of the following.

1.  The Outlook Today window includes all of the following except?
    a.  Calendar
    b.  Contacts
    c.  Autoresponder
    d.  Tasks

2.  To compose a new message, the cyber professional clicks:
    a.  Reply
    b.  Forward
    c.  New
    d.  Send/Receive

3.  What feature is accessed to set up a signature?
    a.  File
    b.  Edit
    c.  View
    d.  Tools

4.  To find out if there are any messages in the Inbox, the cyber professional clicks on:
    a.  Favorites
    b.  Receive
    c.  New
    d.  Help

5.  What does the cyber professional do to send a saved document to a recipient?
    a.  Create a folder
    b.  Send an attachment
    c.  Create a signature
    d.  Access Outlook Express

6.  Why might the cyber professional want to include an attachment to an e-mail message?
    a.  To send digital photos to clients
    b.  To send a database to a fellow colleague
    c.  Both a and b
    d.  None of these

7. Besides allowing the cyber professional to send and receive messages, Outlook also provides:
   a. A calendar
   b. A contact list
   c. A tasks list
   d. All of the above

8. What feature does the cyber professional use to send a message that he or she received to other recipients?
   a. Reply
   b. Reply to All
   c. Forward
   d. Recycle Bin

9. The main function of Outlook Express is to allow the cyber professional to:
   a. Receive an e-mail message quickly
   b. Send an e-mail message quickly
   c. Both a and b
   d. None of the above

10. Which of the following statements is true about Outlook's Notes feature?
    a. Notes cannot be printed out.
    b. Notes cannot be saved.
    c. Notes serve as electronic sticky notes.
    d. None of these

11. Which of the following does not appear on Outlook's menu bar?
    a. View
    b. Tools
    c. Help
    d. Send

12. What does the cyber professional click to reply to an e-mail message?
    a. Reply to All
    b. Reply
    c. Both a and c
    d. None of these

13. An e-mail header includes all of the following except:
    a. To
    b. Message body
    c. Cc
    d. Bcc

14. What does the cyber professional use to organize related e-mail messages?
    a. Address Book
    b. Folder
    c. Attachment
    d. Autoresponder

15. What does the cyber professional use to set up a system to send mass e-mail communications?
    a. Distribution List
    b. Address Book
    c. Return Receipt
    d. Autoresponder

# CHAPTER 10
## A CONTACT AND TIME MANAGEMENT SYSTEM: MICROSOFT OUTLOOK

## PREVIEW

Key factors in the success of a real estate practice are maintaining records on clients, setting appointments, and keeping track of tasks and activities. Establishing a contact management system and managing activities are essential. This chapter focuses on the features and functions of Microsoft Outlook's contact and time management system.

When you finish this chapter, you will be able to:

1. Understand the use of contact and time management and its benefits.

2. Understand the features and functions of Microsoft Outlook's contact and time management system.

3. Set up a personal contact and time management system.

4. Become acquainted with other commercial contact and time management systems.

## KEY TERMS

| | |
|---|---|
| *ACT!*® | *Journal* |
| *Address Book* | *Notes* |
| *Calendar* | *Tasks* |
| *distribution list* | *voice e-mail* |
| *GoldMine*® | |

# 10.1 How Microsoft Outlook Can Benefit the Cyber Professional

To achieve success, the cyber professional must have some form of a contact management and time management system. With these systems, the cyber professional can:

1.   Access appointments for the day, week, or year.

2.   Set up appointments so they do not conflict.

3.   Complete a to-do task list.

4.   Keep notes.

5.   Keep track of ongoing activities with clients.

6.   Maintain an organized list of contacts.

8.   Establish a group e-mail list for the dissemination of marketing materials.

9.   Access vital information about clients.

# 10.2 Getting Acquainted with Outlook

Microsoft Outlook is more than an e-mail software program. It also allows the cyber professional to establish an address book, create a distribution list of contacts, and manage his or her time and appointments. Outlook is very versatile and easy to use. This section describes the different parts of these systems and how they can be used in the practice of real estate.

---

### PUTTING IT TOGETHER

Microsoft Outlook can be used to maintain a list of contacts and keep track of appointments.

# 10.3 Creating Contacts, Notes, and Journal

This section discusses three features available in Outlook: Contacts, Notes, and Journal.

## Contacts

You can take advantage of Contacts to inserts information about prospects, present clients, past clients, and service providers. It can be used as a master list of all contacts made in the practice of real estate. Each time you identify a contact, you can add information about the person for your future reference. Features within Contacts allow you to:

- Add general contact information that includes full name, job title, company name, business address, home and business phone numbers, business fax and mobile numbers, e-mail address, web page address, and a place for notes.

- Add detailed contact information that includes department, office, profession, nickname, spouse's name, birthday, and anniversary.

- View activities that include e-mail correspondence with the contact.

- Use an autodialer that offers options for redial and speed dial.

- Flag items for follow-up.

- Write a letter to a contact.

- Add a contact to a task.

- Record journal entries for a contact.

- Connect to a contact using Microsoft's NetMeeting®.

- Send e-mails and Word documents to contacts.

- Find a contact capability.

- Place contacts in different categories, such as business, family, personal and private.

- List contacts alphabetically.

- Edit and delete capabilities.

- Import capabilities from other systems.

- Export and synchronize capabilities to other types of systems.

- Use nonduplicating contacts capability.

- Display maps to contacts.

- Create a mail merge.

### *PUTTING IT TOGETHER*

The contact file can include detailed information about clients. Maintaining a list of contacts is essential for success in real estate.

## Notes

Using **Notes,** you can write down thoughts, ideas, or follow-up tasks. You can see the notes on the window pane by clicking the Notes icon. To see all of the postings, click the View feature and then Notes List. You can also organize the notes in order to view them by category. You can color-code the notes to better organize them in terms of priority or category. You can edit and delete notes at any point. Another important feature of notes is that they include a time stamp, which can be used to establish important notification verifications.

### *PUTTING IT TOGETHER*

Notes in Outlook are basically electronic sticky notes.

## *Journal*

The **Journal** is used as an electronic paper trail for ongoing conversations and actions that have taken place with a contact. You can use the journal to help refresh your memory about a recent action and to document various activities related to a contact. To begin creating a journal, click Journal. The feature will ask for the subject, the type of entry, the start time, the duration, and a section for a memo or a statement about the action. The journal entry can be used to automatically record e-mails and documents for contacts. It also has an edit and a delete function. Journal entries can be viewed in chronological order, by category, by contact, or by type.

---

### *PUTTING IT TOGETHER*

The Journal can serve as an electronic paper trail.

---

# 10.4 Creating a Calendar and Tasks

You can utilize additional features of Microsoft Outlook: Calendar and Tasks.

## *Calendar*

Managing time is another significant aspect of being a successful cyber professional. The **Calendar** serves as a time management tool to help keep track of meetings, appointments, and other obligations. With this feature, you can schedule your commitments on a calendar.

Clicking Calendar starts this feature. The calendar can be viewed by the hour, day, month, or year. To enter a new appointment, click New. A calendar will appear for the current date. The dialog box will ask for the subject of the appointment, the location, the start time, the end time, a reminder with an alarm feature, and an area for a memo. By clicking Recurrence, you can program an appointment or event that occurs on a regular basis. You can also mark the priority as High or Low importance.

Another helpful feature is being able to find appointments by category or to organize all appointments by category. By clicking Go to Today, you will see the current date. A Reminder system with an alarm may also be used. Other features include being able to send an e-mail requesting a meeting with another networked Outlook user. He or she can accept or decline via e-mail. Appointments can be edited and deleted.

---

### PUTTING IT TOGETHER

The cyber professional can use Calendar to set and view appointments by the hour, day, week, or year.

## Tasks

Being able to identify and complete tasks is important to the success of a real estate practice. To make sure all details are taken care of, some kind of system is necessary. **Tasks** provides a way to record personal and work-related errands and track them through completion. Many cyber professionals do not have a secure and reliable method for identifying and keeping track of tasks. The Tasks feature in Outlook solves that problem,

To create a Task, simply click New, then New Task. The New Task screen will appear. The dialog box requests the subject of the task, due date, start date, status of the task, priority of the task, and amount completed in terms of a percentage. It also has a reminder feature by date and time. An alarm is programmed into the operation. Often different tasks are required on a recurring basis, which you can also record using Tasks.

Another unique feature is the ability to assign a task to a personal assistant. To do this, you create a Task Request. Once the task has been assigned, you can ask the recipient to send a status report when the task is complete. Tasks can be set up and viewed in terms of categories. This process can help you stay on top of all mandatory actions required by contract law. In the Views menu, you can identify tasks in terms of simple list, active list, next seven days, overdue tasks, responsible person, completed task, and task timeline. All of these points can be critical to a successful real estate transaction. You can even color-code overdue tasks. You can build reminders into the system, including having an alarm sound when you need to do something. In the advanced options, you can record the number of hours daily and weekly. Once the tasks have been set up, you can can print them out as hard copy. You can edit and delete all of the items, as with other features.

---

### *PUTTING IT TOGETHER*

Tasks can be used as an electronic to-do list.

# 10.5 Other Contact and Time Management Systems

This section provides a brief discussion of three other contact and time management systems: ACT!, GoldMine, and TOP PRODUCER.

## *ACT!*

**ACT!** is an e-mail program that offers the following amenities: the ability to manage all customer information in one system, to keeping track of schedules and activities, to create and send personal letters, and to send faxes and e-mail messages. This program can also be integrated with Microsoft Outlook and Microsoft Word, as well as downloaded to handheld devices such as PDAs or phones.

ACT! can be downloaded for a free trial at http://www.act.com. The web site gives information about the features of the program and has a demo available for previewing. Ordering is available online through the web site. Like other software programs, it is often upgraded with new features. ACT! is more complicated to use than Outlook and offers more features than the cyber professional may really need.

## *GoldMine*

**GoldMine** is another commercial contact and time management system. It offers even more features and functions then Outlook and ACT!. Its features include a complete tracking system, a client retention system, document management, and many automated processes that allow the user to automatically scheduling appointments and send customized e-mail messages. This program can be purchased as a stand-alone system. To learn more about GoldMine, go to http://www.frontrange.com. One unique aspect of this system is those features that address the needs of real estate professionals. It also allows for integration with QuickBooks: Pro. GoldMine includes special templates that help the agent to better collect and organize contacts. GoldMine also offers the following features:

- Document and Campaign Management
- Opportunity Management
- Team-Based Collaboration
- Forecasting

### TOP PRODUCER®

Another major contact and time management system used by some real estate agents is TOP PRODUCER. It offers an advanced system designed specifically for real estate professionals. To learn more about this system and to download a demo, go to http://www.topproducer.com.

---

**PUTTING IT TOGETHER**

Common commercial contact and time management systems include ACT!, GoldMine, and TOP PRODUCER.

# 10.6 Computer Applications

In this section, you will learn more about using Microsoft Outlook.

**SKILL MASTERY EXERCISE 1**

Using the Address Book and Contact system. The **Address Book** holds e-mail addresses for the cyber professional to use as a reference and as a tool for setting up an e-marketing campaign. It is a convenient tool that saves the cyber professional time and effort. The user can find a recipient, click the name, and begin composing an e-mail message. To set up the Address Book, complete the following steps:

1.  Start Outlook. Select Address Book on the Tools menu.

2.  To enter a new contact, click New. Insert the information you would like to keep about this contact. (You do not need to enter data in every field.)

3.  To find a contact, select Find People. Enter the contact's name. All of the information you inserted will appear.

You can print or export a list of the contacts to other devices. You can use a contact's information to create an e-mail and to dial his or her phone number. You can edit or delete contact information at any time.

Refer to the following illustrations used in the process described above.

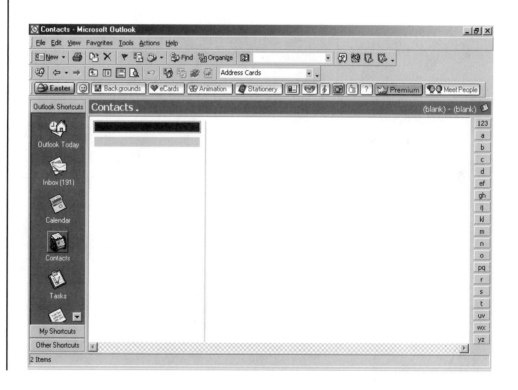

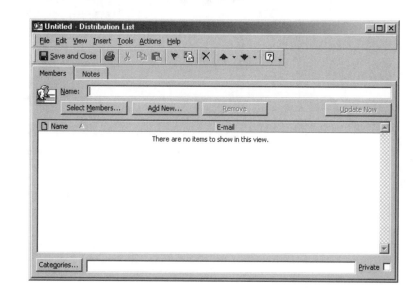

**SKILL MASTERY EXERCISE 2**

Setting up a distribution list. The **distribution list** is a list of selected contacts organized as a special group. The user can access this list to send out one e-mail message to all of the people in the group. The user can send an e-mail message to all of the contacts on the list for everyone to see or send the message as a blind carbon copy that only the recipient can see. To set up the distribution list, complete the following steps:

1. Start Outlook. Select Distribution List from New.

**Select Name**

Show Names from the: | All Groups

Type Name or Select from List:

New...    Properties    Find...

OK    Cancel    Help

**Add New Member**

Display Name:

E-mail address:

Address type: | Internet Address

☐ Add to contacts

OK    Cancel

**Untitled - Distribution List**

File Edit View Insert Tools Actions Help

Save and Close

Members    Notes

Name:

Select Members...    Add New...    Remove    Update Now

| Name | E-mail |
|------|--------|
| | There are no items to show in this view. |

Categories...    Private ☐

2. Enter the name of the group; for example, First-Time Buyers or Investors.

3. Click Select Members. A list of the user contacts will appear.

4. Choose the names of contacts that you want to include or enter new names in the Add New box.

5. Input whatever information you want from the Notes tab.

6. Click Save and Close.

**SKILL MASTERY
EXERCISE 3**

Using the Task feature. The cyber professional uses the Task feature to write down the different activities and/or actions he or she needs to complete. To activate the Task feature, complete the following steps:

1.  Start Outlook. Click Task.

2.  Click New and select Task.

3.  Enter the name of the task next to *Subject*.

4.  Enter the due date and the start date.

5.  Enter the status and priority of the task and the percentage complete

6.  Click the Reminder box if you want to activate this feature. Click the alarm button if you want to hear the sound when a reminder comes due.

7.  Identify the contacts and categories at the bottom of the screen to identify the recipient of the task.

8.  Add any instructions or comment about the task to be executed.

9.  Click Save and Close.

The task you entered will appear when you select the Task feature from Outlook Today. Refer to the following illustrations used in the process described above.

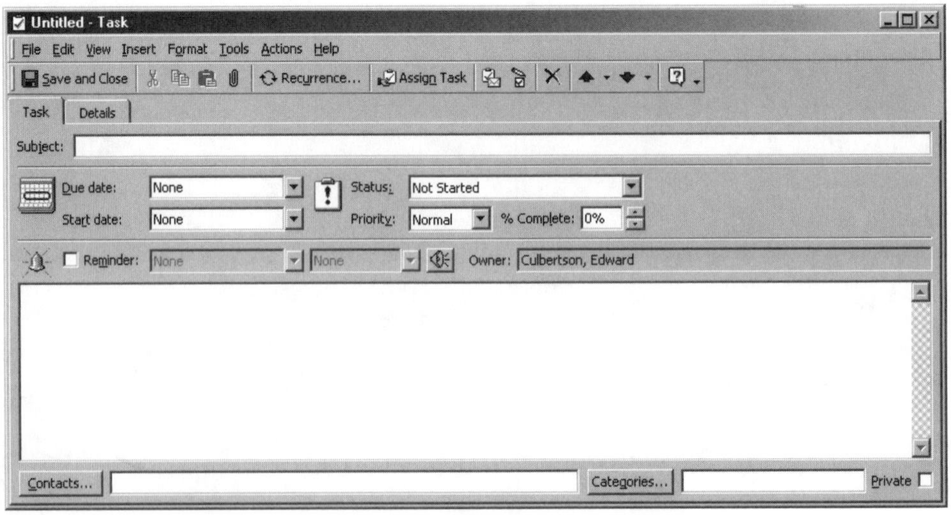

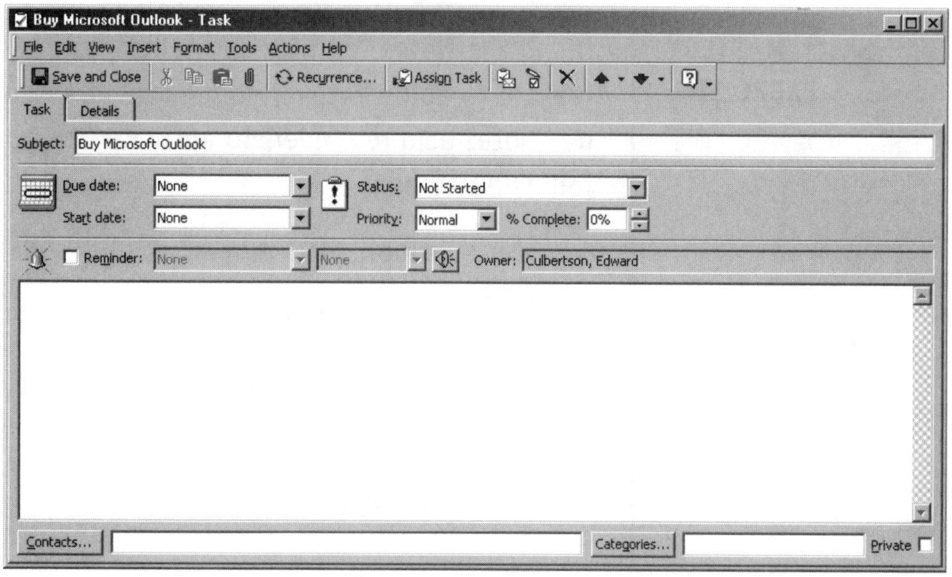
Buy Microsoft Outlook - Task
File Edit View Insert Format Tools Actions Help
Save and Close
Recurrence...
Assign Task
Task
Details
Subject: Buy Microsoft Outlook
Due date: None
Start date: None
Status: Not Started
Priority: Normal
% Complete: 0%
Reminder: None
None
Owner: Culbertson, Edward
Contacts...
Categories...
Private

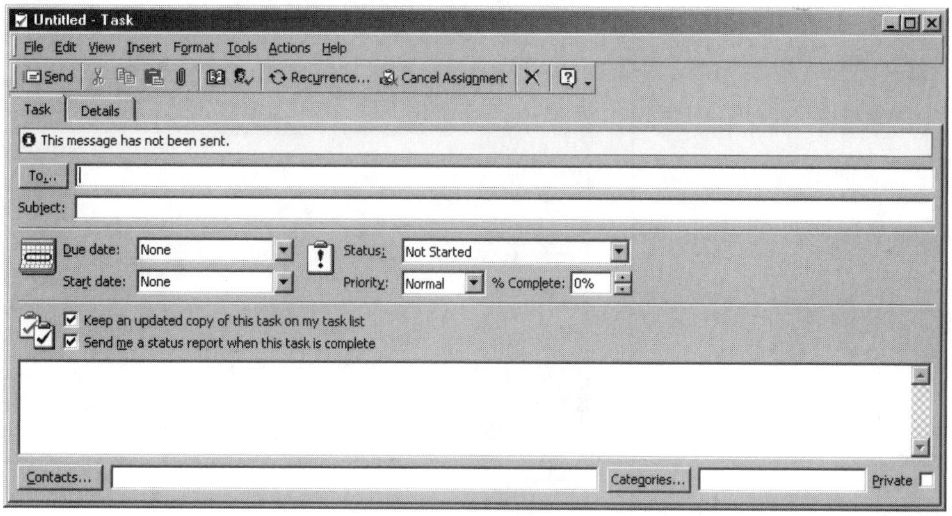
Untitled - Task
File Edit View Insert Format Tools Actions Help
Send
Recurrence...
Cancel Assignment
Task
Details
This message has not been sent.
To...
Subject:
Due date: None
Start date: None
Status: Not Started
Priority: Normal
% Complete: 0%
Keep an updated copy of this task on my task list
Send me a status report when this task is complete
Contacts...
Categories...
Private

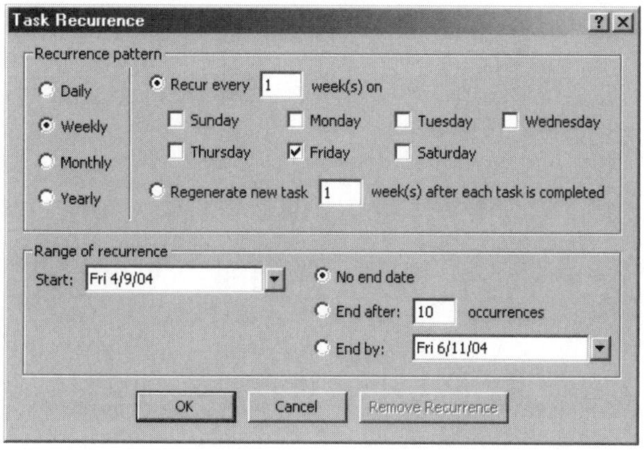
Task Recurrence
Recurrence pattern
Daily
Weekly
Monthly
Yearly
Recur every 1 week(s) on
Sunday
Monday
Tuesday
Wednesday
Thursday
Friday
Saturday
Regenerate new task 1 week(s) after each task is completed
Range of recurrence
Start: Fri 4/9/04
No end date
End after: 10 occurrences
End by: Fri 6/11/04
OK
Cancel
Remove Recurrence

**SKILL MASTERY
EXERCISE 4**

Using the Notes feature. The cyber professional uses the Notes feature to add whatever comments he or she chooses. He or she can use Notes as a reminder. To activate the Notes feature, complete the following steps:

1. Start Outlook. Click Notes.

2. Click New and select Notes.

3. Enter information in the note provided.

4. Click Outlook Today.

The notes you created will appear.

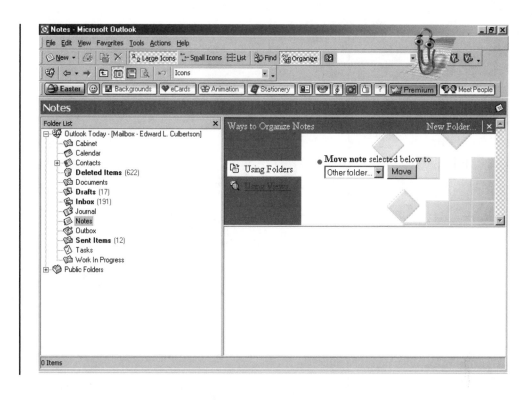

**SKILL MASTERY EXERCISE 5**

Using the Journal feature. The Journal feature is used to keep a running log of all activities related to a given contact or group. To set up the Journal, complete the following steps:

1. Start Outlook. Click Journal.

2. Click New and select Journal Entry.

3. Enter the name of the journal item next to *Subject*.

4. Enter the Entry type.

5. Select the Start time and Duration.

6. Enter information about the topic in the body of the journal.

7. Select the name of the contact and category.

8. Click Save and Close.

The item you entered will appear when you select the Journal feature.

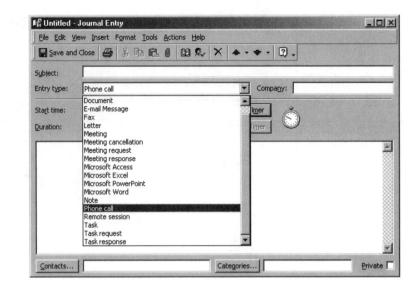

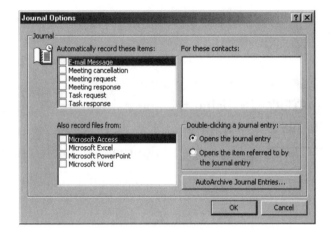

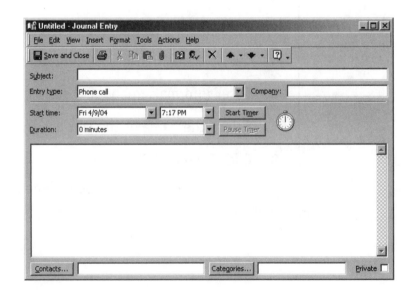

**SKILL MASTERY
EXERCISE 6**

Using the Calendar feature. The Calendar feature can be used as a time management system. It can be used to record appointments on a daily, weekly, or monthly basis or throughout the year. The start time and length of appointments can be added as well. The subject and location of the appointment, along with comments, can be included. Events that recur on regular basis can also be added. Scheduled appointments can be sent via e-mail to others, printed as a hard copy, or synchronized to a personal digital assistant (PDA). The Calendar can be viewed any time or any place using an Internet connection. To set up the Calendar, complete the following steps:

1. Start Outlook. Click Calendar.

2. Click New and select Appointment.

3. Enter the subject and the location.

4. Enter the start time and the end time of the appointment.

5. Make sure a check mark is selected in the Reminder box.

6. Enter information about the appointment in the appointment window.

7. Click the exclamation mark button on the toolbar if the appointment is of high importance. Click the down arrow button on the toolbar if the appointment is of low importance. Selecting neither high nor low leaves the option unchanged.

8. Select Categories to help organize all appointments.

9. Select Contact if the appointment is applicable to a specific person.

10. Click Save and Close.

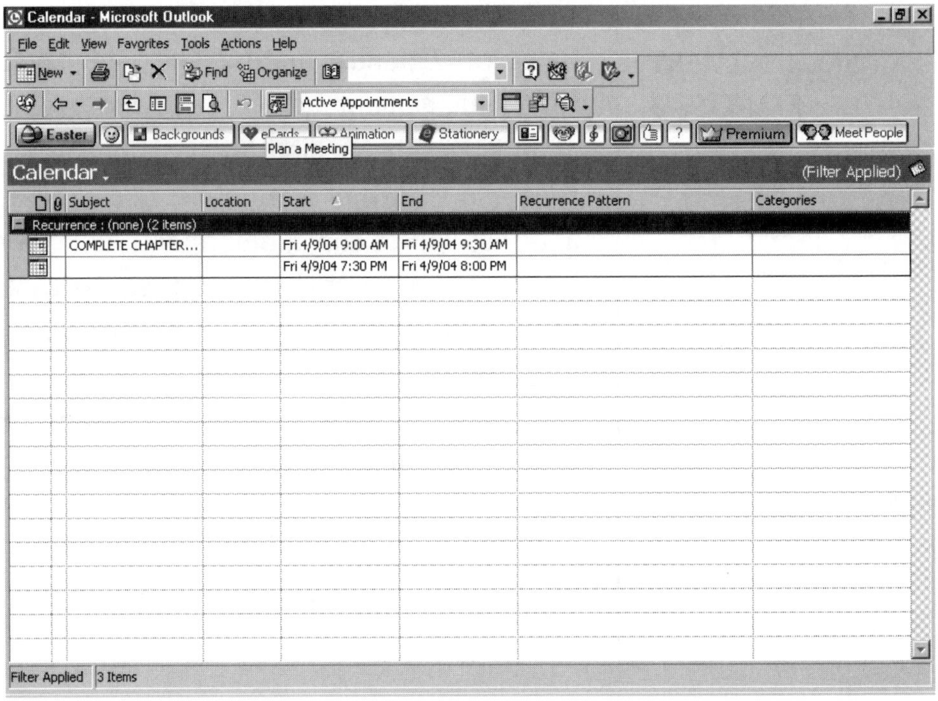
Calendar - Microsoft Outlook
File Edit View Favorites Tools Actions Help
New
Find
Organize
Active Appointments
Easter
Backgrounds
eCards
Animation
Stationery
Premium
Meet People
Plan a Meeting
Calendar
(Filter Applied)
Subject
Location
Start
End
Recurrence Pattern
Categories
Recurrence : (none) (2 items)
COMPLETE CHAPTER...
Fri 4/9/04 9:00 AM
Fri 4/9/04 9:30 AM
Fri 4/9/04 7:30 PM
Fri 4/9/04 8:00 PM
Filter Applied
3 Items

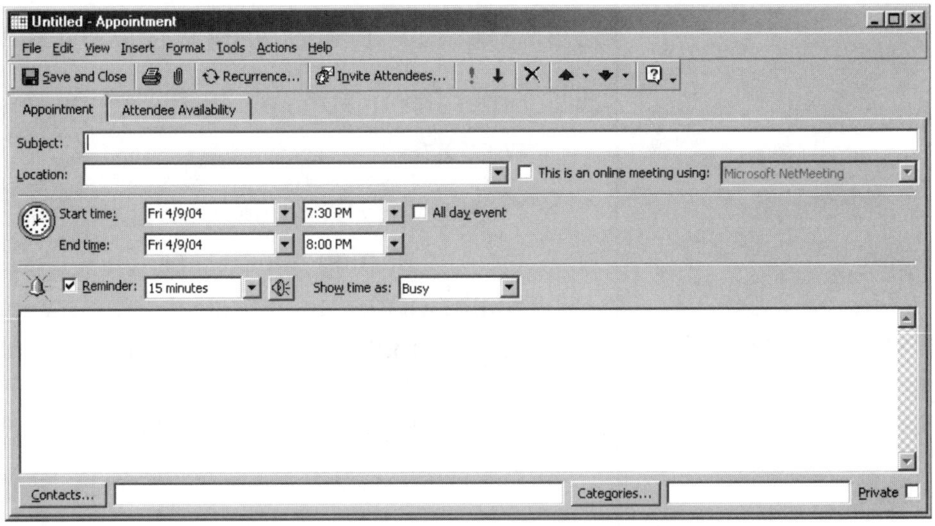
Untitled - Appointment
File Edit View Insert Format Tools Actions Help
Save and Close
Recurrence...
Invite Attendees...
Appointment
Attendee Availability
Subject:
Location:
This is an online meeting using:
Microsoft NetMeeting
Start time:
Fri 4/9/04
7:30 PM
All day event
End time:
Fri 4/9/04
8:00 PM
Reminder:
15 minutes
Show time as:
Busy
Contacts...
Categories...
Private

Calendar - Microsoft Outlook

File  Edit  View  Favorites  Tools  Actions  Help

New ▾ | 🖨 | 📋 ✕ | 🔍 Find 🗂 Organize | 📖 | [          ] ▾ | 🔲 🔍 🔩 🔳 ▾

🌐 | ⬅ ▾ ➡ | 📂 🔳 📄 🔍 | ⟲ 🔲 | Events [          ] ▾ | 🗓 📑 🔍 ▾

| 🌐 Easter | ☺ | 🖼 Backgrounds | eCards | 🐰 Animation | 📄 Stationery | 📧 🔳 📷 🔳 ? | 📬 Premium | 👁👁 Meet People |

## Calendar .                    [Send Greeting Cards in your mail]                    (Filter Applied) 📖

| 📄 | 📎 | Subject | Location | Recurrence ... | Duration | Recurrence Pattern | Categories |
|---|---|---|---|---|---|---|---|
| | | | | There are no items to show in this view. | | | |

Filter Applied | 3 Items

Untitled - Meeting

File  Edit  View  Insert  Format  Tools  Actions  Help

📧 Send | 🖨 📎 | 📖 🔩 | ↻ Recurrence... 🔩 Cancel Invitation... | 🔳 ⬇ | ✕ | ? ▾

Appointment | Attendee Availability

◉ Show attendee availability
○ Show attendee status

| All Attendees |
| 📧 Culbertson, Edward |
| Type attendee name here |

Saturday, April 10, 2004

10:00 11:00 12:00 1:00 2:00 3:00 4:00 5:00 6:00 7:00 8:00 9:00 10:00 11:00    1:00 2:00 3:00 4:00

Invite Others... | Options ▾       ☐ Tentative  ■ Busy  ■ Out of Office  ⧄ No Information

≤< | AutoPick ▾ | >≥

Meeting start time: [Fri 4/9/04] ▾ [7:30 PM] ▾

Meeting end time: [Fri 4/9/04] ▾ [8:00 PM] ▾

The appointment you entered will appear when you select the Calendar feature.

**Appointment Recurrence**    ? X

**Appointment time**

Start: [7:30 PM ▼]    End: [8:00 PM ▼]    Duration: [30 minutes ▼]

**Recurrence pattern**

○ Daily        Recur every [1] week(s) on:
● Weekly
○ Monthly      ☐ Sunday    ☐ Monday    ☐ Tuesday    ☐ Wednesday
○ Yearly       ☐ Thursday  ☑ Friday    ☐ Saturday

**Range of recurrence**

Start: [Fri 4/9/04 ▼]    ● No end date
                         ○ End after: [10] occurrences
                         ○ End by: [Fri 6/11/04 ▼]

[ OK ]    [ Cancel ]    [ Remove Recurrence ]

---

**Calendar - Microsoft Outlook**    _ ⑧ X

File  Edit  View  Favorites  Tools  Actions  Help

[New ▼] [🖨] [] [X] [Find] [Organize] [📇]                    [▼] [?] [] [] [].

[] [⇦ ▼ ⇨] [] [] [] [] [↺] [] [Recurring Appointments ▼] [] [] [].

[Easter] [☺] [Backgrounds] [eCards] [Animation] [Stationery] [] [] [] [] [] [?] [Premium] [Meet People]

**Calendar .**                                          (Filter Applied)

| 📄 ‖ Subject | Location | Recurrence Pattern | Recurrence ... | Recurrence ... | Categories |
|---|---|---|---|---|---|
| There are no items to show in this view. | | | | | |

Filter Applied    3 Items

# 10.7 Advanced Topics

Outlook offers even more features than those presented in the chapter. Additional features include the following:

## *Voice E-mail*

Software is available to send and listen to e-mail messages, although both parties must have the software. This feature can be utilized on any computer that is connected to the Internet and that is set up for voice e-mail. An illustration of the screen is as follows:

## *Outlook 2003 with Business Contact Manager*

This program is an enhanced version of Microsoft Outlook. The special features include:

- Managing business contacts
- Tracking sales opportunities
- Running reports to measure results of activities
- Organizing and accessing all contacts in one place
- Importing data from ACT!

- Creating personalized newsletters and mailings with tracking capability

- Exporting data to a PDA.

## OneNote 2003

This is a new product from Microsoft that allows the user to capture, organize, and reuse notes. The user can organize notes to his or her liking.

## Synchronization

Another valuable feature of Microsoft Outlook is that the data can be downloaded or synchronized with other devices and software programs. For example, the cyber professional can download all contacts and appointments from Outlook to a PDA. Similarly, information or contacts entered on the PDA can be added to Outlook. A process known as synchronization accomplishes this. Data from other software systems, such as ACT!, can be imported or exported to Outlook.

## Open Access

With the appropriate software, the cyber professional can use a remote computer or laptop to access a "home computer" for information. He or she often needs information that is on the home computer to complete a task. Using the software program Laplink® or pcAnywhere™, the cyber professional can access his or her home computer from any remote location.

---

### PUTTING IT TOGETHER

Outlook can be used to import or export data to other devices or programs.

# RESOURCES FOR FURTHER STUDY

http://nami.videoprofessor.com/411/course_outlook2002.php?ID=403 &K=133788

This site offers a tutorial on how to use Outlook.

http://office.microsoft.com/home/office.aspx?assetid=FX01085793

This site provides product information, answers to frequently asked questions, and tips on how to use Outlook.

http://www.computertim.com/howto/category.php?topic=outlook

This site gives tips on how to best utilize Outlook.

http://www.act.com/

This is the home page for ACT! software.

http://www.frontrange.com/goldmine/

This is the home page for GoldMine software.

http://www.topproducer.com

This is the home page for the TOP PRODUCER software suite.

http://www.smartcontactmanager.com/scm_home.shtml

This is a new contact management program that works with Pocket PC and PDAs. It also works with Microsoft Word, Outlook, and Excel. A free 30-day download is available at this site.

# SELF-ASSESSMENT

To determine the extent of knowledge you acquired in this chapter, choose the correct answer for each of the following.

1.  What is the purpose of the Outlook Today window?
    a.  To show an overview of all Outlook Activities
    b.  To show a list of contacts in the Outlook program
    c.  To show appointments only for the day
    d.  To show tasks only for the day

2.  What is the main difference between Outlook and Outlook Express?
    a.  Outlook Express is more complicated and harder to use.
    b.  Outlook Express has more bells and whistles.
    c.  Outlook Express is a condensed version of Outlook.
    d.  There is no difference between Outlook and Outlook Express.

3.  When the cyber professional wants to e-mail information to a select group, what does he or she use?
    a.  Address Book
    b.  Distribution list
    c.  Contacts
    d.  Appointments

4.  When using the Calendar feature, what can the cyber professional see?
    a.  Daily activities
    b.  Weekly activities
    c.  Monthly activities
    d.  All of the above

5.  What can the cyber professional use to organize his or her e-mail messages?
    a.  Address Book
    b.  Distribution list
    c.  Folder
    d.  Favorites List

6.  What feature of Outlook does the cyber professional use to insert information about clients?
    a.  Contacts
    b.  Notes
    c.  Journal
    d.  None of these

7. What does the cyber professional click to add a prospect to the Address Book?
   a. New appointment
   b. New contact
   c. New event
   d. New reminder

8. The best way to locate a contact in Outlook is to access the:
   a. Help feature
   b. Delete feature
   c. Find feature
   d. Sent feature

9. Where are new e-mail messages found?
   a. Outbox
   b. Inbox
   c. Recycle Bin
   d. Draft file

10. What can the cyber professional do to have Microsoft Outlook on his or her computer?
    a. Download the program from the Internet
    b. Purchase and install it
    c. Buy a computer with it already preinstalled
    d. All of the above

11. Which of the following is a feature of Outlook?
    a. Calendar
    b. Tasks/Notes
    c. Journal
    d. All of the above

12. What feature does the cyber professional use to keep an ongoing account of conversations and activities?
    a. Calendar
    b. Journal
    c. Reminders
    d. Tasks

13. What feature can the cyber professional use to set up an event that needs to be accomplished at a certain time?
    a. Notes
    b. Calendar
    c. Tasks
    d. All of the above

14. What feature does the cyber professional use to set up an electronic paper trail for a seller or buyer?
    a. Journal
    b. Notes
    c. None of these
    d. Both a and b

15. In addition to Outlook, what is another contact and time management system?
    a. GoldMine
    b. ACT!
    c. Both a and b
    d. None of these

# CHAPTER 11
## CREATING REAL ESTATE FLYERS WITH MICROSOFT WORD AND PUBLISHER

## PREVIEW

**Two important tasks for the cyber professional are to promote real estate products and to promote him- or herself. This chapter explains how to use Microsoft Word and Microsoft Publisher for creating and designing a professional real estate flyer and a personal brochure.**

**When you finish this chapter, you will be able to:**

1. **Describe the benefits of Microsoft Word and Publisher to the cyber professional.**

2. **Understand the special features and functions of Microsoft Word and Microsoft Publisher.**

3. **Create a real estate flyer that can be used to promote a home.**

4. **Create a personal marketing brochure that can be used to promote yourself to the real estate community.**

## KEY TERMS

| | |
|---|---|
| *AutoShapes* | *tables* |
| *clip art* | *WordArt* |
| *hyperlink* | |

# 11.1 How Microsoft Word and Publisher Can Benefit the Cyber Professional

By learning the special features and functions of Word and Publisher, the cyber professional will be able to:

1. Save time and money by not having to pay graphic designers to create professional-looking flyers.

2. Create a professional-looking promotional flyer as a hand-out or an advertisement or for distribution to group e-mail lists.

3. Create flyers used for a listing presentation.

4. Insert digital photos of properties into real estate flyers.

5. Create a personal brochure for promoting business.

# 11.2 Special Features and Functions of Microsoft Word

Designing, creating, and producing a professional-looking real estate flyer is easy to do with Microsoft Word. The special features the cyber professional uses include the following:

- **WordArt.** This feature is used to create text with special shapes and designs. Text can be formatted in perspective (as if it has depth), as a shape, or in other ways often found in logos or brochures.

- **AutoShapes.** This feature is used to insert predrawn shapes into a document. Some of the options include:
  - Lines
  - Basic Shapes
  - Block Arrows
  - Flowcharts
  - Stars and Banners
  - Callouts

Another aspect of Word is being able to insert special features into a document. The following items can enhance the quality of documents:

- Pictures. This option allows the cyber professional to insert photos of homes. The photos come from a digital camera, or pictures are downloaded from the Internet.

- Tables. **Tables** can be used to organize information in a document

- Hyperlinks. This tool is used to embed a **hyperlink** into a document. A hyperlink is an element in an electronic document that links to another place in the same document, to an entirely different document, or to a web site. Inserting an e-mail address or a URL into a document saves the recipient time and effort.

- Clip Art. **Clip art** is a collection of images that can be inserted into documents. It can be found in a clip art library in Word, on CDs, and on the Internet. When designing a document, the cyber professional can insert these pictures into a document, adding variety and excitement.

## PUTTING IT TOGETHER

WordArt can be used to create text in special shapes and designs in flyers and brochures. Clip art can be used to make documents more exciting.

Using the features just described, the cyber professional should be able to create a flyer similar to this:

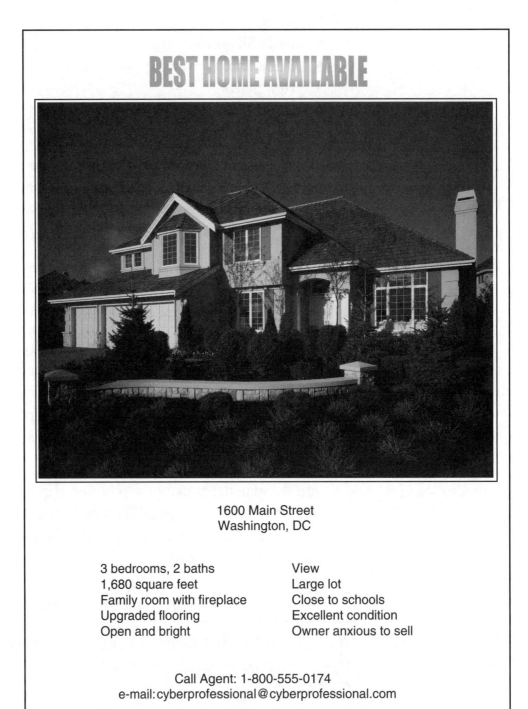

**BEST HOME AVAILABLE**

1600 Main Street
Washington, DC

3 bedrooms, 2 baths      View
1,680 square feet        Large lot
Family room with fireplace   Close to schools
Upgraded flooring        Excellent condition
Open and bright          Owner anxious to sell

Call Agent: 1-800-555-0174
e-mail:cyberprofessional@cyberprofessional.com

# 11.3 Computer Applications

This section explains how to use some of the special features just mentioned . Then to demonstrate your skill, you have the opportunity to create a flyer that includes the features presented here.

**SKILL MASTERY EXERCISE 1**

Using WordArt. To use WordArt, complete the following steps:

1.  In Word, click Insert on the menu bar.

2.  Click Picture.

3.  Click WordArt.

The screen should look like this:

4.  Select a WordArt style and press OK. The screen should look like this:

5.  Key *BEST HOME AVAILABLE* in the WordArt text box and press OK.

**SKILL MASTERY
EXERCISE 2**

Using AutoShapes. Complete the following steps:

1.  In Word, click Insert on the menu bar.

2.  Click Picture, then AutoShapes.

The screen should look like this:

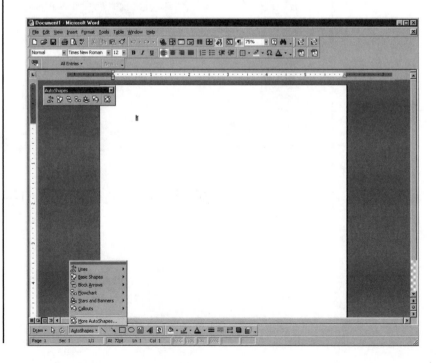

3.  Select a rectangle from the bottom of the screen.

4.  Place the pointer in the middle of the screen. (The pointer is a crosshair.)

5.  Draw a 5 x 7 rectangle: Point to the inside top left corner of the figure. Press and hold the mouse button while dragging down and to the right until the shape reaches the size you want. You can use the horizontal and vertical rulers on the screen to determine the size of the rectangle. (This rectangle is used as a placeholder for a photo.)

The screen should look like this:

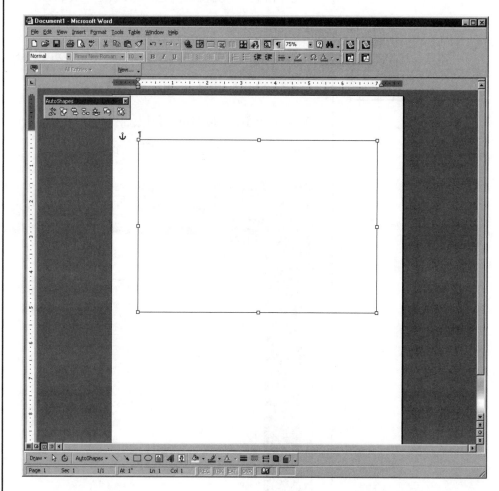

Once a pattern is inserted, it must be moved and resized to fit the document. To do this, you can click and drag the figure to the desired size and location. This may take some practice, but it is easy to master.

**SKILL MASTERY EXERCISE 3**

Inserting a photo into a document (assuming a photo was downloaded from a digital camera and saved to a file). Complete the following steps:

1.  In Word, click Insert on the menu bar.

2.  Click Picture and then From File.

3.  Select the photo you want to use from My Documents or from a floppy disk, a CD-ROM, a DVD-ROM, or another storage device. Press Insert.

The photo should appear on the screen.

**SKILL MASTERY EXERCISE 4**

Inserting a table into a document. Complete the following steps:

1.  In Word, click Table on the menu bar.

2.  Click Insert, then Table.

The screen should look like this:

3.  Select the number of columns (2) and rows (5) you want for the table.

A table with two columns and five rows should appear on the screen, as shown below.

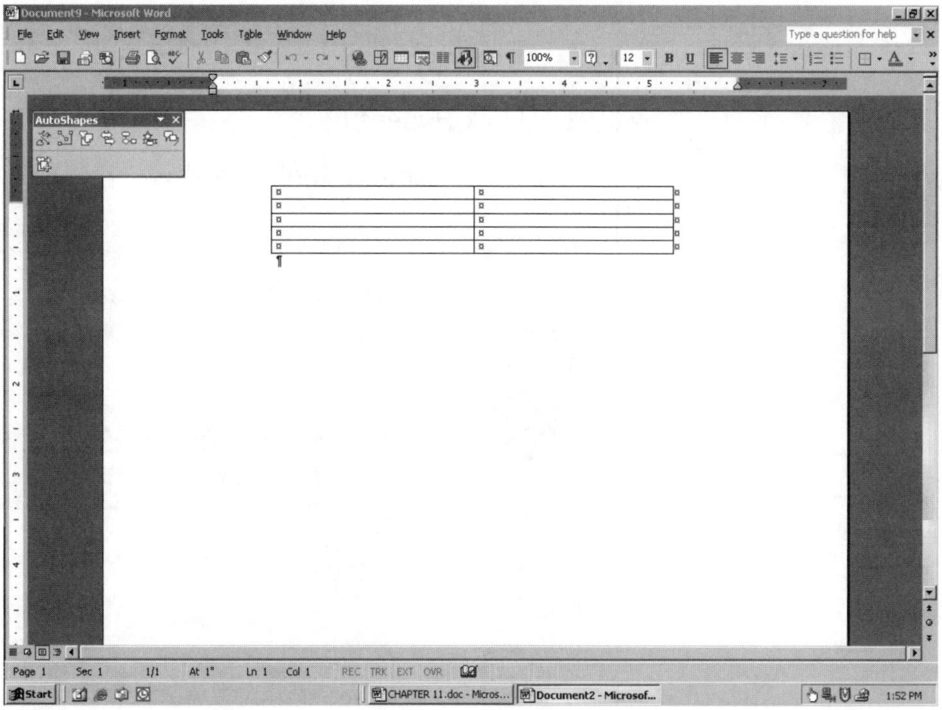

**SKILL MASTERY
EXERCISE 5**

Inserting a hyperlink into a document. Complete the following steps:

1. In Word, click Insert on the menu bar.

2. Click Hyperlink.

The screen should look like this:

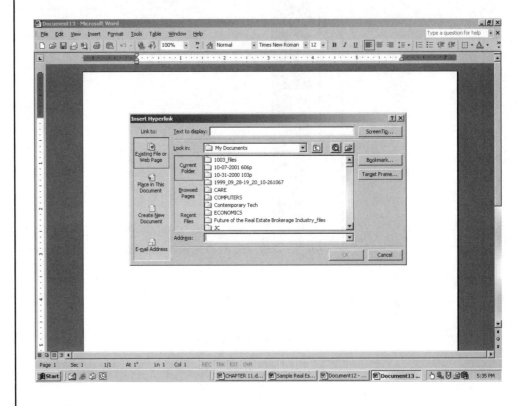

3. Click E-mail Address.

4. Key your e-mail address in the Address Bar and click OK

Your e-mail address should now be shown in blue. When the user clicks the hyperlink, he or she will be taken directly to a blank e-mail screen with your e-mail address already inserted.

## Culminating Exercise

Now you can apply the skills you just learned. Create a real estate flyer making use of WordArt and AutoShapes. Also insert a photo, a table, and a hyperlink. Use other formatting tools as well to create a professional-looking document.

# 11.4 Background of Microsoft Publisher

Publisher is another program available from Microsoft. It is used for simple office and home publishing. With Publisher, the cyber professional can design, create, and publish professional marketing and communication materials; for example, flyers, posters, banners, postcards, and brochures. It allows the cyber professional to create more sophisticated documents than he or she can with Word. Publisher includes many of the tools found in Word, such as bold, italic, and underline. This software can be purchased separately or as part of Microsoft's Small Office Business Edition 2004 and Office Professional Edition 2003. Becoming proficient with the program takes some time and practice. The intent here is not to cover the entire program, but to concentrate on how to make a personal marketing brochure.

---

### *PUTTING IT TOGETHER*

Publisher offers the cyber professional a way to create professional marketing and communication materials. It goes beyond what Word can do.

# 11.5 Special Features and Functions of Publisher

The following is a brief discussion of features of Publisher.

***Publisher Toolbar.*** The toolbar is much like those used in other Microsoft software programs. It includes the following features:

- File
- Edit
- View
- Insert

- Format
- Tools
- Table
- Arrange
- Windows
- Help

***The Wizard.*** This tool guides the user through the process of creating a document. All the user needs to do is follow the cues of the wizard and fill in whatever information is requested. The wizard takes the user through the entire process step by step.

---

### PUTTING IT TOGETHER

The wizard guides the user in creating publications. All the user has to do is follow the cues and fill in the requested information.

# 11.6 Computer Applications

This section shows you how to create a brochure using Publisher.

**SKILL MASTERY
EXERCISE 1**

Creating a personal brochure. Complete the following steps:

1. In Publisher, click File, then New.

The screen should look like this:

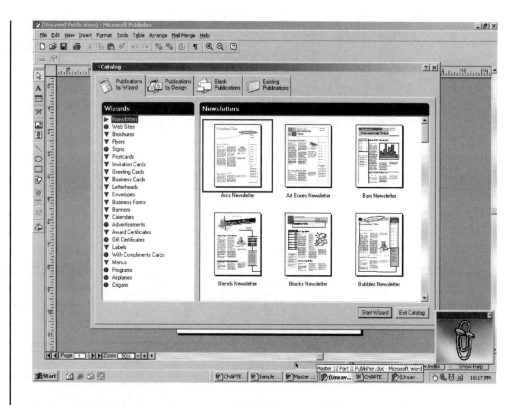

A catalog of options appears, including newsletters and brochures. The text below explains how to create a brochure. The user has several options when constructing a brochure. They include Publications by Wizard, Publications by Design, and Blank Publications. This exercise uses Publications by Wizard.

2.  Select Brochures under Wizards.

Several different brochure options appear. They include the following:

- Informational

- Price List

- Event

- Fundraiser

Only the Informational type will be covered here.

3.  Select the Bars Informational slide. It looks like this:

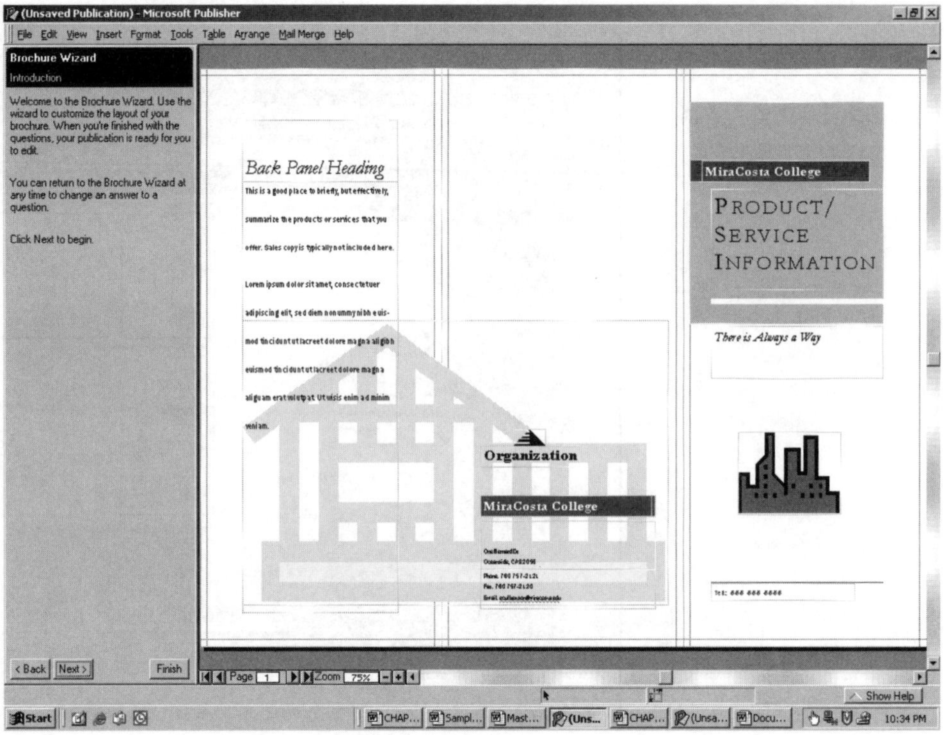

4.  Click Color Schemes and choose Mist. Press Next.

5.  Select letter size (8.5 x 11) and number of panels (3).

6.  Select No for Placeholder and press Next.

7.  Select No for Form and press Finish.

8.  Click inside each of the categories and add the information related to the description.  The categories include these:

    •  Back Panel Heading and information about what you do

    •  Product/Service Information

    •  Name of Organization

    •  Address, Phone, and E-mail

    •  Logo

The brochure will have two pages. Page 1 should look like this:

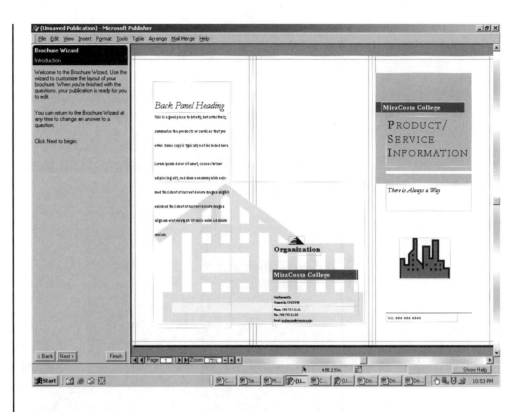

## Page 2 should look like this:

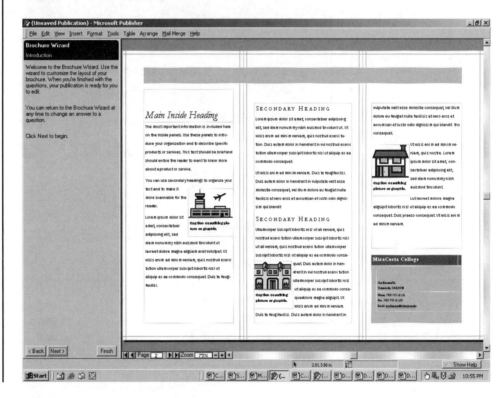

9.  Select each category and fill in whatever information you want to include in your personal brochure.

An example of a brochure appears below.

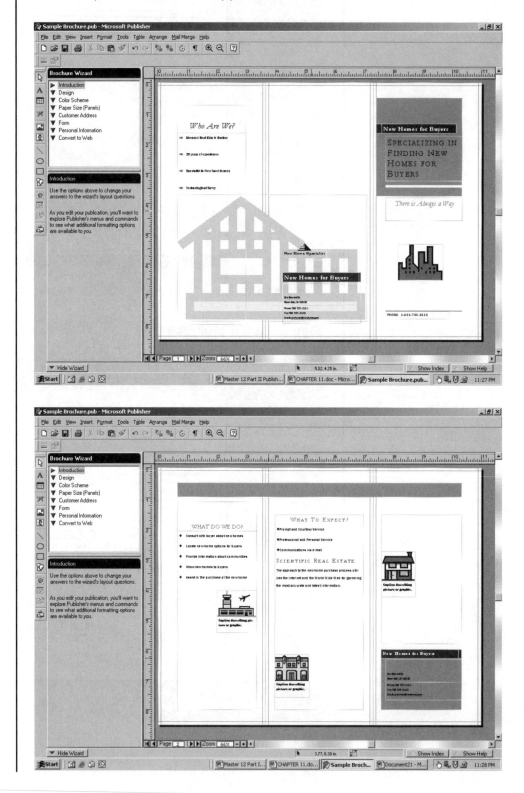

## Culminating Exercise

Now you can apply the skills you just learned. Using the previous illustration as an example, create a brochure in Publisher. Personalize the brochure so you could use it as a cyber professional.

# 11.7 Advanced Topics

Publisher can be used to create other marketing pieces. These are described here.

**Newsletters.** Another option in Publisher is the ability to create newsletters for publication and distribution via the Internet.

**Postcards.** Publisher allows the cyber professional to create postcards that can be used for mailers or for distribution over the Internet.

**Business Cards.** The cyber professional can use Publisher to design, create, and print professional-looking business cards.

**Flyers.** The cyber professional can create a variety of flyers, including Informational and Special Offer.

# RESOUCES FOR FURTHER STUDY

http://nami.videoprofessor.com/411/course_word2002.php?campaignID=2731
This site offers instruction on how to use Microsoft Word.

http://www.ag.ohio-state.edu/course_offerings/outlines/Create%20Brochures.htm
A seminar designed to show how to create flyers and brochures using Word.

http://www.hp.com/sbso/productivity/office/brochure.html
This Hewlett-Packard site gives examples of how to create flyers using Word and Publisher, and even offers downloadable templates.

http://nami.videoprofessor.com/411/course_publisher2002.php?campaignID=2731
This site offers instruction on how to use Publisher.

http://desktoppub.about.com/od/publisher/
A tutorial on how to use Publisher.

http://www.seniortechcenter.org/reference_library/software/intro_to_ms_publisher.php
This site provides some basic background on Publisher.

http://www.officetutorials.com/publishertutorials.htm
A tutorial on how to use Publisher to create flyers and brochures.

http://www.freedownloadscenter.com/Search/microsoft_publisher.html
Publisher can be downloaded from this site.

# SELF-ASSESSMENT

To determine the extent of knowledge you acquired in this chapter, choose the correct answer for each of the following.

1. The cyber professional can produce real estate flyers using which program?
   a. Microsoft Windows
   b. Microsoft Word
   c. Microsoft Publisher
   d. Both b and c

2. What special tool in Microsoft Word can the cyber professional use to create real estate flyers?
   a. AutoShapes
   b. WordArt
   c. Hyperlinks
   d. All of the above

3. Which of the following statements about WordArt is true?
   a. It is used to create text with special shapes and designs.
   b. It is used to insert predrawn shapes into a document.
   c. It is a feature of Publisher.
   d. None of these

4. Examples of AutoShapes include all of the following except:
   a. Rectangle
   b. Oval
   c. Lines
   d. Hyperlinks

5. Which of the following statements about a table is not true?
   a. The cyber professional can decide on the number of rows and columns.
   b. A table can be used to organize information in a document.
   c. Tables can be created using the Wizard in Publisher.
   d. Both a and c

6. What is an advantage of adding a hyperlink to a document?
   a. It allows the recipient to go directly to a web site.
   b. It allows the cyber professional to insert photos in documents.
   c. It offers convenience for the recipient.
   d. Both a and c

7. To insert a hyperlink, what does the cyber professional access?:
   a. File
   b. Insert
   c. View
   d. Edit

8. Which program is best for creating real estate flyers?
   a. Microsoft Word
   b. Internet Explorer
   c. Microsoft Publisher
   d. Microsoft Windows

9. Which of the following statements about clip art is not true?
   a. It is available on the Internet.
   b. It is text on a page that a person clicks to go to another page.
   c. It is a collection of images that can be inserted into documents.
   d. It is available in Word.

10. All of the following are options for a brochure except:
    a. Informational
    b. Event
    c. Fundraiser
    d. Announcement

11. The main function of the wizard in Publisher is to:
    a. Serve as a guide
    b. Make the task of creating a publication easier
    c. Save time
    d. All of the above

12. All of the following colors are offered in Publisher's Color Schemes except:
    a. Burgundy
    b. Mist
    c. Black Forest
    d. Bluebird

13. Which of the following statements about Microsoft Publisher is not true?
    a. It comes preinstalled on all computers.
    b. It can be purchased as part of Microsoft Office Small Business Edition 2003.
    c. It can be purchased as part of Microsoft Office Professional Edition 2003.
    d. It can be purchased as a stand-alone software program.

14. Using Microsoft Publisher, the cyber professional can create all of the following except:
    a. Catalogs
    b. Business cards
    c. Postcards
    d. Spreadsheets

15. By learning how to use Microsoft Word and Publisher, the cyber professional:
    a. Can promote his or her real estate business
    b. Doesn't have to pay a graphic designer to create real estate documents
    c. Create his or her own real estate documents
    d. All of the above

# CHAPTER 12
## MAKING REAL ESTATE PRESENTATIONS: MICROSOFT POWERPOINT®

## PREVIEW

The consumer has become accustomed to the best technology has to offer. Keeping this in mind, the cyber professional should do everything possible to give his or her clients what they expect. The purpose of this chapter is to highlight the features and functions of Microsoft PowerPoint so the cyber professional can learn to create multimedia presentations for seminars and for web sites.

When you finish this chapter, you will be able to:

1. Describe the benefits of Microsoft PowerPoint to the cyber professional.

2. Explain how multimedia presentations can be used in real estate.

3. Understand the features and functions of PowerPoint.

4. Produce a multimedia product with PowerPoint.

## KEY TERMS

| | |
|---|---|
| *animation* | *Slide Layout* |
| *handouts* | *Slide Show* |
| *outline* | *Transition Effects* |
| *Slide Design* | |

# 12.1 How Microsoft PowerPoint Can Benefit the Cyber Professional

Being able to produce PowerPoint presentations will show the cyber professional's expertise in using technology. Using Power-Point, the cyber professional will be able to:

1. Create multimedia presentations that can be used to conduct seminars for sellers and buyers.

2. Create multimedia presentations that can be used to distribute information over the Internet.

3. Create special presentations that can be used on web sites for informational purposes.

4. Create an operational web site in lieu of purchasing a commercial web site.

# 12.2 Production

Professional multimedia presentation software used to be rather difficult to use. With PowerPoint, anyone who is willing to learn the program can produce professional multimedia presentations. PowerPoint has many uses for the cyber professional. One application is to create presentations to give to potential clients. These presentations can be given at seminars on a wide variety of real estate topics; for example, a seminar on the advantages of home ownership. (This example will be illustrated later in the chapter.)

In addition to seminars, the cyber professional can create Power-Point presentations on CDs about any number of topics. The CDs can be duplicated and distributed to prospects, clients, and past clients. Presentations can also be sent via e-mail to a distribution list or used to create an electronic newsletter. Another application of PowerPoint is to set up a laptop presentation at a trade show. This presentation can be programmed to run automatically so people see it when they walk by a booth. PowerPoint can also save presentations in a web-viewable format, which is readable by a web browser. This topic is covered in the next two chapters.

## PowerPoint

PowerPoint is easy to use and is an effective tool for communicating information. PowerPoint, like other software programs, has gone through numerous versions, resulting in a better program for the user. PowerPoint is often purchased as a stand-alone product, but it is part of all Microsoft Office Editions 2003. The program is easy to install but requires ample hard disk space.

### PUTTING IT TOGETHER

PowerPoint is part of the Microsoft Office Editions 2003.

PowerPoint has features in common with other Microsoft programs. However, to be able to use the program, the user must learn how to use several new tools.

## Features and Functions of PowerPoint

This section explains the features and functions of PowerPoint.

- New and Open. If you are already working in PowerPoint, you can click New in the File menu to display a new blank presentation. Open is used to open an existing slide show that has already been saved.

- Insert. Insert menu is used to insert information into a slide. This information may be in the form of a document, a table, clip art, a photograph, or a hyperlink. Clip art is typically available either on the hard disk or on the program's install CD. Other clip art files may come from a variety of locations, including the Internet. This feature is often used by cyber professionals to insert pictures of homes that clients can find on the Internet.

- **Slide Layout.** The layouts represent the different options for displaying information on the slides. The choices are Text Layout, Content Layout, Text and Content Layout, and Other Layouts. Determining which one to use depends on the content of the slide. For example, Text Layout is used to add written information only, whereas Content Layout is used to add pictures, graphics, and other features. Features that may be inserted in this type of slide include the following:

  - Table
  - Chart
  - Clip Art
  - Picture
  - Diagram or Organizational Chart
  - Media Clip

  The other categorizes have slides for charts, media clips, and other special options. These layouts give the cyber professional the ability to create more dynamic presentations.

- **Slide Design.** A unique feature of PowerPoint is being able to choose a design template already created by the software. All you need to do is examine each of the options and determine which one is best for the message you are trying to convey. You can choose predesigned templates, color schemes, and even animation schemes. Once you choose a design or color scheme all of the slides in the presentation are changed. This provides consistency and saves you time.

- Background. With this feature, you can customize the background of slides by adding color, a shade, a texture, a pattern, or a picture.

- **Animation.** Being able to add animation is another unique feature of PowerPoint. This gives you the opportunity to animate the text and graphics on the slides. You can apply text animation so text appears on the screen one letter, word, or paragraph at a time. If a slide has more than one level of bullet points, you can animate different levels separately. You can animate shapes. You can also animate objects and text together, or you can animate one but not the other. You should experiment with all of the options before deciding which one to use.

---

## *PUTTING IT TOGETHER*

Many options are available when adding animation to a PowerPoint presentation.

- **Transition Effects**. Transition effects vary the way one slide replaces another, thereby adding variety to the presentation and making more of a visual impact. Transitions include such effects as sliding into view from one of several directions, dissolving from the outer edges or from the center, and checkerboarding across or down.

- New Slide. You click this button each time you want to create a new slide in a slide show. It is accessed by clicking on the New Slide button on the Formatting toolbar or by clicking Insert on the menu bar and then New Slide.

- Help. The Help button found on the menu bar is an important part of the program. It allows you to get answers to questions you may have about different functions of PowerPoint. All you have to do is click Help on the menu bar, then select Microsoft Office PowerPoint Help to conduct a search.

---

## *PUTTING IT TOGETHER*

You can get help in PowerPoint.

- **Outline.** The Outline tab of the Outline/Slides pane allows you to keep track of the progress of the slide show. It is displayed to the left of the slides being produced.

- **Handouts.** When a slide show is finished or before a presentation starts, you may want to provide a handout of the presentation to the recipients. This can be accomplished by clicking View on the menu bar, clicking Master, and then Handout Master. Handouts can include from one to nine slides per page.

- **Slide Show.** When all slides have been created, Slide Show is used to present the individual slides to an audience. To start the slide show with all slides, click Slide Show on the menu bar. You can move to the next slide or previous slide by pressing the right arrow key or the left arrow key located at the bottom of the keyboard. You can also right-click on the screen and click Next or Previous on the shortcut menu. To end a session, press the Escape (Esc) key located at the top left corner of the keyboard.

- Slide Sorter View. In Slide Sorter view, you can display all of the slides created for a presentation. It lets you preview an entire presentation. You can delete slides and change their order.

- Normal View. In Normal view, you can work with a presentation in three way: as a text outline or set of thumbnails, as a slide, and as speaker notes.

- Toolbar. As in other Microsoft programs, the toolbar contains buttons that perform common commands in PowerPoint.

- Header and Footer. A header is a title or information that prints at the top of a slide. A footer is a title or information that prints at the bottom of a slide. You create a header or footer by selecting View, then Header and Footer.

- Text Box. A text box is used to insert text into a document. You insert a text box by clicking the Text Box button on the Drawing toolbar. You can format, resize, and move a text box as you would a graphic object.

- Movies and Sounds. With Power Point, you can insert movie clips and/or sound into a presentation.

---

## *PUTTING IT TOGETHER*

With PowerPoint, you can insert movie clips and music into slide presentations.

- Record Narration. PowerPoint allows users to add narration to a presentation. You might use this feature if you are creating a presentation that people will view on their own machines or if you want to include speaker's comments.

- Rehearse Timings. Rehearse Timings allows you to control the speed of a slide show. You can rehearse the presentation while PowerPoint automatically tracks and sets the timing for you. This way your presentation will incorporate the amount of time you spent on each slide during the rehearsal. This technique lets you spend more time discussing some slides than others.

(Note that not all features and functions of PowerPoint have been presented in this chapter. Only those that can help with the creation of a basic slide show have been discussed. To become more proficient with PowerPoint, you will need additional training.)

# 12.3 Computer Applications

This section demonstrates how to create a simple PowerPoint presentation.

**SKILL MASTERY EXERCISE 1**

Starting PowerPoint and opening a new slide. To start a new Power-Point presentation, complete the following steps:

1. Go to Start, Select Programs, then Microsoft Office. Click Microsoft PowerPoint. The screen should look like this:

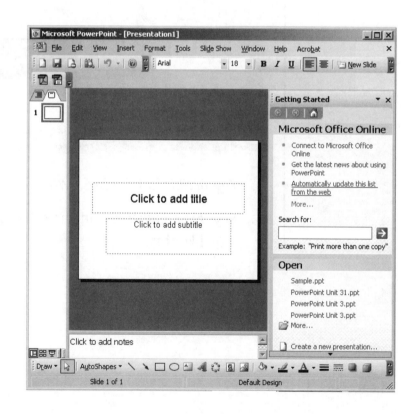

What you see is PowerPoint's program window, which displays the components and features that are common to all Microsoft Office programs, that are unique to Office 2003, and that are unique to PowerPoint.

**SKILL MASTERY
EXERCISE 2**

Creating a Title Slide. Complete the following steps to select and start a Title Slide:

1. From the Format menu, select Slide Layout. You will see thumbnails of a variety of design templates.

2. The screen should look like this:

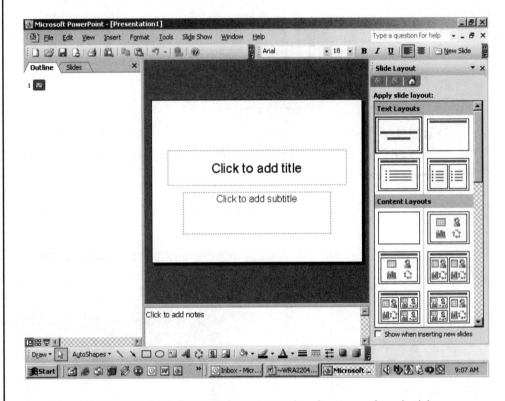

3. Key *BENEFITS OF HOME OWNERSHIP* in the top placeholder.

4. Key *By Ed Culbertson* in the other placeholder. The slide should look like this:

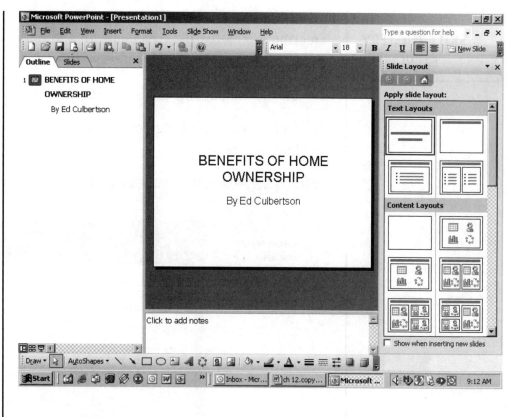

5. Click Save.

**SKILL MASTERY
EXERCISE 3**

Creating a bulleted list in a slide. To add bullets to a slide, complete the following steps:

1. On the Formatting toolbar, click New Slide.

2. From Slide Layout, select the second layout. The slide should look like this:

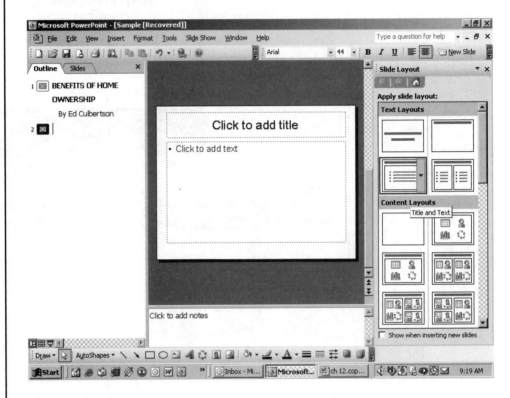

3. Key *BENEFITS* in the top placeholder.

4. Key *Pride of Ownership* in the other placeholder and press Enter. Key *Tax Deductions* and press Enter. Key *Appreciation* and press Enter. Key *Equity Build-Up* and press Enter. Then key *Forced Savings*. The slide should look like this:

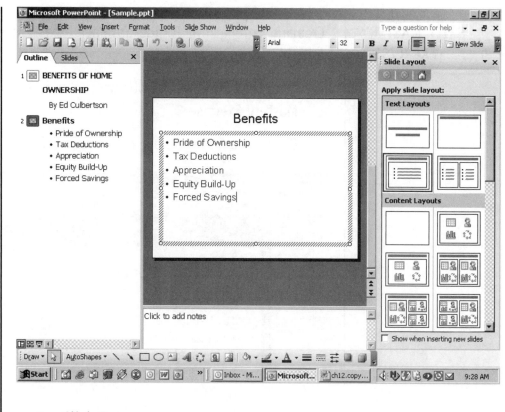

5. Click Save.

**SKILL MASTERY EXERCISE 4**

Creating animation. To add animation to a slide, complete the following steps:

1. Click New Slide and duplicate the slide you created in Skill Mastery Exercise 3.

2. Click Slide Show. Select Animation Schemes.

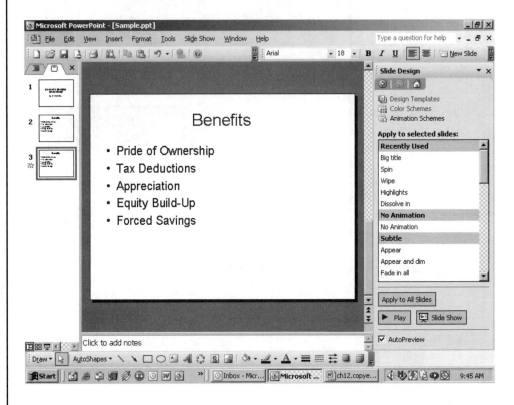

3. Scroll through the animation schemes. As you select various schemes, you will see how they look. Choose one you would like to apply to this screen.

4. Click Save.

(Note that the animation cannot be displayed until the slide show is actually running.)

**SKILL MASTERY
EXERCISE 5**

Creating a slide with clip art. To add clip art to a slide, complete the following steps:

1. Click New Slide. Click Slide Layout. Scroll down and choose the first layout under Text and Content Layouts, shown below:

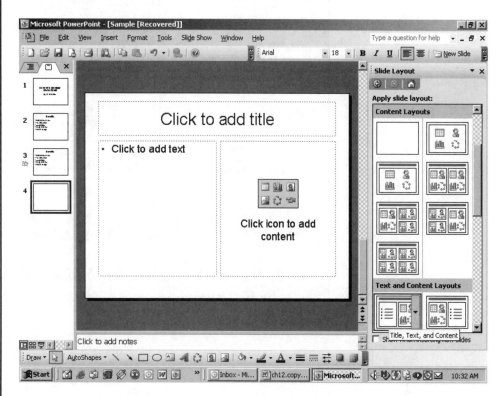

2. Duplicate the slide you created in Skill Mastery Exercise 3.

3. In the last placeholder, click Insert Clip Art. The screen should look like this:

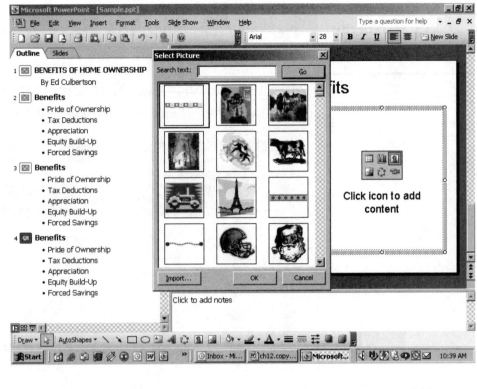

4.  In the search text box, key *business*. Click Go. Double-click on the first picture.

The picture now appears on the slide. It should look like this:

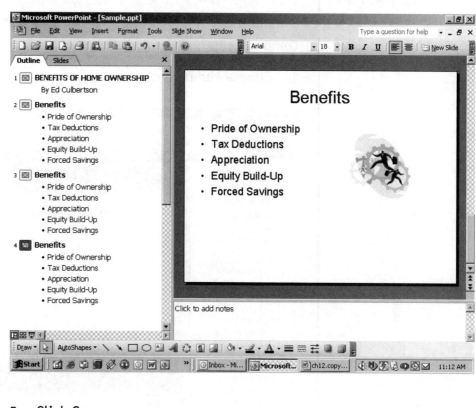

5.   Click Save.

**SKILL MASTERY**
**EXERCISE 6**

Creating a slide with a photo. (You must have a digital photograph available to complete this exercise.) To insert a photo of a home, complete the following steps:

1. Choose the layout shown below.

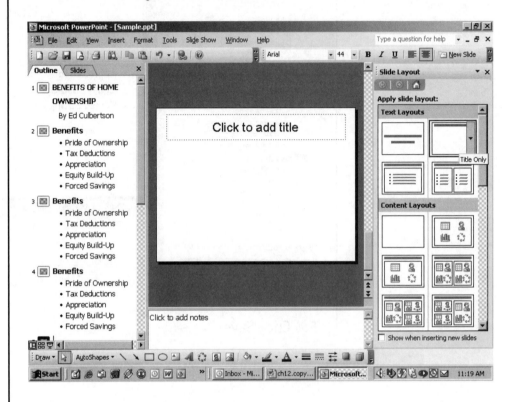

2. In the placeholder, key "Home for Sale."

3. Move your pointer to the space below the placeholder. To insert a picture from a file on your hard disk, removable disk, or network, click Insert, Picture, From File. You can then size the photo to fit the space in the slide.

**SKILL MASTERY EXERCISE 7**

Creating a slide with a hyperlink. To create a slide with a hyperlink, complete the following steps:

1. Click on the layout shown below:

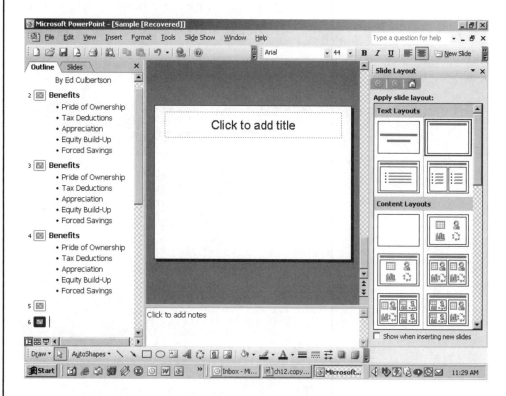

2. In the placeholder, key *Search for a Home,* as shown below.

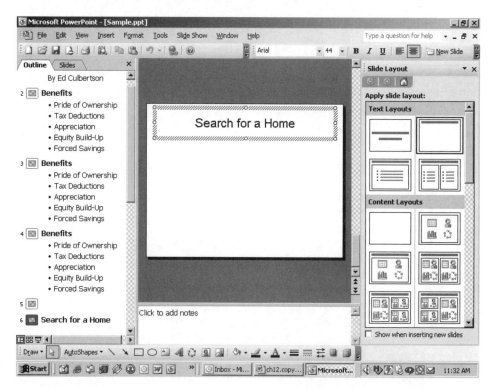

3. Highlight *Search for a Home* by dragging the pointer over the text.

4. Click Insert on the toolbar.

5. Click Hyperlink. Key http://www.realtor.com in the Address box. It should look like this:

6. Click OK. The title in the slide is now highlighted and underlined. It is recognizable as a hyperlink, as shown below.

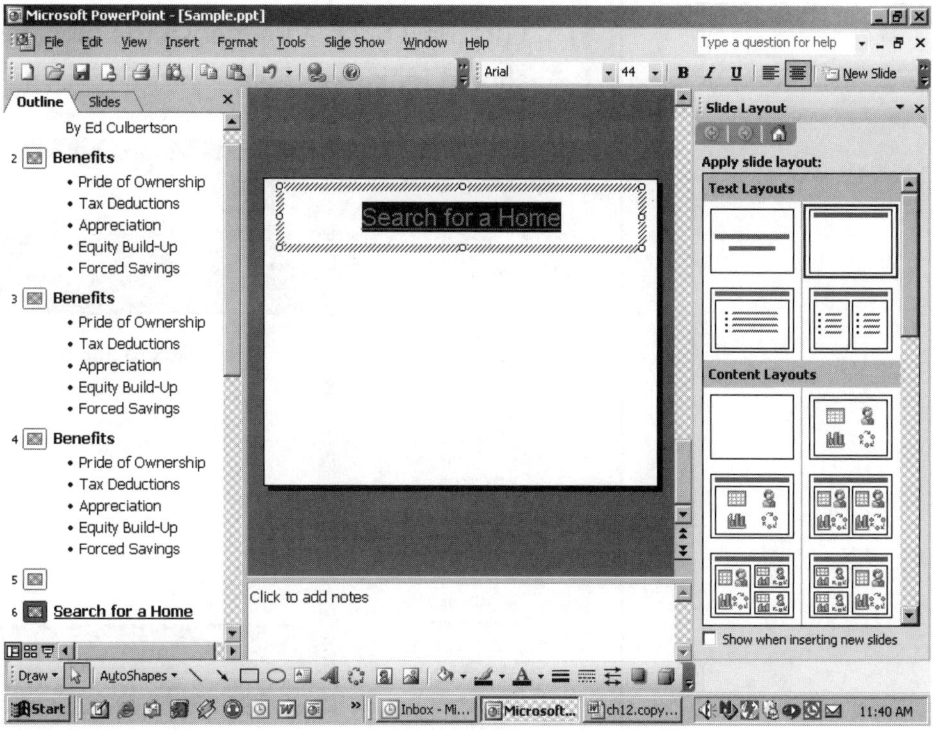

7. Click Save.

(Note that the hyperlink will not be activated until the slide show is actually running.)

**SKILL MASTERY
EXERCISE 8**

Creating a thank-you slide. To create a final slide for a presentation, complete the following steps:

1. Click New Slide and choose the layout shown below. Press OK. It should look like this:

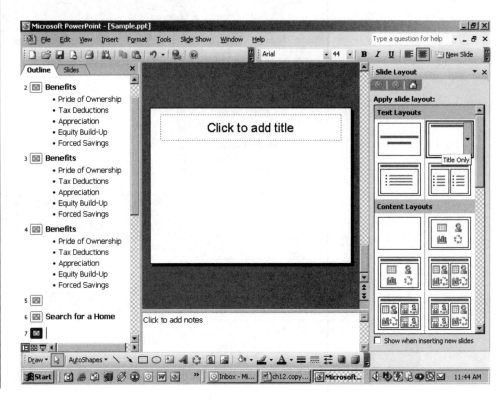

2. Key *THANK YOU* in the placeholder. The slide should look like this:

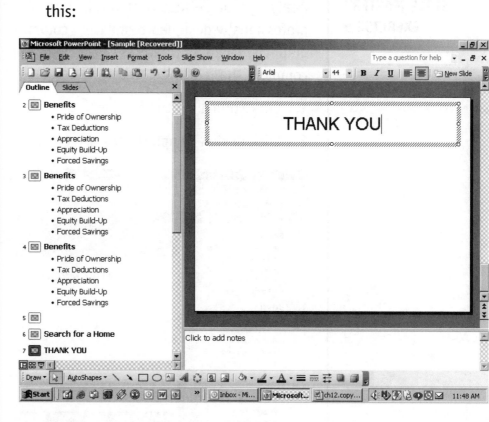

3. Click Save.

**SKILL MASTERY
EXERCISE 9**

Applying a predefined design template. You can use a variety of professionally designed templates (colors, text formats, and graphics) to apply to a presentation. To apply a design template, complete the following steps:

1.  Click Format on the toolbar.

2.  Click Design Template. The screen should look like this:

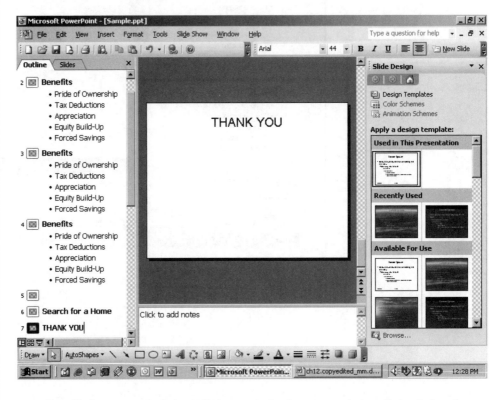

3.  Scroll down and right-click on a design template. Select Apply to All Slides. An example of the design is applied to your slides.

If you chose Ripple, the slides should look like this:

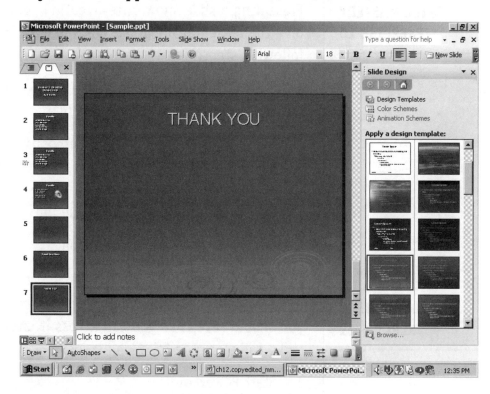

(Note that a design template can be changed at any time.)

**SKILL MASTERY EXERCISE 10**

Presenting a slide show. After creating your slides, you are ready to give the presentation. To set up the Slide Show, complete the following steps:

1. Click Slide Show on the toolbar. Click View Show. The presentation will begin with the first slide.

2. To move to the next slide or previous slide, press the right arrow key or the left arrow key located at the bottom of the keyboard. You can also right-click on the screen and click Next or Previous on the shortcut menu. Continue until the show is complete.

3. Save and close the presentation.

**SKILL MASTERY EXERCISE 11**

Retrieving a slide show presentation. Once a slide show is complete, you should save it so you can access it later. To retrieve an existing slide, complete the following steps:

1. Start PowerPoint.

2. Click File, then Open.

3. Locate the file and click Open.

4. The slides will appear.

## Culminating Exercise

Now you can apply the skills you just learned. Create a PowerPoint presentation pertaining to real estate that contains 10 to 12 slides. Incorporate the features of PowerPoint just presented in the Skill Mastery Exercises.

# 12.4 Advanced Topics

PowerPoint offers many more features than this chapter presented. Additional features include the following:

- Adding 3D animation

- Recording sound to include in a presentation

- Adding video to a presentation

- Utilizing Meeting Minder

- Adding Notes to slides

- Setting up a self-running slide show

- Creating a web page

- Publishing a web page on the Internet

- Using an annotation pen for highlighting points on the slides

- Using the Package for CD feature to send the presentation to others who do not have PowerPoint software

- Printing handouts to distribute to attendees

PowerPoint has even more to offer the cyber professional. It is a tool the cyber professional can use to create striking presentations to impress clients and potential clients.

# RESOURCES FOR FURTHER STUDY

http://nami.videoprofessor.com/411/course_powerpoint2000.php?campaignID=2731

A web site offering instruction on how to use PowerPoint.

http://office.microsoft.com/OfficeUpdate/default.aspx?display-lang=EN

PowerPoint software and updates can be downloaded from this site.

http://office.microsoft.com/home/office.aspx?assetid=FX01085797

The home page for PowerPoint offers instruction and a trial version of the software.

http://www.ga.k12.pa.us/curtech/powerwk.htm

This site offers a tutorial on how to use PowerPoint, with numerous illustrated examples.

# SELF-ASSESSMENT

To determine the extent of knowledge you acquired in this chapter, choose the correct answer for each of the following.

1.  PowerPoint can be used to:
    a.  Create presentations for real estate seminars
    b.  Create presentations that can be duplicated onto CDs
    c.  Create web presentations
    d.  All of the above

2.  To start PowerPoint, the cyber professional:
    a.  Clicks Start, then Programs
    b.  Clicks File, then Open
    c.  Clicks File, then New
    d.  None of these

3.  PowerPoint may be purchased:
    a.  As a stand-alone product
    b.  As part of all Microsoft Office Editions 2003
    c.  Both a and b
    d.  None of these

4.  With which program does PowerPoint have things in common?
    a.  Word
    b.  Windows
    c.  Publisher
    d.  All of the above

5.  To create a new slide show, the cyber professional clicks:
    a.  Edit
    b.  File
    c.  View
    d.  Insert

6.  All of the following features can be incorporated into a Power-Point presentation except?
    a.  WordArt
    b.  AutoShapes
    c.  Office Assistant
    d.  Hyperlinks

7. Choices for different types of Slide Layouts include:
   a. Text Layouts
   b. Content Layouts
   c. Text and Content Layouts
   d. All of the above

8. What is involved with changing a slide design?
   a. Each slide must be changed individually.
   b. The slides cannot be changed once the program is begun.
   c. All slides change automatically.
   d. None of these

9. To start a slide show, the cyber professional:
   a. Clicks File, then New
   b. Clicks Insert, then Picture
   c. Clicks Slide Show on the menu bar
   d. Clicks Start, then Programs

10. Which of the following features can be inserted into a slide?
    a. Table
    b. Picture
    c. Organization Chart
    d. All of the above

11. What is the purpose of including animation in a PowerPoint presentation?
    a. To add excitement to the program
    b. To distract the audience
    c. So the presenter can impress the audience with his her PowerPoint skills
    d. Animation serves no useful purpose.

12. Which of the following views is not available in PowerPoint?
    a. Slider Sorter view
    b. Normal view
    c. Continuous view
    d. Slide Show view

13. Why is a hyperlink included in a PowerPoint presentation?
    a. To allow viewers to access a web site
    b. To add color
    c. To distract the audience
    d. To impress the audience

14. What should the cyber professional do after he or she has created a presentation?
    a. Delete it
    b. Save it
    c. Store it in the Recycle Bin
    d. Send it to a client

15. What is an advanced feature and function of PowerPoint?
    a. Record Narration
    b. Package for CD
    c. Meeting Minder
    d. All of the above

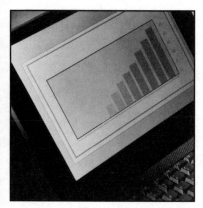

# CHAPTER 13
## UNDERTANDING WEB SITES

## PREVIEW

The next two chapters of the text are devoted to web design and development. This chapter concentrates on the basics of web sites. Having a web presence on the World Wide Web is a must for the cyber professional. With a domain name and a web site, the cyber professional will be able to create a new dimension fo productivity and profitability.

When you finish this chapter, you will be able to:

1. Describe the importance of having a web presence.

2. Describe terminology pertaining to web site development.

3. Explain the concept of domain names and hosting.

4. Discuss different types of web designs and layouts.

5. Describe several web development software programs.

## KEY TERMS

| | |
|---|---|
| *domain name* | *sticky* |
| *hierarchical* | *viral* |
| *home page* | *vortal* |
| *hosting* | *web pages* |
| *portal* | *web site* |
| *secondary pages* | *webmaster* |
| *splash page* | *WYSIWYG* |

# 13.1 How a Web Presence Can Benefit the Cyber Professional

To compete in the real estate industry today, a real estate professional needs to have some form of electronic recognition. By having a web presence, the cyber professional:

1. Can achieve technological credibility.

2. Can conduct business anytime, anywhere in the world.

3. Can provide relevant real estate information to potential prospects who use the Internet.

4. Can communicate with the e-consumers via e-mail, newsletters, and instant messaging.

5. Can assist clients in processing selling and buying paperwork.

6. Has a business presence like that of large organizations.

# 13.2 Setting Up a Web Presence

To have a presence on the Internet, you first need to understand some basic fundamentals about web development. One of the first things you must do is select a domain name. A **domain name** is the unique name that identifies an Internet site. Domain names always have two or more parts separated by periods. The part on the left is the most specific, and the part on the right is the most general. The name should reflect your organization or personal name so potential customers know how to contact you.

After choosing a domain name, you need a way to get the domain name available on the Internet. To do this, you need to contact a **hosting** service. It most cases, you pay for this service, as you do for an ISP. Hosting will be discussed in more detail later in the chapter.

## *Web Definitions*

Typically, when you decide you want a web site, you discuss the matter with a systems analyst. You discuss the purpose of the site and how you want it organized. A major player in developing a web site is a programmer. His or her primary role is to write background programs for the pages related to the site. In some cases, this individual has extensive training and education in computer engineering and applications. The programmer starts the web development process. Along the way, other professionals, such as a multimedia specialist or a graphic artist, may become involved. Once the web site is up and running, another major player steps into the picture. This individual is responsible for the overall operation of the web site and is known as the **webmaster.**

The webmaster's tasks include editing, monitoring, evaluating, and maintaining the site. What the webmaster does or does not do can have an impact on how successful the web presence proves to be for the cyber professional.

## *Web Site*

The term *web site* is often confused with the term *web page*. They are different. A **web site** is a collection of web pages that collectively represents a company or an individual on the World Wide Web. A web site needs to have some form of identification to distinguish itself from other sites on the Web. Each site has a unique address. A system called DNS (Domain Name System) assigns these addresses, like unique telephone numbers in the yellow pages. A web site is given identification so it can be found on the World Wide Web. Each registered web site is assigned a URL. A typical web site address begins with *http://,* which represents the type of protocol that is used. The next part of the address, *www,* stands for World Wide Web, followed by a period. Next is the actual domain name of the operation, such as *realtor.* The final part of the address is the extension. Since there are millions of URLs, they are categorized into several areas. A common designation is *com.* An example of a complete URL address is http:// www.realtor.com. In advanced browsers, *http://* is usually not needed to access the Internet. Often a URL will include more specific information from a special file. This additional file includes the forward slash symbol (/). Another example of a URL is as follows: http:// www.nahrep.org/Calendar/calendar.html.

Within each web site are individual pages containing whatever information you choose. These individual pages are called **web pages.** A web site often contains multiple pages. The first page to appear on a web site is the **home page.** This is the first page that a web user encounters. The design and organization of the home page often determines whether a user will continue to explore the site. Therefore, the home page is very important because "First impressions are lasting impressions." A user who accesses a web site that makes a poor first impression may not bother to delve deeper or may decide not to return to the site.

A webmasters may decide to create a **splash page,** which is an opening page that a user must click on to enter the web site. This page serves as an inducement to get the user to enter the site and see what it has to offer. As with the home page, the splash page must look professional in order to lure users into the site.

## PUTTING IT TOGETHER

A web site may include a home page, a splash page, and web pages.

Webmasters try to make a site "**sticky**." This implies that the user will *stick* with the site to get the information they want easily and quickly. The webmaster tries to design a site that is "**viral**," or contagious, so the user will get hooked on the site and return time after time. The user may even bookmark the web site for future reference.

### *PUTTING IT TOGETHER*

Web sites should be "sticky" and "viral."

Another goal of webmasters is to make a site a "one-stop site." This is a web site where all relevant information about a topic is located. In the case of real estate, it may include information about homes for sale, finance, maps, communities, schools, and more. The webmaster tries to make a site a **portal.** This term is used to describe a web site that is intended to be the first place people see when using the Web. For example, a portal may open the door to the entire real estate process. The user doesn't need to go anywhere else. A **vortal** is a specialized portal that serves a particular organization or interest group; for example, real estate. All of the pages beyond the splash page or home page are called the **secondary pages.**

In review, a user inputs a URL, then a splash page may appear, followed by the home page and the secondary pages.

### *PUTTING IT TOGETHER*

A one-stop web site implies that everything a user wants is on one web site.

# 13.3 The "Big Two" Considerations

One of the first steps in the web development process is to select an appropriate name that best represents the message you want to convey about your business. The second step is to engage a host that will service the web site.

## *Domain Names*

A domain name is the name of the operation. It usually indicates what the site represents or what the site does. Each user must have a specialized domain name—just like a social security number. The domain name identifies one and only one entity. There are millions of domain names, and the options for choosing one are limitless. The .com domain name has over 9 million entries. Domain names have top-level names that delineate different areas of business and government. Some examples of these are as follows:

- com represents commercial and personal sites
- edu represents the field of education
- gov represents different aspects of the government
- mil signifies the military
- net signifies anything related to different types of networks
- org represents nonprofit entities
- biz signifies anything related to the field of business
- pro indicates anything related to a profession
- info represents the dissemination of information for commercial or personal reasons
- name signifies a personal web site

Domain names may also indicate the country from which the site originates. Some examples include:

- ca for Canada
- uk for the United Kingdom
- to for Tonga
- us for the United States

As the Internet gets crowded with domain names, more top-level names will be added. This is similar to what happened when there were more toll-free numbers than the 1-800 exchange could cover. So the 877 exchange was added.

***Domain Name Selection.*** Choosing a domain name requires some consideration and research. Before choosing a domain name, consider what you are trying to portray. What do you want to be known for, or what do you do? Being descriptive will help consumers find your business. You should also choose a name that is short and to the point. With millions of web sites on the Internet, you must think seriously about how users can recognize you. The maximum length of a domain name usually is 26 characters.

Consider the following points:

- What is the potential viewer's point of view?

- What name would make a viewer want to visit this site?

- Does the name have a connection to the purpose of the business?

- What are some keywords that suggest what the site represents?

- Is the name similar to other sites? Is the name confusing?

- Is the name politically correct and appropriate?

---

### PUTTING IT TOGETHER

Choosing a domain name requires some consideration and research.

***Use a Business Name or a Personal Name?*** Another important decision is whether you should use a personal name or a business name. Each has advantages and disadvantages. If you use a personal name, it may get lost in the Internet's maze of millions of domain names. At the same time, it provides recognition and ownership. A business domain name that is descriptive of what you do could be picked up by a search engine, resulting in your being found among the millions of names. A solution for this dilemma is to acquire both a personal and a business domain name.

***Is the Domain Name Available?*** Once you have chosen a domain name, you must determine whether that name is available for use on the Internet. There can be only one name per person. If someone else has chosen the same name, you must choose another one. You may be surprised to learn that other people have thought of the same name you did.

You can easily determine if a domain name is available by going to one of several web sites. One often-used site is http://www.register.com (see page 263). After accessing this web site, key in the proposed domain name to see if it is available. In many cases, you can use a name, but with a different top-level domain name. In other words, instead of using *com,* you might try *net.* Changes to a domain name can also be made by adding a hyphen (-) or an underscore (_) after any part in the name. Note that an underscore is often overlooked and hidden from view and thus may not be a good choice.

If a domain name is available, you may decide to purchase the name before someone else acquires it. The fee varies from company to company. A domain name can be acquired for one year or more. You can also purchase as many domain names as you want. If you are not ready to launch a full web site but want to hold a particular name, you can pay a fee and reserve the name for the future. This way, no one else can buy the name; you have reserved it.

Once you have chosen and paid for a domain name, it belongs to you as private intellectual property—like a copyright or patent. If the fees are not paid, the domain name will go back on the open market for others to acquire. Another way to acquire a particular name is to buy it from someone who already owns it and is willing to sell.

### *PUTTING IT TOGETHER*

Selecting a domain name is important because it represents you for business purposes.

Changing a domain name can be expensive and may result in lost marketing efforts. Choose wisely and stick with your domain name.

## *Hosting*

Without a host to house, service, and maintain a web site, nothing would appear on the Internet for potential clients to view. Basically, hosting is renting space for your online business. Choosing a host is

Courtesy of register.com

## PUTTING IT TOGETHER

To determine whether a domain name is available, go to http://www.register.com or http://www.networksolutions.com.

similar to choosing an ISP. When choosing a host, you may want to consider the following:

- Cost. There may be a set-up fee and a monthly fee thereafter to service the site. Costs vary, so make sure you know what you're paying for. The price is contingent upon the features. Doing some comparison shopping can save you time and money in the long run. Most host companies offer several plans (basic, standard, and upgraded) depending on your needs. Fees are charged by the month or year. Often discounts are available for paying fees several years in advance. You may be able to set up an account so the fee is paid automatically via credit card or online banking.

- Tech Support. This may be the most important consideration when deciding on a host. Will the host company be available for assistance in the event of a failure? Is there a toll-free number to call for help? Is tech support prompt? Do they treat you well?

How often is the system down? Does tech support include 24/7/365 assistance via phone or e-mail?

- Reputation. How long has the host company been in business? What do others say about the service it provides? Will the company be in business if the economy changes?

- Services. What is the host company offering for the fee? Some services may include the following:

  1. Virus protection and security

  2. Multiple e-mail accounts

  3. Fast connection speed (bandwidth)

  4. Statistical reports such as Internet traffic reviews

  5. Special code capability for advanced programming

  6. Custom domain name at no extra charge

  7. Free marketing

  8. Free web builder

  9. Money-back guarantee

  10. No banner ads or pop-ups

  11. Free site promotion

  12. Free message board

  13. Free counters and trackers

  14. Free guestbook services

Many companies provide hosting. Therefore, you should do some research. The following web sites may be helpful in selecting a host:

- http://www.hostbyte.com

- http://www.web-host-search.com

***Web Design Rules.*** Every webmaster has a list of rules for developing a web site. Different sources have different rules, and rules have a tendency to change. However, most webmasters adhere to some generally accept guidelines:

- Take time to plan the web site.

- Consider the target audience.

- Make the site easy to access and navigate.

- Grab the audience's attention.

- Include pertinent and accurate information.

- Keep the site simple.

- Use white space effectively.

- Keep bandwidth in mind.

---

### PUTTING IT TOGETHER

When designing a web site, keep it simple.

**Web Design Mistakes.** There is no such thing as the perfect web site. The best a webmaster can do is to avoid mistakes in web development.

Many studies have been conducted and many books have been written on what not to do when building a web site. The following list includes some common mistakes:

- The site cannot be viewed on a browser.

- The content is slow to load.

- The site contains broken hyperlinks.

- Information is not accurate or reliable.

- Users cannot navigate the site effectively.

- The site has too many bells and whistles.

- The site contains irrelevant information.

- There is no way to contact the web site.

- The site contains spelling and grammar errors.

- The site looks amateurish and unprofessional.

- The site is "under construction."

- The site misuses multimedia.

- The site contains outdated information.

- The site uses poor typography.

- The content is too long.

- The content is illogical and misplaced.
- The site contains long scrolling pages.

---
### *PUTTING IT TOGETHER*
---

Do not include too many bells and whistles on a web site.

***Web Design Architecture.*** The organization and structure of a web site can determine whether a viewer will stay in a site once they find it. The site must have a certain feel or sense about it to make it "sticky." If the site is well organized and easy to use, it will attract potential clients. There are several ways to organize a web site. This section will discuss a few elementary designs.

---
### *PUTTING IT TOGETHER*
---

Web sites need to have balance, unity, and consistency to make them effective.

***Hierarchical.*** As the name implies, this style starts with the most important part of a web site, with links to categories and subcategories organized in a logical manner. It looks like this:

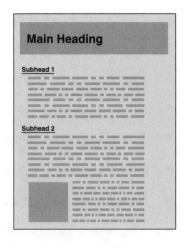

***Horizontal.*** This horizontal or linear style starts with the home page and then sequentially goes to secondary pages in a logical manner. In this type of web page, you often find three buttons for navigation, similar to this:

***Vertical.*** This style starts with the home page and then sequentially goes to secondary information in a vertical position. The first screen of information is most important. Readers scroll down the page to view the secondary information.

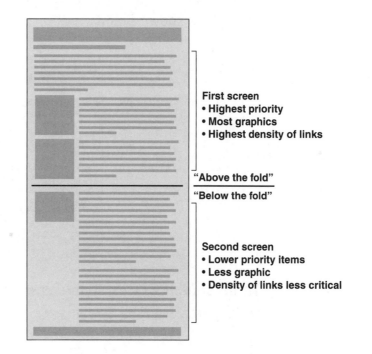

**H-Shape.** This style is in the shape of an *H,* with the home page positioned in the middle. This allows the viewer to decide what secondary page to choose next instead of following a linear fashion.

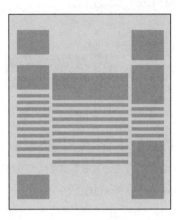

**Two Columns.** This style divides a home page into two equal parts. An example is shown below:

**Three Columns.** This style shows the home page divided into three equal parts. It looks like this:

***Sectional.*** This style is divided into several sections. It looks like this:

Other styles are possible as well. Styles for web sites change as often as styles of clothing change. Keep your web page up to date so it doesn't appear outmoded or obsolete.

---

### *PUTTING IT TOGETHER*

Web site design includes numerous styles.

***Web Design Content.*** The content of a web site is also important in capturing and keeping a viewer's attention. Careful planning is required. The goal is to keep viewers at your web site for at least 60 seconds. Important questions to ask yourself include the following:

- What do I do?

- What am I offering?

- What can you expect from me?

- Who am I?

- How can I be contacted?

The answers to these questions are critical for getting the viewer to delve further into your site. But once the viewer decides to do that, the site still has to meet his or her expectations. Secondary pages should include additional relevant information. Try to create a one-stop web site. Additional pages could include free information related to the following:

- Buying and selling process

- Home selection options

- School and community information

- Economic and real estate news

- Mortgage information

- Interest rates

- Legal information

- Surveys and contests

- Search engines

- Maps

As important as it is to include essential information, it is just as crucial not to include too much information. Other features you may consider adding include the following:

- Guest book

- Option for follow-up

- Privacy statement

- Security assurances

- Lead capture and tracking

- Autoresponder

- Fair Housing logo

---

### *PUTTING IT TOGETHER*

All web sites should include the Fair Housing logo.

---

***Commercial Web Development Software Systems.*** Another resource for developing a web site is web development software. No special programming knowledge or skill is required. A web site can be constructed on the fly. However, the learning curve may be an issue. *What you see is what you get* (**WYSIWYG**) is the software's main advantage. Tutorials are available, as well as how-to books. Several different software packages are available for purchase. Some web development software is part of a suite of systems, or the software may be bought individually. This section will discuss several of the more well-known products.

**FrontPage.** FrontPage is a stand-alone product developed by Microsoft. It has been available for many years and is quite popular. With some training and a review of tutorials, you can construct a professional-looking web site. This software allows you to build a home page from scratch. It provides a step-by-step process to creating a web site. It utilizes several different themes and templates. With the help of a wizard, you can build a complete web site. One key advantage of FrontPage is that it provides prepackaged templates. In place of HTML, you use the FrontPage Editor, which serves as an editing tool for writing script. To get more information about this product, go to http://www.microsoft.com/frontpage.

At this site, you can view a demo and order a trial version. Also available at this site is information on training and on purchasing the program. Key features found in FrontPage include the following:

- Designing a Web Site
- Developing a Web Site
- Developing a Data-Driven Site
- Publishing a Site
- Maintaining a Site

**Dreamweaver.** Dreamweaver is a stand-alone product produced by Macromedia. It, too, has been available for several years. It is one part of a suite of web development products offered by Macromedia. One feature of the software includes walking the user through the major web phases of a web site. Other features include these:

- Planning
- Design
- Development
- Publishing
- Maintenance

More information about Dreamweaver can be found at http://www.macromedia.com. The site offers a free 30-day trial.

***GoLive®.*** GoLive is another professional web development program. It is produced by Adobe. It interfaces with other Adobe products—Adobe® Photoshop®, Adobe® Illustrator®, and Adobe Portable Document Format (PDF). GoLive offers HTML as well as WYSIWYG. It is a stand-alone product that can be installed easily. It features a wizard to help the novice web site developer, and it is considered to be very intuitive. Numerous books and tutorials are available to help in the creation of complex and sophisticated web sites. More information on this software can be found at http://www.adobe.com. The site also offers a free 30-day trial.

At his site, the user can view a demo and order a trial version. Also available at the site is information on training and on purchasing the program.

---

### PUTTING IT TOGETHER

Several web development software programs include Microsoft Front-Page, Macromedia Dreamweaver, and Adobe GoLive.

***Templates.*** Templates are designs that have been preconstructed. This eliminates the need for you to build a web site from scratch. By using a well-designed template, you can speed up the construction process and end up with a more professional-looking web site.

***Custom-Designed Sites.*** A custom-designed web site, maintained by a webmaster, is the ultimate goal for the real estate professional. These sites include the latest in technology and show a high level of sophistication. Numerous companies are available to provide this service. The cost to build and maintain a custom site may be rather expensive.

# RESOURCES FOR FURTHER STUDY

http://www.hostbyte.com

This is a one-stop web site that offers a comprehensive list of hosting companies.

http://www.web-host-search.com

This site contains a directory of and guide for web hosts.

http://www.otterhosting.com

This site provides information on how to choose a web-hosting company.

http://www.web-hosting-space.com

This site features a web-hosting directory of some of the top companies, plus reviews.

# SELF-ASSESSMENT

To determine the ex.tent of knowledge you acquired in this chapter, choose the correct answer for each of the following.

1. To have a presence on the Internet, the cyber professional must have:
   a. An ISP
   b. A web host
   c. A webmaster
   d. Both a and b

2. A web site gives the cyber professional:
   a. 24/7/365 accessibility
   b. The ability to compete with larger organizations
   c. A web presence
   d. All of the above

3. What is the main difference between a web site and a web page?
   a. There is no difference.
   b. A web site is part of a web page.
   c. A web page is part of a web site.
   d. A web site costs more than a web page.

4. What is the first page that usually appears on a web site?
   a. Home page
   b. Web page
   c. Secondary page
   d. Portal

5. A top-level domain name includes all of the following except?
   a. edu
   b. mil
   c. gov
   d. con

6. What is a commercial web development software?
   a. Dreamweaver
   b. FrontPage
   c. GoLive
   d. All of the above

7. What is a major advantage of commercial web development software?
   a. No need for programming knowledge
   b. Ease of construction
   c. Use of predesigned templates
   d. All of the above

8. When choosing a host company, the cyber professional should consider:
   a. Service fees
   b. Technical support
   c. Reputation
   d. All of the above

9. A web site can be established by:
   a. Developing your own
   b. Hiring a web site developer
   c. Using web development software
   d. All of the above

10. Which of the following is a design layout for a web page?
    a. Hierarchical
    b. Diagonal
    c. Bottom-up
    d. Top-to-bottom

11. Who is responsible for maintaining a web site?
    a. Graphic artist
    b. Programmer
    c. Webmaster
    d. Systems analyst

12. What is the most important consideration for designing a web site?
    a. Cost
    b. Target audience
    c. Ease of access
    d. Speed of access

13. Which of the following should not be a consideration for a web site?
    a. Ease of access
    b. Speed of access
    c. Ease of navigation
    d. All of these should be considered

14. What is an important part of domain name selection?
    a. Cost
    b. Type of extension
    c. Use of capital letters
    d. Simple and descriptive name

15. What is a major design flaw for a web site?
    a. Too complicated
    b. Too much content
    c. No white space
    d. All of the above

# CHAPTER 14
## BUILDING A WEB SITE

## PREVIEW

This chapter follows up on Chapter 13 by discussing several types of web development companies available to the cyber professional. The main focus of the chapter, however, is demonstrating how to build a free web site through Yahoo. The final part discusses how a web site can be serviced.

When you finish this chapter, you will be able to:

1.  Describe two methods for constructing a web site.

2.  Identify several web site development companies.

3.  Compare the advantages and disadvantages of a paid site to a free site.

4.  Construct a free real estate web site.

5.  Describe how to evaluate, promote, and maintain a web site.

## KEY TERMS

| | |
|---|---|
| *Composer* | *lead capture* |
| *guestbook* | *lead generation* |
| *hitometer* | *meta tags* |
| *Hypertext Markup Language (HTML)* | *tags* |
| | *traffic reports* |

# 14.1 Web Site Development

This section of the chapter discusses how to build a working web site. The basis of the World Wide Web is **Hypertext Markup Language (HTML)**. This language is a file format standard that allows documents to embed text formatting information as well as hyperlinks. Hyperlinks allow the web page designer to provide one-click access to other web pages.

## *Hypertext Markup Language (HTML)*

HTML is the formatting language used by web page designers. Developing a web page using HTML requires an understanding of **tags**. Each tag represents an action or a command to be used by the browser reading the page. A tag is used to describe how an element of a web page should look or behave. By understanding what tags mean, you can develop a web page from scratch. You must plan the web page first, then begin to construct the page using the appropriate tags.

This section provides only a brief introduction to developing a web page with HTML. Complete courses on this topic are available through many training institutions. Below are some common tags used in HTML:

- <HTML>
- <HEAD>
- <TITLE>
- <BODY>
- <HR>

---

## *PUTTING IT TOGETHER*

---

A special formatting language called HTML is used to create web pages.

In most cases, tags are used in pairs, with an opening tag and a closing tag. The closing tag includes a forward slash (/) immediately before the tag name. For example, a standard HTML file begins with <HTML> and ends with </HTML>. The slash indicates the end of the HTML code. The same application would be used for <TITLE></TITLE>; any text within these two tags will be interpreted as the title of the web page.

An example of how to use tags for a web site might look like this:

<HTML>

<HEAD>

<TITLE>The New Home Locator</TITLE></HEAD>

<BODY>Specializing in Finding New Homes for Buyers</BODY>

</HTML>

```
Insert HTML                                    [x]
Enter HTML tags and text:
 <HTML>
 <HEAD>
 <TITLE>The New Home Locator</TITLE>
 <BODY <Specializing in Finding New Homes for Buyers</BODY>
 <HTML/>




              Example:   <i>  Hello World!  </i>

                                  [ Insert ]   [ Cancel ]
```

For more information on using HTML, refer to books on the topic or try tutorials found through search engines. An example of a free tutorial can be found at http://www.echoecho.com/html.htm.

If you wanted to see the HTML code from another web site, you could go to the Netscape browser, click View on the toolbar, and then select HTML Source. This would reveal all of the HTML code used in building the web site. To locate the HTML code in the Internet Explorer browser, click on View, then Source. Examples of HTML code follow.

By viewing HTML code on other sites, the cyber professional can gain insight on how to improve his/her own site.

```
New Home Locator [file:/.../New_Home_Locator.html] - Composer

File  Edit  View  Insert  Format  Table  Tools  Window  Help

New   Open   Save   Publish  Browse  Print   Spell   Image   Table   Link

<!DOCTYPE html PUBLIC "-//W3C//DTD HTML 4.01 Transitional//EN">
<html>
<head>
  <title>New Home Locator</title>
  <meta http-equiv="content-type"
 content="text/html; charset=ISO-8859-1">
  <meta name="author" content="Joe Blow">
</head>
<body>
The New Home Locator<br>
<hr width="100%" size="2">Specializing in Finding New Homes for Buyers<br>
</body>
</html>
```

```
Normal   Show All Tags   <HTML> Source   Preview
                         Done loading page
```

After constructing a web page, the developer can preview how it will look on the Internet. The next step is publishing the web page on the Internet by utilizing a feature called Web Publisher.

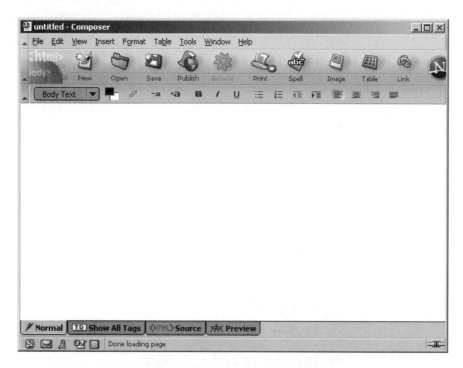

Developing a web site from a blank page using HTML can be complicated and involve extensive training. Most of the programs discussed in this chapter do not require any knowledge of HTML.

## Netscape Composer

Another approach to developing a web site is to use a feature called **Composer**. It is found in the Netscape browser. This feature does not require any knowledge of HTML. All the developer has to do is use several web authoring tools. By clicking on Window, then Composer, the following screen will appear:

Now the cyber professional is ready to start creating the web page. He or she can refer to a tutorial found in Netscape.

## Commercial Web Site Development Companies

An alternative to the do-it-yourself method is to contract with a company that specializes in producing web sites for real estate professionals. These sites have the feel and sense of a customized site but at a much lower price. These sites are usually built using templates with built-in features. There is no need to learn HTML or advanced programming or to buy any software. All the user needs to do is add the features that best fits the message he or she is trying to convey.

Commercial developers usually have a one-time set-up fee, charging on a monthly basis thereafter. Often an additional up-front fee can include a domain name. Sometimes discounts are offered or the monthly fee is reduced if the user pays on an annual basis.

A major advantage of this type of site is that the user can control and direct the site with a password. The user can pick and choose the type of information he or she wants to include in the site. Most systems offer sample reports and information. All that is necessary is to personalize the data so it looks like a custom web site.

Many companies offer these semi-customized web sites. Some companies have been around for many years, and new companies are entering the marketplace on a regular basis. Deciding which company to choose requires some research. Criteria to consider when selecting a web development company include the following:

- Reputation and reliability
- Longevity
- Cost
- Contractual obligations
- Services
- Inclusion of a domain name
- E-mail and aliases
- Free reports and statistics
- **Lead capture**
- **Traffic report** and analysis
- Innovation and scalability
- Training and tech support

Another way to learn about web development companies is to check with other real estate professionals for references. You also might check out each company's web site to see how it looks and the impression it makes.

# 14.2 Commercial Sites

This section will examine several commercial sites available to real estate professionals.

## *REALTOR.com*

This is the registered web site for the National Association of REAL-TORS® (NAR). Over a million listings are presented on this site for the general public to view and inspect. This site averages over 5 million visits per month. It is the starting point for most Internet Empowered Consumers. Since REALTOR.com has high visibility, the real estate professional should examine how this site can benefit his or her real estate practice.

NAR offers two types of web sites to member REALTORS®. One is the Standard web site, which looks like this:

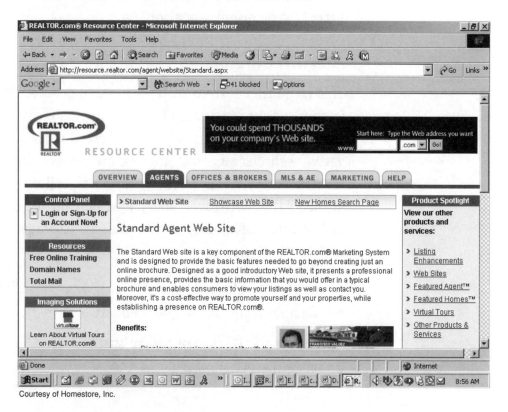

Courtesy of Homestore, Inc.

The other is the Showcase web site, an advanced web site with more features. It looks like this:

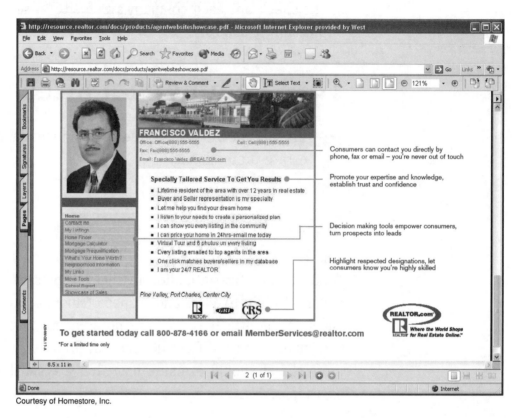

Courtesy of Homestore, Inc.

Both sites have many features that can benefit the real estate professional. More information on these sites can be found at http://www.resource.realtor.com.

## Advanced Access

This is another system with national exposure. The basis of this system is pre-established templates that are used as the core of individual web sites. The goal of Advanced Access is to provide attractive, innovative web designs that are comprehensive, information-rich sources for consumers, home buyers, and home sellers. Two levels of web sites are available with over 900 pages of content-rich information about real estate. Level one is the Classic Package. Some of its features include the following:

- Choice of hundreds of styles, colors, and graphics

- Complete control of the web site

- Automatic Client Follow-up system

- Lead Generation tools

- Featured Properties

- E-mail Property Listings

- Property Update Center

- School Information

- Community Links

- Resource Center

Examples of the Classic Package looks like this:

Web site screen capture provided by ADVANCED ACCESS, Anaheim, California

The other option is the Premium Design, which is a custom web design and web site. You receive a domain name, web design services, web site hosting, and several other optional features. There is a one-time set-up fee and a monthly charge for web hosting. Lower rates are offered for up-front one- and two-year options.

Getting started with Advanced Access is simple, allowing the cyber professional to be up and running in little time. To obtain more information about Advanced Access, go to http://www.advancedaccess.com.

## Homes.com®

This site is similar to REALTOR.com in that it is a beginning point for consumers to use in locating properties on the Internet. In addition to listing properties for sale, it offers information about moving, neighborhoods, mortgages, and more. A key offering is the opportunity to identify a registered real estate professional in a selected area. Homes.com also offers a templatelike web site called the Agent Advantage. Web site layouts include several themes, such as Classic and Franchise styles. Homes.com offers a full-service program that can be used to capture leads. The web site also has site management tools available to the user in controlling what and how the site is arranged. Some of the major features include:

- Own domain name

- **Lead generation**

- Up to five e-mail accounts

- Toll-free member services support

- Personalized photo and logo

- Flyer generator

- Audio and video upload capability

- Virtual and video tour support

- National "search for homes" database

- Registration with major search engines

Many other features are also included. For more information, go to http://www.homes.com. You can register for a free trial web site. There is a set-up fee and an option to purchase additional software. Coaching opportunities are available as well. Another unique feature of Homes.com is the ability to download information about properties on to handheld devices such as PDAs. Free downloading of software is available.

# 14.3 Free Web Site Development Systems

The beginning real estate professional may wish to save on cost by developing a free web site that offers free hosting. Numerous options are available on the Internet. Free sites include the following:

- GeoCities: http://www.geocities.yahoo.com (discussed in more detail later)

- Angelfire®: http://www.angelfire.lycos.com

- Homestead®: http://www.homestead.com

- Tripod®: http://www.tripod.lycos.com

To begin constructing a web site, go to any one of the sites listed above and follow the directions. Some of the sites are easier to comprehend than others.

Learning how to construct a web site can help you gain a basic understanding of web construction and design. A typical sequence follows:

- Construct a free web site from several sources.

- Construct a web site using commercial software.

- Purchase a paid web site with hosting.

- Hire a professional webmaster to custom-build a web site.

An advantage of starting with a free site is, obviously, the cost. Hosting is free as well. These amenities can be very helpful in the beginning stages of a real estate practice. Another benefit is the fact that the cyber professional has an opportunity to experience and learn about web sites. Given this basic background, the cyber professional is in a better position to move to the next level of web construction if he or she so chooses. Building a free web site will be covered in the Computer Applications section of this chapter.

One disadvantage of this method is the time and effort it can take to create a professional-looking web site. Another disadvantage is the fact that the domain name includes the brand of the site, which means the URL may be a distraction because it is long. The URL may also connote a personal and nonprofessional feel to users. Sites also include banner advertisements and information about other companies trying to attract business.

Many companies provide free web sites with hosting for personal as well as business uses. This may seem like a generous offer, but there is a catch: the free web site contains advertisements from a variety of vendors. The web site URL also includes the name of the company, meaning it is advertised to the clients of the web site. Another factor is that the cyber professional may discover that the web site has limited options in terms of what he or she needs. Each of these web site development companies offers additional options for a fee.

The downside of this process is that it takes time and effort to learn how the programs work. The cyber professional should consider whether this is worth the effort. Would it be better to hire someone to develop a web site and, instead, devote the time to serving clients in the buying and selling of real estate?

Additional web sites that offer free web development are discussed next. Many options are available on the Web. To find even more, you can conduct a search using the keywords *free web site*.

## Tripod

Tripod is a web development site offered by Lycos. It is easy to use. Tripod doesn't require knowing or being able to use HTML. An entire web site can be constructed with the built-in Site Builder that allows for fast and effortless editing. Numerous professional web designs are available, and photos can be loaded to the web site. Tripod also includes the option of adding hit counters, a **guestbook**, maps, weather, news, and more. To begin using this program, go to http://www.tripod.lycos.com.

## Angelfire

Angelfire offers free web site development through Lycos. To create a web site, a user must sign up with Lycos. Once the user has established an account and password, he or she can begin building a web site. Instructions are fairly easy to follow. Web construction may vary from less than an hour to several hours. Some of the features of Angelfire include these:

- No set-up or monthly fee

- 20 MB of disk space

- 1 GB of monthly bandwidth

- Inclusion of ad on the web site

- Free blog builder

- Free site-building tools with tutorial

- Free uploading of file and images

By paying a fee, the user can get more options and higher capacities. To find out more about Angelfire, go to http://www.angelfire.lycos.com.

## GeoCities/Yahoo

Later in the chapter, this site will be used to demonstrate how to construct a free web site.

---

### PUTTING IT TOGETHER

The cyber professional has several options for building a free web site.

---

# 14.4 The Web Site Development Process

In most real estate circles, having a professional real estate web site and an Internet presence is expected. Where to start presents professional and financial dilemmas. Should the beginning professional start at the top and get the best and most expensive technology available, or should he or she work up to the top? Presented below is logical sequence of events that may occur with a new real estate professional.

```
┌─────────────────────────────────────────┐
│ Step 5: Custom Business Web Site         │
│     Professional webmaster               │
├───────────────────────────────────────┐ │
│ Step 4: Commercial Business Web Site   │ │
│     REALTOR.com                        │ │
│     Advanced Access.com                │ │
│     Homes.com                          │ │
├─────────────────────────────────────┐ │ │
│ Step 3: Self-Made Business Web Site  │ │ │
│     HTML programming                 │ │ │
├───────────────────────────────────┐ │ │ │
│ Step 2: Self-Made Business Web Site from Software │ │
│     FrontPage                      │ │ │ │
│     Dreamweaver                    │ │ │ │
│     GoLive                         │ │ │ │
├─────────────────────────────────┐ │ │ │ │
│ Step 1: Self-Made "Free" Business Web Site │
│     Tripod                       │ │ │ │ │
│     Angelfire                    │ │ │ │ │
│     GeoCities                    │ │ │ │ │
└─────────────────────────────────────────┘
```

Most cyber professionals start at the bottom with a free web site they create themselves and work toward a custom web site. Progressing to higher levels may depend on the success of the cyber professional's practice and the results he or she achieves from the web site.

# 14.5 Computer Applications

This section discusses how to create a free web site with free hosting. The web development service offered by GeoCities is used to demonstrate how to create a preliminary web site. After completing this exercise, you will have an operational web site you can use for business. Note that this is a beginning site that will suffice in the early stages of a real estate practice. As you advance in your career, you may find that a more sophisticated web site better serves your needs.

## GeoCities

GeoCities is a web development system that allows you to construct a personal or business web site by following specific guidelines. This section will walk you through the process, as described below.

1. Start Internet Explorer. Key *http://geocities.yahoo.com* in the address window. The web page should look like this:

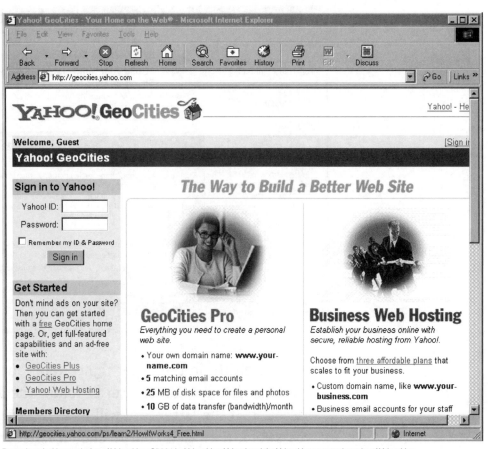

2.  Click the "free" link under "Get Started" in the left-hand column.
    The new web page should appear like this:

Reproduced with permission of Yahoo! Inc. ©2004 by Yahoo! Inc. Yahoo! and the Yahoo! logo are trademarks of Yahoo! Inc.

3.  Click **Sign Up** in the upper right. Now you will need to sign in if
    you are already a Yahoo user or follow the directions to set up an
    account. If the latter, you will be asked to create a Yahoo ID and
    password. Note that your ID should reflect the type of business
    you are pursuing; for example, *thenewhomelocator*. This is
    because your ID will be part of your business URL – in this case,
    http://www.geocities.com/thenewhomelocator. Make sure you
    save the ID and password for future use. You will also be asked to
    furnish an e-mail address. Consider a Yahoo e-mail account as
    well.

After setting up a Yahoo account, you will be asked to "choose a topic" to determine the type of ads that will appear on your web site. (Yahoo is able to offer this free web hosting service by selling ad space on free sites. If you do not want ads to appear on your site, you have the choice of selecting one of Yahoo's premium web hosting services for a monthly fee.)

4. Click Build Your Web Site Now.

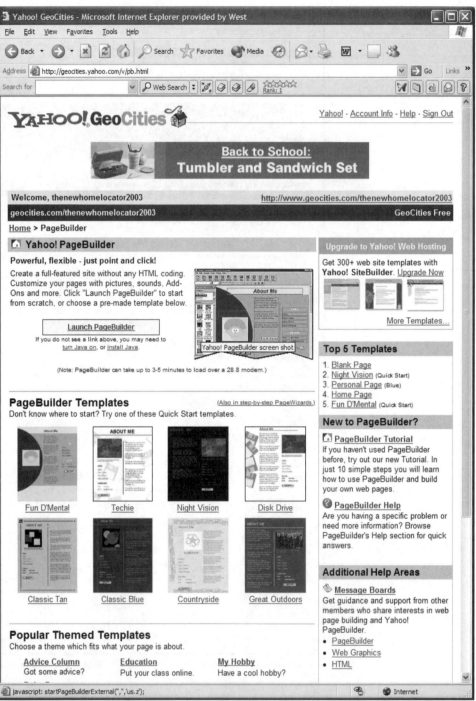

5. Click Yahoo! PageBuilder and then click PageBuilder Tutorial in the right-hand column. Go to the next level. The tutorial will lead you through the ten steps of building a web site:

- Start with a new page

- Selecting a background

- Adding a page title image

- Adding text

- Adding a picture

- Adding an e-mail link

- Adding a paragraph of text

- Adding links to other web sites

- Adding a counter

- Saving and viewing your page

6. Now you are ready to Launch PageBuilder and follow the steps outlined.

When finished, you should have a basic web site. If any problems arise, refer to the tutorial for assistance.

# 14.6 Web Site Servicing

Once the cyber professional has constructed a web site and arranged for a web host, his or her work is not done. The web site must prove to be profitable, which takes effort. This section discusses some of the factors that can be helpful in this endeavor.

## *Web Promotion/Web Marketing*

With millions upon millions of web sites on the World Wide Web, how can the cyber professional get noticed? This is no easy task. Many professionals and businesses have a full-time staff working to achieve visibility on the Internet. Basically, there are two main approaches to promoting a web site: doing the task independently or having it done commercially.

***Self-Promotion.*** Once the cyber professional has a domain name and a web address, his or her next step is to let others know. The cyber professional can take the following steps:

1. Put the URL address on these items:

   a. Business cards

   b. Personal brochures

    c. Signs

    d. Flyers

    e. Promotional materials

    f. Advertising pieces

    g. Distribution lists

    h. Newsletters

    i. Banners

    j. Stationery

2. Submit the URL to search engines and directories. In general, there are about ten free top search engines. To find out how to submit a URL to a web site, go to http://www.submit-it.com. The site will ask for keywords that best describe the web site, a title of the web site, a brief description of the web site, the URL, the contact name, and the contact e-mail address. The cyber professional can choose which search engine to use. The following site offers information to help the cyber professional stay abreast of changes in search engines: http://www.searchenginewatch.com.

***Professional Promotion.*** Along with conducting self-promotion, the cyber professional may want to hire a professional promotion service. In some cases, commercial web sites offer this service as part of the contract. They also may assess an extra charge for handling promotion.

One way to achieve a presence on the Internet is to have the URL submitted to search engines and directories. As mentioned previously, the cyber professional can handle this by himself or herself. Studies show that heavy traffic on a web site is the result of the site being submitted to a search engine. The submissions can be time-consuming to do, and they may or may not be received. Special rules may apply to the submission process. Often the regulations change as well. Therefore, it may be advantageous for the cyber professional to have a full-time professional service handle this duty. Many companies are in this business, and they offer many plans for the service. Some companies guarantee certain results; others do not.

This is not a one-time process. It is an ongoing task that requires many submissions and constant monitoring to be effective. Initially, most companies submit their URL to over 400 different search engines.

Then the companies focus on the main engines for regular submissions. Keywords called **meta tags** are often used to get the attention of the automated web searching programs. Once the keywords are "grabbed," they get selected for display. The meta tags include keywords such as *real estate, luxury, beach, estate, first-time buyer,* and *empty nester.* The list can be endless, but the meta tags must be descriptive to be grabbed by the computerized searching tools.

Popular search engines that get a lot of traffic include the following:

- Google
- AOL Search
- iWon®
- Dogpile®
- HotBot
- Ask Jeeves®
- WebCrawler®
- Overture
- EarthLink

To get placed on some of the top search engine requires submission be done manually instead of automatically. This is called paid placement or paid listing. Some search engines charge by the number of hits received, called pay per click.

The top companies notify the user each time his or her site is submitted and send a report on how the web site ranked on the search engine. These companies usually charge a one- time set-up fee and a monthly charge thereafter. Most require contracts for certain time periods.

***Building Links to Your Site.*** You can build links to your web site through word of mouth. Whenever possible, you should ask permission to link with other worthwhile web sites. This will, in effect, expand your sphere of influence and your visibility. You may link with the local board, mortgages companies, title companies, escrow companies, and moving companies. Avoid linking with the "wrong" sites! Once linked, check the links on a regular basis to make sure they remain credible and to ensure that they still work. Remember, judgments are made by the company people keep. This includes hyperlinks!

## Web Monitoring and Management

Many beginning cyber professionals believe that just having a Web presence is enough. This mentality does not work in the electronic era. The cyber professional must keep his or her web site up to date.

Some of the questions to ask in this key area include:

- Does the site work?

- Is it producing results?

- How do you know?

- Where does the business come from?

- Who are the viewers?

- Is there a connection between sales and the web site?

Many of these questions and issues can be solved by implementing a "traffic report" plan or a site monitor. This service comes with many packaged commercial web sites. These services can also be added to a web site.

Another major role of monitoring is to be sure that the content on the web site:

- Is accurate.

- Is relevant.

- Is reliable.

- Is up to date.

- Is fresh.

- Is technically functional.

- Takes into consideration size of graphics.

- Takes into consideration speed of loading.

- Takes into consideration quality of content.

The cyber professional also needs to make occasional changes to the web site to indicate to frequent users that the web site is current and attended to on a regular basis. Some webmasters change the look and feel of a site to reflect the seasons/holidays or the mood of the country or world. Care should be taken to not offend a particular group, however.

Adding a feedback form or a survey to the web site can help the cyber professional determine whether the web site is doing what he or she intended. Some web sites have contests and even gifts to keep viewers returning.

Another feature often added to a web site is a **hitometer**. This device keeps track of all hits, or instances of people connecting, that come to the site. On some web sites, this meter is visible; on others, it is hidden. Most experts advise that it be hidden so users cannot see how inactive (or, for that matter, how active) the site is.

Some companies are available to analyze a web site to determine whether it is effective and functional.

### PUTTING IT TOGETHER

A hitometer keeps track of how many users visit a web site.

## Buying into the Web Site Program

Having a web site is not like having a pet project; it is not just an image thing. Just saying "I have a web site" will not prove to be profitable. Having a web site is serious business and requires a commitment if it is going to be productive. It is taking on an added responsibility. Complete the following assessment to determine your level of commitment for having a web site.

## WEB SITE COMMITMENT ASSESSMENT

Read each statement. Circle the number that best reflects your reaction to the statement , with 5 being the highest and 1 being the lowest. Then add up your score and compare it to the summary to determine your level of commitment.

---

1. I have researched the topic of web development.        (1 2 3 4 5)

2. I have the resources for creating and maintaining       (1 2 3 4 5)
   a web site.

3. I have the time to spend on a web site.                 (1 2 3 4 5)

4. I have the knowledge base needed to work with           (1 2 3 4 5)
   a web site.

5. I have made a commitment to working with a              (1 2 3 4 5)
   web site.

---

**Summary**

| Category | Total Score |
| --- | --- |
| Very Committed | 20-25 |
| Somewhat Committed | 15-19 |
| Neutral | 10-14 |
| Not Committed | Below 10 |

# RESOURCES FOR FURTHER STUDY

http://www.webmonkey.com

This site gives information on how to construct a web site.

http://searchenginewatch.com/webmasters

This site provides tips on how to submit a web site to a search engine.

http://www.promotionworld.com

This site gives tips on how to promote a web site.

# SELF-ASSESSMENT

To determine the extent of knowledge you acquired in this chapter, choose the correct answer for each of the following.

1. A major disadvantage of a free web site is that it is:
   a. Easy to construct
   b. Less expensive
   c. Has a long and complicated URL
   d. Has limited exposure

2. A major advantage of a commercial web site is that it:
   a. Costs less
   b. Allows the cyber professional to use his or her own domain name
   c. Has a long URL
   d. Is difficult to construct

3. All of the following are free web site development systems except?
   a. GeoCities
   b. Angelfire
   c. Advanced Access
   d. Tripod

4. Which of the following is a commercial web site?
   a. Advanced Access
   b. Homes.com
   c. REALTOR.com
   d. All of the above

5. What is the first tag usually used in an HTML file?
   a. <Body>
   b. <Head>
   c. <Title>
   d. <HTML>

6. Which of the following is not a tag used in an HTML file?
   a. <TITLE>
   b. <PARAGRAPH>
   c. <BODY>
   d. <HR>

7. Which symbol indicates the end of an HTML tag?
   a. (<)
   b. (>)
   c. (</)
   d. (/>)

8. Which program can be used to construct a web site without the use of HTML?
   a. Composer
   b. Messenger
   c. Windows
   d. Internet Explorer

9. Which of the following programs offers a free web site with hosting?
   a. Angelfire
   b. Tripod
   c. GeoCities
   d. All of the above

10. Which of the following is an example of an add-on to a web page for GeoCities?
   a. Guestbook
   b. Links
   c. News and Weather
   d. All of the above

11. What is the main objective of a hitometer?
   a. To track how many users viewed the site
   b. To track who visited the site
   c. To track when users visited the site
   d. All of the above

12. What does the cyber professional use to connect to another web site from the home page?
   a. Hyperlink
   b. Template
   c. Hitometer
   d. Guestbook

13. The toolbar in GeoCities includes all of the following features except?
    a. Textbox
    b. Background
    c. Template
    d. Hyperlinks

14. To promote a user domain name, the cyber professional submits the name to a:
    a. Search Engine
    b. Webmaster
    c. Programmer
    d. Guestbook

15. Once constructed, a web site must be
    a. Promoted
    b. Monitored
    c. Evaluated
    d. All of the above

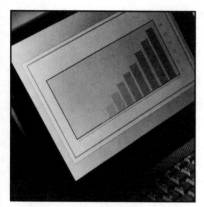

# CHAPTER 15
## COMPUTER ENHANCEMENTS

## PREVIEW

This final chapter discusses computer enhancements that are beneficial to the cyber professional. The chapter begins with a discussion on handheld devices and the Tablet PC, describing the features and functions of each. Also discussed in this chapter are specialty phones, digital cameras, camcorders, scanners, webcams, and global positioning systems and how they can be used by the cyber professional. The essentials of a home and mobile office are also covered. The chapter ends with a short section on the impact technology has on users.

When you finish this chapter, you will be able to:

1. Describe how a handheld device can be used to enhance a real estate practice.

2. Describe the Tablet PC and indicate how it can be used by the cyber professional.

3. Explain how a digital camera, a scanner, a webcam, a camcorder, and specialty phones can be used in the practice of real estate.

4. Describe the components in a typical home and mobile real estate office.

5. Describe the potential impact of technology on the user.

## KEY TERMS

| | |
|---|---|
| *camcorder* | *scanner* |
| *digital cameras* | *synchronization* |
| *handheld* | *Tablet PC* |
| *personal digital assistant (PDA)* | *Virtual Assistant (VA)* |
| | *webcam* |
| *Pocket PC* | |

# 15.1 Handheld Device

Real estate professionals today often use a handheld device called a **personal digital assistant (PDA)** as part of their arsenal for success in real estate. A PDA is any small handheld wireless device that provides computing and data storage capabilities. This handheld computer is a relative newcomer to the Internet world. In the beginning, the cost was prohibitive for most users. As is typical in the technology industry, the price is now reasonable for most cyber professionals. Because of competition in the field, many choices are available. Not only has the cost of the handheld come down, but its capacity and efficiency has skyrocketed.

## What Is It?

Basically, a **handheld** device has many of the same features and functions of a desktop but is limited in terms of capacity. The main advantage of the handheld is its small size, allowing it to be carried in a pocket. Since the handheld is like a regular computer, it has a processor, an operating system, and memory and storage capacities. Software similar to that used in PCs is also available for handhelds but in condensed versions. Handhelds can also be used wirelessly for sending and receiving e-mail messages and for accessing web sites.

## *How a Handheld Device Can Benefit the Cyber Professional*

Most real estate professionals are out of the office a great deal and do not have access to a computer. With a handheld, the cyber professional can take care of most tasks that would otherwise be accomplished in the office. Some of those tasks include the following:

- Accessing contact information
- Using the Address Book
- Using the appointment calendar
- Creating a to-do list
- Creating a reminder list
- Taking Notes
- Receiving and sending e-mail messages
- Using instant text messaging
- Connecting to web sites
- Accessing a Multiple Listing Service
- Creating documents
- Synchronizing with a desktop PC
- Calculating loan information
- Tracking business expenses
- Locating stored files and documents

Other miscellaneous tasks include these:

- Listening to music
- Reading e-books
- Playing games
- Using a voice recorder

Special components have been designed for the handheld. Some of these include the following:

- Digital Camera
- Global Positioning System (GPS)
- Printer
- Scanner
- Keyboard

## *Types of Handhelds*

In general, handhelds fall into one of two categories based on their operating system. The most common are handhelds with Palm OS™ and Windows CE. Each one has different features, functions, and software applications. Due to the small size of the handheld, only the most useful features and functions are included in their capabilities.

---
### *PUTTING IT TOGETHER*
---

Handhelds are useful to the cyber professional while he or she is away from the office. They allow the cyber professional to do many of the same tasks he or she could accomplish in the office.

### The Pocket PC

Like Microsoft Windows, Pocket PC includes Programs, Settings, Find, and Help. Typical features and functions found in a Pocket PC include the following:

- Today. This feature allows the user to get a quick overview of the activities and tasks for the day.

- Calendar. This feature is similar to Outlook. It shows appointments on a daily, weekly, monthly, or yearly basis.

- Contacts. This feature includes addresses of business and personal contacts. It is similar to the Address Book in Outlook. In fact, through a process called **synchronization**, the contacts from Outlook can be downloaded to a PDA. (Names of contacts must be input by hand initially.)

- Inbox. The inbox holds all incoming e-mail messages. It is similar to other e-mail inboxes.

- Internet Explorer. This feature allows the user to access web sites. There is a fee for this service, and the PDA must have a modem. This action can be conducted wirelessly if the service is available. Often complete Internet web sites are not available. Some services provide clips, or basic information, from selected web sites, such as the news, stock market reports, and sports.

- MSN Messenger. This feature allows the user to exchange text messages with other users.

- Pocket Excel, Word, and PowerPoint. These condensed versions perform most of the tasks of the original programs.

### The Palm PDA

Typical features and functions of the Palm include the following:

- Calendar

- Contacts

- Notes

- To-do List

- Calculator

- Games

Typically, both types of handhelds have similar features and functions. The main difference is the type of program available for use.

## *Typical Specifications*

Like a desktop computer, handhelds have computer hardware specifications. One major factor is processor speed. As technology advances, so does the speed of the handheld processor. Current levels are in the range of 400 MHz. Memory for RAM can be as high as 64 MB. Other factors include the following:

- Display quality

- Battery life

- Durability

- Weight and size

- Ability to use wireless networks

- Ability to attach accessories (phone, digital camera, GPS, printer, scanner)

- User interface (pen and touch, keyboard, handwriting, character recognition)

- Warranty

## *Typical Software Applications*

Not all software works with both systems. Most software programs to date have been written for the Palm operating system. However, some programs can be used interchangeably. Common Pocket PC software programs include these:

- Microsoft Word, Excel, PowerPoint, Money, Internet Explorer, Outlook, Streets, and Media Player

- ACT!

- Maps

- Games and entertainment

- Language translation

- Phone book

- Memo pad

- City time and world clock

Common Palm handheld software includes the following:

- Quickoffice Premier for Palm OS

- Mobile Word 2004

- Mobile Excel 2004

- Mobile Money 2004

- Pocket Quicken

- Solitaire

## Manufacturers

The major manufacturers of handhelds include the following companies:

- Hewlett-Packard/Compaq

- Dell

- Sony

- Toshiba

With handhelds continuing to grow in popularity, more manufacturers are entering the market.

---

### PUTTING IT TOGETHER

The most significant decision when choosing a handheld is whether to go with the Palm O S or Windows CE system.

## Considerations When Purchasing

The cyber professional must consider several factors when deciding whether to buy a handheld. Criteria discussed previously also apply here; for example, capabilities and features. A main consideration, however, is deciding whether to buy a Palm OS or Windows CE. As was already mentioned, more software is available for the Palm than the Pocket PC. This may be an important factor for some cyber professionals. On the other hand, if the user likes the Windows operating system and is familiar with its programs, the Pocket PC may be preferred. Another important factor is memory expandability. Both systems are comparable in price. The dimensions and capacities of each system are similar as well.

The main factor may be whether the cyber professional really needs a handheld and how often he or she will use it. People often purchase handhelds with good intentions, then forget to bring them, lose them, or find them stolen. The cost of handhelds has dropped, but they start at a few hundred dollars and go up from there. For a handheld to be fully serviceable, the user must buy a modem and subscribe to a service, which charges a monthly fee.

---

### *PUTTING IT TOGETHER*

The handheld can be a useful tool for the real estate professional who is committed to using it.

## *Tablet PC*

This relatively new device goes beyond the typical laptop or notebook. The **Tablet PC** is a computer much like a laptop, but it has many features that make it unique. It is thin; lightweight; flexible; and, most of all, versatile. The Tablet PC can replace notebooks, handhelds, daily planners, spiral notebooks, and sticky notes. It combines electronic devices and paper-and-pen actions into one system. Another unique asset about the Tablet PC is that it operates on a version of Windows XP Professional.

The Tablet PC screen can rotate to meet the needs of the user. The landscape position can be used for note taking; the portrait position, for PowerPoint presentations. The Tablet PC can be purchased in two versions. The most common is the convertible version with the integrated keyboard. The slate version uses a docking station with the host desktop PC. With the slate version, the user can synchronize with the desktop PC, detach the Tablet PC, and go. This version provides a mobile device that can be used anywhere and anytime.

---

### *PUTTING IT TOGETHER*

The Tablet PC operates Microsoft Windows XP Professional.

---

The Tablet PC has many uses and special features, including the following:

- Windows Journal. This feature allows the user to take handwritten notes on the screen by using a digital pen. The user can convert these notes to text, save them, or e-mail them. This is often called handwriting recognition.

---

### *PUTTING IT TOGETHER*

The cyber professional can write on the screen and convert it to text.

- Input Panel. With this feature, the cyber professional uses the on-screen keyboard for taking electronic notes. Another aspect of input panel is being able to dictate to the computer and then having the speech converted to text. This is often called speech recognition.

---

## PUTTING IT TOGETHER

The Tablet PC uses handwriting and speech recognition software.

- Annotation. This allows the user to use a special digital pen for commenting on documents in handwriting. The user can then save and e-mail the annotations.

- MSN Messenger. The user can download this program to the Tablet PC and use it to communicate with clients.

- Wireless connectivity. This feature is built into the Tablet PC, meaning it can connect to wireless networks for Internet access, allowing the user to send and receive e-mail messages.

- Digital Pen. This special pen is used as a mouse on a PC. It also allows handwritten information to be converted to text.

- Collaboration. This feature allows the user to annotate documents from Microsoft Office 2003 and Microsoft Outlook. He or she can then e-mail these changes to staff and colleagues.

- Help and Support Center. Troubleshooting information is available through the Help button; live help, from the Support Center.

- Tutorial. A built-in tutorial is available on the menu bar.

- Downloads. Free Tablet PC downloads, as well as updates, are available.

***Tablet PC Manufacturers.*** The Tablet PC is available from the following sources:

- Acer: http://www.acer.com

- Toshiba: http://www.toshibadirect.com

- Fujitsu: http://www.fujitsupc.com

A picture of a typical Tablet PC from Toshiba is shown here:

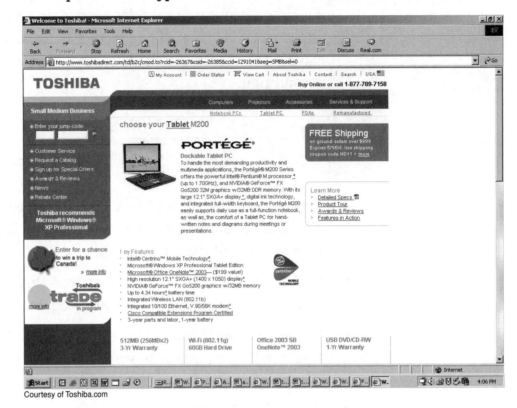

Courtesy of Toshiba.com

The Tablet PC can be purchased online from manufacturers or any of the technology sources shown here.

| | | | |
|---|---|---|---|
| acer | Acer | Insight | Insight |
| BEST BUY | Best Buy | jr.com | J&R |
| buy.com | Buy.com | MICRO CENTER | Micro Center |
| CDW | CDW | WAREHOUSE | Microwarehouse |
| CIRCUIT CITY | Circuit City | Motion Computing | Motion Computing |
| COMPUSA | CompUSA | PC Connection | PC Connection |
| datavision.com | Datavision | PCMall | PC Mall |
| electrovaya | Electrovaya | TOSHIBA | Toshiba |
| FranklinCovey | FranklinCovey | ViewSonic | ViewSonic |
| Fry's Outpost.com | Fry's Electronics | WalkAbout | WalkAbout Computers |
| FUJITSU | Fujitsu | ZONES | Zones, Inc. |

***How the Tablet PC Can Benefit the Cyber Professional.*** The Tablet PC may be the one-stop electronic device. Given its special features and functions, the cyber professional can do the following:

- Eliminate the need for a laptop and handheld computer

- Eliminate the need for a spiral notebook, a daily planner, and sticky notes

- Create real estate forms and fill them out using a digital pen

- Jot down handwritten to-do lists, tasks, activities, and appointments and have them automatically converted to text as you write

- Conduct an interview with a seller or buyer by writing notes and facts on the Tablet PC screen

- Respond to e-mail messages in handwriting for personal attention

- Use speech recognition software to dictate to the computer, then have it converted to text

- Have a lightweight and versatile computer that performs the tasks of a desktop PC

- Be able to use most of the Microsoft Office applications and Windows XP Professional

# 15.2 Other Computer Enhancements

The cyber professional can make use of additional technology in his or her career. Some of these items are discussed here.

## Specialty Phones

The marketplace offers a wide variety of telephones. Deciding which brand to buy and which plan to subscribe to can be a challenge. An important consideration of the cyber professional is how the phone will best serve his or her real estate practice. Obviously, taking and receiving calls is a basic issue. Beyond that, however, the cyber professional will want to be able to access the Multiple Listing Service while in the field. Since staying in touch with clients is so important, having the ability to communicate via e-mail and/or instant messaging may also be of utmost importance.

Many specialty phones have an address book with direct dialing. They include many of the same services available on home and business phones, such as redial, call forwarding, conferencing, and caller ID. Some also have the capacity to link with Microsoft Outlook and Lotus Notes. Also featured on some phones are the same attributes found on the handheld. One popular model even includes the ability to take digital pictures and then share them wirelessly. This option allows the cyber professional to instantly send photos of new listings to clients. With the Chat feature and instant messaging, communication can take place in the field. This gives the cyber professional a competitive edge and makes a difference in situations involving multiple offers.

A dilemma for the cyber professional is whether to carry around a telephone and a handheld or acquire a phone that includes both.

Several specialty phones on the market address this issue. For instance, Treo™ from Hanspring has the Palm OS organizer built into it. It also includes a keyboard below the screen for text messaging. Another useful tool available for text messaging is BlackBerry. This wireless handheld requires a monthly service fee.

## *Digital Cameras*

The 35 mm camera faces a challenge from new technology, **digital cameras.** A disadvantage of the 35 mm camera is that pictures must be taken to a photo shop for processing. In a culture of "I want it now," this necessity may be a nuisance. With a digital camera, however, the user can see and, in some cases, produce pictures instantaneously.

This section does not discuss the technology behind the digital camera. Instead, the focus is on the implications of digital camera use for the real estate professional.

Today most real estate appraisers use a digital camera when completing typical real estate appraisal reports. The advantage to using a digital camera is that the appraiser can take pictures onsite, download them to a PC, incorporate them into a report, and instantaneously transmit the photos and report electronically. This process saves time, money, and effort. The real estate professional can also make use of a digital camera when working with clients in the selling and buying of homes.

***How a Digital Camera Can Benefit the Cyber Professional.*** The cyber professional can take advantage of the following by using a digital camera:

- A digital camera is useful in the listing process. The cyber professional can take pictures of a property and then add them to a web page.

- The cyber professional can use digital pictures to create flyers and other marketing materials.

- The cyber professional can transfer digital pictures via e-mail to potential buyers.

- The cyber professional can store digital pictures for future reference.

- The cyber professional can use digital pictures as evidence if legal issues arise.

These are just a few of the benefits of digital cameras. The cyber professional's creativity will determine other uses.

***Types of Digital Cameras.*** Digital cameras can be a stand-alone product, or, as previously mentioned, they can be built into a PDA or telephone. They come in different sizes. The miniature ones are small enough to put in a pocket; larger sizes offer more advanced options. Many different models of digital cameras are available, each offering different capabilities. Although many brands are available, some of the more popular manufacturers include the following:

- Olympus

- Sony

- Canon

- Hewlett-Packard (HP)

- Kodak

- Nikon

***Considerations for Purchase.*** An important question for the cyber professional to ask is "Do I really need a digital camera?" The answer may depend on his or her budget and the cost of the camera. Is a digital camera necessary in order to be profitable? Once these questions are answered, the cyber professional should consider the following factors:

- Cost. The cost of a digital camera begins in the $100 range and can run over $1,000.

- Size and Weight. The size may be small enough to fit into a pocket or purse or large enough to require a special case.

- Zoom. There are two kinds of zoom: optical and digital. Optical zoom uses lenses and positioning to zoom. Digital zoom uses processing to enlarge a portion of an image. Optical zoom is preferable to digital zoom.

- Resolution and Pixels. These factors also determine the quality of pictures. Many of the lower-end cameras have below 1.0 megapixels; some of the more expensive cameras offer more than 6.2 megapixels.

- Storage and Memory Card Reader. This determines how many pictures can be stored on the camera at a time and what memory storage format is used. There are several competing standards. Special attachments can be added to cameras to increase the storage capacity; several different kinds are available, including a Memory Stick offered by Sony. Once pictures are stored, they can be scanned into the computer for future use.

- Transfer Speed. Transfer speed is how fast images from a digital camera can be uploaded to a PC. There are a variety of common connection standards: USB, USB2, and FireWire.

- Software. A digital camera comes packaged with computer software. This software can range from transfer utilities to photo editing suites.

- Batteries. This critical element is often overlooked. The size and type as well as durability are key factors. Some batteries are rechargeable.

Of special note is the fact that pictures taken with an ordinary 35mm camera can be converted to digital format and placed on CD-ROMs. This can easily be accomplished at most photo development centers.

---

### *PUTTING IT TOGETHER*

The cyber professional must consider a variety of factors when deciding whether to purchase a digital camera.

## *Camcorder*

A **camcorder** is a combination camera/VCR that allows the cyber professional to film live images. He or she can then incorporate these images into a web site for potential buyers to view. Basically, there are two types of camcorders: analog and digital. Although digital camcorders are more technologically advanced, they are not always the best choice. Digital camcorders can be very costly depending on the specifications and the size. Most analog camcorders use compact VHS videotapes and need special equipment to convert to use on a PC. The other types are classified as DVs, meaning digital video. Newer on the market are DVD models.

With the digital camcorder, the cyber professional can transfer the film directly into a PC via USB2 or FireWire. This connection standard allows quick video transfer to a PC for storage and future use. This process is known as video streaming.

Some camcorders also serve as digital cameras, using the same memory modules as digital cameras in some cases.

Once the cyber professional has stored the film, he or she can tap into the images and post them on a web site for potential buyers to view. Another way the cyber professional can use a camcorder is to create a welcome message to display on a web page. A camcorder can also be used to record testimonials from past clients or to explain some fact of the real estate process. There are many possibilities for using a camcorder in a real estate practice.

## *Scanner*

The **scanner** is another useful tool for the cyber professional. Its primary use is to read and translate regular photos and documents into a form the computer can use. The cyber professional can use the scanned pictures in business materials such as flyers and brochures.

Scanners are usually one of two types: a flatbed scanner or a fed scanner like a copier. The advantage of a flatbed is that the top of the scanner can be lifted to allow pages from a book to be scanned.

The price of scanners is relative inexpensive but depends on specifications such as resolution, size, and speed of transmission.

Learning how to operate a scanner is relatively simple. The trick is getting the right dimensions for the image and then deciding where to store the file and how to retrieve it. Some computer skill is necessary to make scanned material look professional.

A scanner can be purchased as a stand-alone machine. Many brands are available that offer a variety of features. A scanner may also be one feature on a machine that includes a printer, fax machine, and copier as well—an all-in-one device.

## Webcam

A **webcam** is a simple video camera that connects to a computer and allows the user to view video using the Internet. It looks like a digital camera, and it is located on the computer screen. When a webcam is connected and when the right type of software is used, the cyber professional can broadcast live presentations and conduct net meetings or conferences. If the user on the other end has a similar compatible device, the two can communicate via the Internet. The cyber professional can use this tool to communicate directly with clients or prospects. The cyber professional can use a webcam to capture pictures of a house for sale from a satellite. Webcams can be used to show live pictures of just about anything.

Webcams are generally inexpensive but depend on the specifications. Several brands are available for purchase.

## Global Positioning System (GPS)

A Global Positioning System (GPS) may be the answer for real estate professional who have to show properties in unknown areas. This system allows the user to locate almost any place on Earth via satellites. Common trade names include NeverLost® and OnStar®, which is found in newer model vehicles. A GPS can be purchased separately at a modest price and added to a compatible PDA. This service does, however, require a monthly service fee. An alternative to this service is software that can be purchased for a given area and then downloaded to a PDA or laptop.

## *Typical Home Office Network*

Since many real estate professionals conduct business at home, they may find it necessary to have their home office wired for maximum performance. Often the cyber professional has a desktop, a laptop, and even a PDA at his or her disposable without any of them working together in a coordinated fashion. With a home network, all of the electronic devices are coordinated to work together without the need for the cyber professional to buy additional equipment. In a networked home office, all of the equipment is tied to function well together. For example, given the right equipment, all computers in a household can have an Internet connection. This can also be done wirelessly. The most common application is to have all computers connected to one printer, one scanner, one copier, and one fax machine.

The equipment required to network a home office is relatively inexpensive but does require some technical knowledge to coordinate all of the devices. Another benefit of a networked home office is being able to access the home office when not physically there. This can be accomplished using special software that allows one computer to connect with another—even from a distance. Software programs such as pcAnywhere™ and Laplink can make this happen. Windows XP also provides this capability.

## *Typical Mobile Office System*

Most real estate professional are out in the field dealing with potential prospect, but they must be accessible. This can be accomplished with the right equipment. Equipment necessary to conduct business on a 24/7/365 basis includes the following:

- A cellular telephone with answering service, call forwarding, caller ID, and text and instant messaging

- A cellular phone that allows access to a Multiple Listing Service

- A laptop computer that has the proper software for conducting business, such as being able to write contracts and check credit reports

- A PDA that provides pertinent information when necessary

- A portable printer and scanner

With all of these devices, the cyber professional is always accessible. He or she can act quickly when the need arises.

# 15.3 Communication Tools

The real estate professional may find instant messaging and discussion groups helpful in his or her career. Each of these is discussed briefly.

## *Instant Messaging (IM)*

Instant messaging (IM) is a useful tool that allows the cyber professional to contact clients without having to pay long-distance telephone rates. IM is conducted live from a computer, a telephone, a PDA, or a BlackBerry device. It is simple to set up and to use. Some programs, such as the one offered by Yahoo, are free, but other programs, such as BlackBerry, require a service charge. IM can be wireless, or it can be connected via a cable, DSL, or a modem.

## *Discussion and Chat Groups*

Another way to communicate with clients is to establish a discussion group or chat session. This can be done for free by setting up an account with Yahoo. In a discussion group, each member of a transaction could be included in the group, allowing all of the members to communicate with one another. Messages pertaining to the progress of a transaction could be posted on a message center. The scheduling of events or activities could also be posted. If necessary, a conference session could be set up so all of the parties involved could participate. This would eliminate expensive telephone calls and save time.

## *Weblogs*

This relatively new form of Internet communication allows webloggers to post their thoughts and ideas as they would in a journal. Others can access the site and post their impressions as well. Using a weblog, the cyber professional can communicate with clients, support services, and the community of real estate professionals.

## *Virtual Assistant (VA)*

Michael Russer, also known as "Mr. Internet," had the foresight to recognize that not all individuals are interested in working with technology or reinventing the mousetrap. He also realizes that real estate professionals are in the business of selling real estate, not being a webmaster or a master of technology. Therefore, he established a system known as the **Virtual Assistant (VA).** This VA concept implies that many real estate professionals would rather hire someone else to do the technical work than take the time to learn or do the work themselves. The VA system is "technology for hire." Once a real estate professional knows what he or she wants in the way of technology, he or she can put the request up for bid from a host of VAs who are highly capable and who are willing to provide the services requested. The real estate professional accesses the VA web site and states what he or she wants done. The registered VAs contact the real estate professional for more details and then bid on the tasks. To learn more about how the VA works, go to the following web sites:

- http://www.virtualassistant.com
- http://www.elance.com

# 15.4 Technology and Information Overload

Recent studies have shown that computers, the Internet, e-mail, and cell phones can cause depression, exhaustion, anxiety, sleep disturbances, and difficulty in decision making and concentration. All of these factors tend to rob the user of time. The term for this predicament is new economy depression syndrome (NEDS). Studies have also indicated that reading e-mail messages has added more to people's workload. Instead of the elimination of work, there has been an actual increase in work!

Research on the topic of information overload is only just beginning. How the public reacts to this phenomenon remains to be seen.

There has been a backlash in terms of spam and pop-ups. In the future, there may be a technology tune out, a TTO.

The cyber professional should watch that he or she doesn't get too deeply involved in technology, resulting in a technology knockout (TKO). The cyber professional should also avoid going overboard with technology since it just might overwhelm the Internet user. Other types of annoyances include spyware and adware. These programs can rob the user of valuable disk space and even pertinent personal information.

## RESOURCES FOR FURTHER STUDY

More information about handheld devices can be found at the following web sites:

- http://www.handango.com

- http://www.pocketgear.com

- http://www.avantgo.com

- http://www.ebookdirectory.com

- http://www.cewindows.net

- http://www.developerone.com

- http://www.pocketrealestate.com

- http://www.igo.com

- http://www.palmgear.com

Courtesy of AvantGo.com

- http://www.microsoft.com/windowsxp/tabletpc/default.asp

This site is useful for learning more about the Tablet PC. It even gives a live demonstration.

- http://www.webex.com

This site can help with setting up a webcam connection between parties so that they can communicate live and even see each other. A free trial is available.

# SELF-ASSESSMENT

To determine the extent of knowledge you acquired in this chapter, choose the correct answer for each of the following.

1.  What is the device most often used by real estate professionals today?
    a.  Scanner
    b.  Webcam
    c.  PDA
    d.  Camcorder

2.  A PDA is best described as a/an?
    a.  Miniature computer
    b.  Organizer
    c.  Personal Digital Assistant
    d.  All of the above

3.  What is the major advantage of a handheld over a laptop?
    a.  Size
    b.  Capability
    c.  Weight
    d.  Both a and c

4.  Handhelds have more capacity and capability than a:
    a.  Desktop
    b.  Laptop
    c.  Notebook
    d.  None of these

5.  The Pocket PC is based on what platform?
    a.  Windows CE
    b.  OSX
    c.  Linux
    d.  Opera

6.  What is a major benefit of the handheld?
    a.  Has many of the same features and functions as a PC
    b.  Is faster that a desktop
    c.  Is faster than a laptop
    d.  None of these

7. What is the main advantages of the Palm OS over the Pocket PC?
   a. More available software
   b. More memory
   c. A faster processor
   d. More storage

8. Who is a manufacturer of Tablet PCs?
   a. Acer
   b. Toshiba
   c. Fujitsu
   d. All of the above

9. What is the major advantage of a digital camera over a 35 mm camera?
   a. Costs less
   b. Is lighter
   c. Takes better pictures
   d. None of these

10. What can digital photos be used for?
    a. To create real estate flyers
    b. To create brochures
    c. To post on a web site
    d. All of the above

11. What does an all-in-one device refer to?
    a. A scanner and a printer
    b. A copier and a scanner
    c. A printer and a fax machine
    d. A scanner, a copier, a fax machine, and a printer

12. What is an advantage of a home network?
    a. Requires more equipment
    b. Requires less equipment
    c. Can be done wirelessly
    d. Both b and c

13. Specialty phones often include features that are similar to
    a. A handheld
    b. A laptop
    c. A desktop
    d. None of these

14. What is the idea behind the Virtual Assistant?
    a. It is "technology for hire."
    b. It was developed by Michael Russer.
    c. Real estate professionals prefer doing their own technical work.
    d. Both a and b

15. What is a result of technology and information overload?
    a. Depression
    b. Anxiety
    c. Sleep disturbance
    d. All of the above

# EPILOGUE

Technology is never static. It continually improves upon itself in a relatively short period of time. The Internet and the World Wide Web, when compared with the telephone and television, have saturated the market in record time. These systems are available everywhere in the world.

Significant advances have been made in computer hardware and software. The increase in speed and capacity of the computer is nothing short of phenomenal. Software is increasing productivity at an unheard-of rate. And the good news is that prices have dropped in most cases. As a result, the number of users all over the world is reaching its full potential.

It should be noted that the technologically savvy user can never rest. One must continually look to the horizon just to keep up. The same may be said of the real estate industry. In this ever-growing field, one must continually look to the horizon just to keep up.

At the time of this book's publication, new and better systems are being developed. Soon wireless connections for the Internet will be commonplace. The author will attempt to update this book as expeditiously as possible to keep the cyber professional well informed.

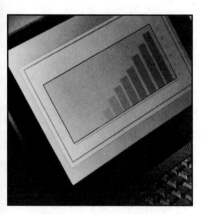

# APPENDIX: REFERENCE GUIDE TO OTHER OPERATING SYSTEMS AND SOFTWARE PACKAGES

## Introduction

Time is a very important element for the Internet empowered real estate agent as well as for the Internet empowered consumer. The Internet empowered consumer will form opinions and rate a real estate agent on how quickly the agent responds with pertinent information during the home buying and/or selling process. If the Internet empowered consumer requests information at 11 a.m., the Internet empowered real estate agent, using advanced software tools, should respond within minutes—an hour at the most. The non-Internet empowered real estate agent may take several hours or up to a day. The reduction in response time, the reduction in the utilization of paper-based forms, and the increase in efficiency ultimately shortens the sales cycle and makes the Internet empowered real estate agent a powerful salesperson.

Today's modern real estate professional uses hardware and software tools from a variety of manufacturers. Most people think of Microsoft as being the biggest and sometimes only provider of software and computer-related productivity tools. In fact, for today's Internet enabled real estate professional, many other computing and technology platforms and software packages provide opportunities for sales cycle automation, contact management, and cutting-edge productivity.

This Appendix features computer operating systems and software packages with a non-Microsoft focus. The Appendix should serve as a reference guide for Internet enabled real estate professionals who want to use and/or learn about alternative computer-based productivity solutions. Two main computer operating system platforms are discussed—the Apple Macintosh operating system and the Linux operating system.

You should gain an understanding of the origins of both of these computer operating systems. This allows you to come away with the decision-making information you need to make software and hardware choices as a future Internet empowered real estate agent.

When choosing a computer operating system and its respective software and hardware, there is never a wrong choice. Your choice should provide the specific tools and features you need to solve problems and make business processes work effectively and profitably.

The following section includes a brief history of Apple Computer and the Apple Macintosh operating system. The term *operating system* and the acronym *OS* are interchangeable. They both refer to the same thing—computer operating systems. They will be used interchangeably in this Appendix.

After the discussion of the Apple Macintosh, the Appendix provides a brief history of the Linux operating system. The Appendix also highlights non-Microsoft- produced alternative software packages that can be run on all three major operating system platforms—Macintosh OS (Mac OS X is the latest Macintosh OS in production), Microsoft Windows, and Linux.

# Desktop/Laptop Computing

## *Apple Macintosh Computing Platform*

The Macintosh computer is manufactured and marketed by Apple Computer, Inc., in Cupertino, California. It has been one of the most successful personal computer platforms in history. The Macintosh has a loyal following of users who like its easy-to-use and easy-to-learn user interface.

Apple Computer started building computers in the mid-1970s and produced the first successful mass-market computer called the Apple II. After a visit to Xerox's PARC research laboratory in Palo Alto, California, Steven Jobs, Apple's founder, became convinced that the easiest interface for a computer user to use would be a graphical user interface, more commonly known as a GUI. GUI-based operating systems are dominant today's. With a GUI-based operating system, a user clicks certain objects on the computer screen using a pointing device (usually a mouse) to direct the computer to perform certain operations. This method of controlling the computer is easier to use than the traditional command-line input method. The command-line input method requires the user to memorize a series of commands that the he or she then keys into the computer to perform certain operations.

In 1984, Steven Jobs and Apple Computer launched the first version of the Macintosh computer. The original Macintosh was a simple, easy–to-use, and powerful personal computer. It was a breath of fresh air to those who were used to using non-GUI command-line operating systems, such as Microsoft's MS-DOS. The Macintosh was heralded as a major innovation in the computer world because of its intuitive, easy-to-use GUI. Using the Macintosh GUI, computer users could easily learn how to use a computer. Even children who had no exposure to computers could be trained to use a Macintosh quickly and easily.

Over the years, Apple Computer has developed many different models of the Macintosh. Macintosh computers come in high-performance business desktop and laptop versions, as well as consumer, student, and home user versions.

Many real estate professionals prefer the Apple Macintosh computer over a standard PC. They like the Macintosh platform because they can achieve a high level of productivity in a short amount of time. The time it takes them to become proficient in controlling the Macintosh operating system and applications is very short. Most applications that run on a Macintosh computer have similar user interfaces. A user who becomes familiar with a single Macintosh computer program can learn other applications with relative ease because of the intuitive nature of the operating system and the similar user interfaces among the programs.

The operating system of the Macintosh computer is commonly referred to as the Mac OS. As of this writing, the latest version of Mac OS was Mac OS X. The most popular operating system for computers is Microsoft Windows. Of particular interest is the fact that the Microsoft Windows user interface copied many of its features from the Macintosh.

Because of its ease of use and short learning curve, the Macintosh computer has a loyal following of real estate professionals who want an uncomplicated yet powerful computing platform.

## Linux Computing Platform

Linux is a computer operating system that has gained popularity in recent years with consumers and businesses. It is an open-source operating system, which means it may be free for anyone to use and share. Nobody owns it outright. It is maintained, developed, and upgraded by users and developers in industry and education worldwide. They post updates and enhancements to the operating system via the Internet.

Linux is a derivative of an operating system called UNIX. In the early 1990s, a young man from Finland, Linus Torvalds, started to create an open-source version of UNIX, which became known as Linux. The name *Linux* is a composite word made up of the letters *Lin* (from *Linus*) and the letters *ux* (from UNIX). (The word *Linux* is pronounced with a short *i*.) Linux is highly customizable, and new features are relatively simple to add. Since its inception, application development for Linux has been fast and furious. Technology-savvy computer users have made Linux a popular computing platform on the Internet, where it is the dominant operating system for web site server computers.

Linux is very cost-effective. You do not need powerful computing hardware to run it. Linux can run on older models of PCs, such as 386s and 486s. You can turn an old PC into a Linux PC, performing basic office tasks such as word processing, e-mail, and web surfing.

Natively, Linux is a non-GUI operating system. This means that in its native form, Linux requires users to memorize commands that they type into the operating system line by line. Fortunately for Linux, several GUI interfaces have been developed that allow the user to control Linux similarly to the way the Microsoft Windows and Apple Macintosh operating systems are controlled. The GUI interfaces for Linux are used in much the same way as they are for Microsoft Windows and Apple Macintosh. Two of the most popular GUI interfaces for Linux are K Desktop Environment (KDE) and Gnome. The look and feel of these two GUIs resemble Windows and Macintosh; many of the same tools and utilities are included, such as file management, help systems, window management, and configuration management.

Linux has a large following of loyal users and developers, yet the amount of mainstream software available for the Linux platform is small when compared to Windows and Macintosh. Many corporations, including IBM, support Linux and create specialized Linux software for their corporate products. Other companies are creating software packages compatible with Linux. These are aimed directly at the small business and home user market. The hope is that consumers and small business owners/managers will realize that Linux has power and flexibility and offers most of the features of the Microsoft Windows operating system environment.

Like other professionals who use computing technology, the Internet empowered real estate agent wants software that is ready to install and run directly from the packaging or download. As a result, several companies sell Linux in user-friendly retail packaging as well as complete downloadable packages. These companies give users the complete operating system that is ready to install from a few CDs or as an executable downloaded file from the company's web site. Some of the better-known companies packaging and selling the Linux operating system include these:

- Red Hat             http://www.redhat.com
- Mandrakesoft      http://www.mandrakesoft.com
- SUSE LINUX       http://www.suse.com/us

Some companies even offer Linux suites targeted to specific end users, such as IT professionals, business users, and home users.

Many software development companies have been transferring some of their most popular Microsoft Windows and Apple Macintosh computer programs over to the Linux computing platform.

Many Linux proponents would like to see Linux become the dominant operating system. After all, it is free to use and own and it can be as powerful as Microsoft Windows and Apple Macintosh (without the higher price). As versatile and popular as Linux is, it still has a long way to go to reach the level of user friendliness and consistent out-of-the-box experience that comes only with time and product maturity, as is the case with Microsoft Windows and Apple Macintosh. With its current worldwide adoption rate, one day Linux may prove to be a threat to Microsoft's domination of the operating system market.

# Alternative Productivity Software Applications for the Internet Enabled Real Estate Professional

The following pages contain an assortment of software packages the Internet enabled real estate professional can use when conducting his or her day-to-day business. The software packages presented are alternatives to the more common Microsoft software packages. Many people are unaware of alternatives to Microsoft software simply because Microsoft dominates the market.

In today's personal computing world, three main computer platform operating systems are widely used. The first one, which also has the largest user-installed base, is Microsoft Windows. The second one, with a much smaller user-installed base yet with an extremely loyal following, is Apple's Macintosh OS. The third one, with a growing user population, an increasing worldwide market share, and increasing consumer acceptance, is the Linux operating system.

The Internet empowered real estate agent can use software packages on any of the three operating systems to enhance and build his or her real estate business. The most common computer operating system platforms are Microsoft Windows and Apple's Macintosh. Therefore, if the Internet empowered real estate agent wants to use Linux, he or she must do some online research. He or she can find the software tools needed for installation and implementation as well as sales consultation from a specialized software and/or hardware store or computer consulting business.

All three operating systems have their upsides. The upside of Microsoft Windows as an operating system is the diversity and availability of software packages. The upside of Apple's Macintosh OS as an operating system is the ease with which the system is mastered. The upside to the Linux operating system is the fact that the overall software and hardware costs can be kept to a minimum.

The Internet empowered real estate agent must be aware of the total cost of ownership, also known as TCO, when selecting a computer operating system. In the real estate agent's day-to-day business operations, TCO refers to the amount of resources required to learn and effectively implement a particular computer operating system and its respective software components. Resources include money spent on computer hardware; money spent on software; hours of training required to master a specific operating system and its GUI; hours of training required to master software; and money, time, and resources spent on hardware and software maintenance and technical support.. Analyzing the potential TCO of a particular operating system is a wise and prudent move on the part of the Internet empowered real estate agent. If the Internet empowered real estate agent makes hardware, software, and operating system choices based, in part, on a comprehensive analysis of the TCO, he or she can take comfort in knowing that the choices were right for his or her needs.

The following section provides descriptions of alternative software products, which can be used in lieu of the Microsoft equivalents. Internet URLs have been provided for each of the software packages listed. At the time of writing, all URLs were fully operational and all links were working. If for any reason the links do not work, try entering the name of the software package into a well-known search engine. Doing so should provide you with an updated URL that you can access for more information..

## *Real Estate Software for the Apple Macintosh*

The following companies produce real estate software in both Macintosh and Windows versions.

### Business Edge Software (Mac/Windows)

### http://www.businessedgesoftware.com

Business Edge Software is a software development company that focuses on producing real estate-oriented software for Windows and Macintosh computers. Its software catalog includes products for working with loan origination and process management, property management, real estate investment analysis, contact management, client prospecting systems, and real estate agent web site creation. Business Edge Software is one of the few real estate-oriented software companies producing multiplatform products. If you are an Internet empowered real estate agent who uses an Apple Macintosh, you should consider this company's products.

## Real Data: Software for Real Estate (Mac/Windows)

**http://www.realdata.com/index.html**

Real Data is a real estate-oriented software company that produces software packages for real estate investors and developers. The company's software helps people construct different types of analysis and make decisions regarding income property, condominium development, and document preparation and reporting for real estate lending processes. The software packages are produced in a multiplatform format so that they work on both Microsoft Windows and Apple Macintosh operating systems.

## Astoundit Software (Mac/Windows)

**http://www.astoundit.com/index.html**

Astoundit Software makes two powerful yet simple-to-use software packages for the Internet enabled real estate professional using a Macintosh operating system.

## Real Introduction (Mac/Windows)

Real Introduction is a software package that allows the real estate agent to create custom interactive software-based presentations. The agent can use these presentations as marketing pieces at sales presentation and open houses. Once the agent has created a presentation on the computer, he or she can distribute it to potential clients via CD and/or DVD. The agent can even have potential customers download a specific presentation from the Internet, using a web site address provided. This program is an effective marketing tool. Anyone who uses an Apple Macintosh computer should consider this package as part of his or her marketing tool kit.

## Real Listings (Mac/Windows)

Real Listings is a software package that helps the Internet empowered real estate agent design customized property listing flyers. As most real estate agents know, professional-looking listing flyers are a key component to the real estate sales process. Real Listings gives the agent the opportunity to keep a library of custom-designed listing flyers on the computer, retrieving and using them as templates for future flyers. The agent can customize a flyer for a particular client, then adapt it for different situations. The software allows computer novices as well as computer experts to create professionally produced listing flyers in no time at all.

## Panoweaver (Mac/Windows)

### http://www.easypano.com

Panoweaver is an easy-to-use software package that allows the Internet empowered real estate agent to create panoramic photographic images with a 180° or 360° field of view. The agent can use Panoweaver to preview a property with his or her client, giving a virtual representation of the property and the surrounding environment. Using Panoweaver, the agent can digitally stitch together individual photographs to create a seamless larger photograph. The result is an image that is panoramic in scope, providing a 180° or 360° view for the client.

## *Office and Business Productivity Software*

### All-in-One "Office" Software Suites

### AppleWorks (Mac)

### http://www.apple.com/appleworks

AppleWorks is a fully integrated productivity suite that targets the small business and home user. It is tightly integrated and offers word processing, spreadsheets, digital painting, digital drawing, the ability to create electronic slide show presentations, and the ability to create and work with databases. This is a useful application for the Internet empowered real estate agent who owns a Macintosh but does not need the power of a software suite..

### Corel® WordPerfect Office Suite 12 (Windows)

### http://www.corel.com/servlet/Satellite?pagename=Corel2/ Products/Home&pid=1047022958453

For the user who wants a comprehensive office productivity suite without the large price tag, Corel WordPerfect Office Suite is the answer. It is significantly cheaper than Microsoft Office. It offers compatibility with Microsoft Office and provides several software modules, which give the same functionality as the modules in Microsoft Office. The suite contains WordPerfect for word processing; Quattro Pro, a spreadsheet application; Presentations, a program similar to Microsoft PowerPoint; and Address Book, which provides easy data access to an electronic client, Rolodex type of filing system.

## ThinkFree Office (Mac/Linux/Windows)

### http://www.thinkfree.com

ThinkFree Office is another office productivity suite. It features a word processing application, a spreadsheet application, and a PowerPoint type of presentation application. The names of these applications are Write, Calc, and Show. The applications are tightly integrated with one another, allowing the user to work seamlessly between them. The user can create documents with full file compatibility to Microsoft Office applications. The user can save documents directly to file formats such as .doc, .xls, and .ppt. ThinkFree Office is cross-platform compatible. It runs on most major computing platforms, including Macintosh, Linux, and Microsoft Windows.

## StarOffice (Linux)

### http://wwws.sun.com/software/star/staroffice/index.html

StarOffice is an extraordinary compilation of Microsoft-compatible business productivity applications. StarOffice Suite has the biggest market share of any office productivity suite on the Linux computing platform. It is also one of the leading office suites on the Windows computing platform for people who want an alternative to Microsoft Office. StarOffice is open source-based software. It is affordable and easy to master. The core applications include word processing, a spreadsheet application, a presentation application, database creation and maintenance, and a drawing application. This is a great choice for the Linux user who wants an office suite backed by a major company (in this case, Sun Microsystems).

## OpenOffice (Mac/Linux/Windows)

### http://www.openoffice.org

OpenOffice is a leading office software suite that shares its underlying heritage with the StarOffice application from Sun Microsystems. It is an open-source, open standards software suite, which allows it to run on all major computing platforms. It is fully compatible with Microsoft Office files. Because of its open software architecture, it is suitable for multilingual support for many different languages. It has the ability to output the user's documents in Adobe's PDF Acrobat® file format, which has become a standard in electronic document distribution. It also has the ability to output graphics the user created using the Macromedia Flash file format, which has become a standard in animated graphic file distribution. OpenOffice is easy to use and entails a short learning curve, especially for people coming from a Microsoft Office background.

OpenOffice includes the following software modules:

- Writer: Writer is a full-featured, powerful word processing package on par with Microsoft Word. It allows the user to create professional-looking documents with relative ease. A person can be up and running quickly and easily, creating a variety of documents including newsletters, brochures, reports, and flyers, as well as content ready for output to the Internet.

- Calc: Calc is a spreadsheet application as powerful as Microsoft Excel. It allows the user to easily manipulate numerical data and turn it into decision-making information. Functionality includes the ability to create data analysis as well as charts and graphs.

- Impress: Impress is an alternative to Microsoft PowerPoint. Creating presentations has never been easier with an open-source software package. Functionality includes special effects, animation, and the ability to catch audiences' attention with colorful drawings and graphics.

- Draw: Draw is an easy-to-use drawing and diagramming program. Draw gives the user the power to create impressive graphics, such as charts, business diagrams, and 3D illustrations.

- OpenOffice Database Tools: These tools give the user the power to create databases that are framed in an easy-to-use spreadsheet-like format. The dBase database format is used for overall compatibility with other database programs as well as legacy database software products.

# Word Processing

## Mellel (Mac)

**http://www.redlers.com**

This word processing package is a good one for the Macintosh-running OS X. It is useful for anyone in a creative or technical field wanting a flexible and feature-laden program. The program has a small memory footprint, meaning it won't consume many of the computer's system resources while running. Mellel offers innovative formatting and text tools that appeal to people in academia as well as industry.

## Nisus Writer Express (Mac)

**http://www.nisus.com**

This word processing package is affordable yet powerful. It has been written for speed and efficiency. It has been optimized to work with Macintosh computers running OS X. It has a user-customizable interface and reads and writes Microsoft Word file formats. It also supports multiple editable clipboards and allows the user to create customized text selections and user-definable keyboard shortcuts. The included document manager makes creating complex documents easy. Macintosh computer aficionados should consider checking out this word processing package.

## AbiWord (Linux/Windows)

**http://www.abisource.com**

AbiWord is well suited to all types of document creation. One of the objectives of AbiWord is to be completely and fully compatible with a multitude of computing platforms. AbiWord can be used with many different language overlays, giving the program a huge potential user base. The wonderful thing about AbiWord is that it is free! This versatile word processor reads and writes word processing files from programs such as Microsoft Word and WordPerfect. It also reads and writes file formats such as RTF (rich text format) files, HTML (hypertext markup language) files, and the OpenOffice and StarOffice file formats.

## Corel WordPerfect (coming soon to Linux)

### http://www.corel.com/servlet/Satellite?pagename=Corel2/Products/Home&pid=1047023021963&trkid=search

Corel software is retooling the WordPerfect word processing package for release onto the Linux computing platform. WordPerfect is a full-featured word processor that competes with Microsoft Word. This release of WordPerfect for Linux is totally updated and was in a product-testing phase as of the writing of this Appendix. Corel is one of many companies committed to developing software for the Linux operating system platform.

## LyX (Mac/Linux)

### http://www.lyx.org

LyX is a unique word processing package in that the developers do not refer to it as a word processor, but as a document processing package. This program allows the user to write and brainstorm ideas on the computer while leaving the details of page layout and formatting to the software. LyX is an open-source software program, which means that it runs on many different computing platforms, including Mac OS X and Linux. LyX has a breadth of features that make it suitable for creating documents as diverse as doctoral theses and letters and memos. The developers call this type of package a "what you see is what you mean" document processor. With this software, you choose a classification or type of document you want to create and the corresponding style you want the document to have. Ideas and thoughts are entered into the program while you brainstorm new ones. The software adds all formatting and styling touches to the document. LyX includes a mathematical equation editor, making this package suitable for people who create documents that include many numerical references. The best part about this package is that it is free.

## Ulysses (Mac)

### http://www.blue-tec.com

Ulysses is another outstanding document processing package. It can import files from Microsoft Word and export completed files to industry-standard RTF files. This program is on the rise and is one Macintosh computer users should look into.

## Database Creation and Maintenance

### FileMaker (Mac/Windows)

**http://www.filemaker.com/index.html**

FileMaker is a mature, stable, and powerful database program. Originally, it was available only on the Macintosh computing platform. It is now available in Microsoft Windows as well. It is very flexible and easy to use. As a key tool for the Internet enabled real estate agent, database creation and management has many uses in the sales environment. FileMaker is an asset because it can quickly be configured for a number of duties, including contact management, real estate property inventory and attributes, and general organizational tasks.

## Utilities

### Adobe Acrobat Reader 6.0 (Mac/Linux/Windows)

**http://www.adobe.com/products/acrobat/readermain.html**

Adobe Acrobat reader is a useful piece of software. It allows the user to view and print Adobe Acrobat PDF files. Acrobat PDF files are the industry-standard file format for electronic document distribution on the Web. Acrobat files allow text, graphics, and pictures to be shared across different computer platforms. This is an essential utility that all real estate professionals should have on their computer.

### QuicKeys (Mac/Windows)

**http://www.cesoft.com**

This program helps you create shortcuts, also known as macros, to automate repetitive tasks done at the computer. If you have text that you input regularly, a Quickey, or macro, can simplify this task. If you launch a certain program often or want to assign specific buttons or icons to repetitive keystrokes, this is a program you should consider.

### SpellCatcher (Mac/Windows)

**http://www.spellcatcher.com**

This software can help you create documents with better user readability. It is best used as a spell checker for e-mail messages, instant messages, and other documents you work with frequently. It can check your spelling in 13 different languages! The program can be configured in different yet flexible ways. It can be configured as an as-you-type and after-the-fact spell checker on existing text selections. It even has a shorthand glossary that allows you to include custom abbreviations for phrases and sentences that you use a lot. Spell-Catcher complements the spell checkers that reside in most word processing, e-mail, and writing applications.

## Operating System Utilities for Linux

These Linux utilities make the Linux operating system experience more like the Windows and Macintosh operating system experience. They are great little software gems that no Linux user should be without.

### Linux Media Player (Linux)

**http://www.forensicgames.com**

This is a digital media player for the Linux operating system.

### RealPlayer (Linux)

**http://www.real.com**

RealPlayer® is a multimedia file player that allows the user to listen to and view audio and video from RealAudio-enabled content on the Internet.

### Acrobat Reader 5.0.9 (English version in Linux)

**http://www.adobe.com/products/acrobat/alternate.html**

This Adobe Acrobat PDF file reading program has been optimized for the Linux operating system. It allows the Linux OS user to view and print PDF files.

### BitDefender (Linux)

**http://www.bitdefender.com/bd/site/products.php?p_id=16**

Every operating system needs a computer virus defense system. This antivirus software has been specifically designed for Linux computing platforms.

### DOS Emulation (Linux)

**http://www.dosemu.org**

This software allows the Linux user to run Microsoft MS-DOS programs on a Linux system. It does this by providing an emulation mode where the MS-DOS programs can be run.

### VideoLAN Client (Linux)

**http://www.videolan.org**

VideoLAN Client is media software that allows the user to view video streams in many different file formats, such as MPEG 1, 2, and 4 as well as DivX and DVD video. It is free to use, and it is an open-source program, meaning it runs on all major computing platforms, including Mac OS X, Linux, and Windows.

### CDRecord (cdrtools) (Linux)
**http://www.fokus.gmd.de/research/cc/glone/employees/ joerg.schilling/private/**

**cdrecord.html**

CDRecord allows the user to create audio as well as data files to recordable optical media. This program is free to download and use. It is another open-source program that runs on most major computing platforms, including Mac OS X, Linux, and Windows. Disc recording programs are necessary for anyone in the real estate sales field. They are an inexpensive way to distribute photos of homes, video virtual tour presentations, and graphical or image content relevant to the sale of homes.

### Quicktime 4 (Linux)

**http://heroinewarrior.com/quicktime.php3**

This program is designed for the easy creation of QuickTime file format movies and videos using the Linux computing platform. Real estate agents may want to take advantage of short digital videos that they can e-mail to clients when marketing homes for sale. Quicktime is another free software package.

### QuickDownloader (Linux)

**http://qdown.sourceforge.net**

This file download management program is useful for coordinating and managing software downloads over the Internet. Downloading software and associated updates is an integral function of modern-day computing. A good download manager makes it easy to recover from interrupted and/or corrupted software downloads.

## *Outliners/Project Management*

### OmniOutliner (Mac)

**http://www.omnigroup.com/applications/omnioutliner**

OmniOutliner is a productivity tool that allows the user to brainstorm ideas while organizing them into an outline. Almost any task—to-do lists, project management, sales and client management, expense management, and note taking organization—can be organized with this outlining program. (Outlining programs are a necessity when it comes to organizing one's thoughts in relation to managing a process.) The interface on this program is easy to use. It takes advantage of all of the attributes of Mac OS X. It excels at list making and basic outlining functionality. This software package allows users to organize their thoughts so they can build upon them to succeed at a specified objective.

## *Charting/Graphing/Business Diagramming*

### OmniGraffle (Mac)

**http://www.omnigroup.com/applications/omnigraffle**

The ability to communicate an idea graphically can be difficult if you do not have the right software tools. OmniGraffle is a specialized business diagramming software package that allows the user to communicate methodologies and processes visually so people can understand ideas more clearly. When done correctly, diagrams and charts can communicate ideas more effectively than the spoken word. Omni-Graffle is easy to use and takes advantage of the special features of the Macintosh operating system.

# Presentation Software

## Keynote (Mac)

**http://www.apple.com/keynote**

Keynote is an advanced professional presentation software package similar to Microsoft PowerPoint. It is designed for Macintosh computers running Mac OS X. Keynote makes it easy to create presentations with beautiful imagery, top-notch thematic accents, charts, tables, and artistically styled text and graphics. Transitions between slides can be done with a 3D flare. With Keynote, the user can create intricate and beautiful animations to complement a presentation. The program is easy to master.

# Graphics/Design/Digital Media

**Content Creation and Distribution**

## *All-in-One Graphic Suites*

### CorelDRAW™ Graphics Suite 12.0 (Windows)

http://www.corel.com/servlet/Satellite?pagename=Corel2/
Products/Home&pid=1047022690654

CorelDRAW Graphics Suite is a full-featured program for small business and graphic design professionals. The core components consist of CorelDRAW, Corel PHOTO-PAINT™, Corel R.A.V.E.™, and other support programs. CorelDRAW is an intuitive drawing, illustration, and page layout program suitable for creating brochures, newsletters, flyers, and other high-impact marketing documents. Corel PHOTO-PAINT is a professional digital imaging and touch-up software package. It is beneficial for the image-editing user who wants the power of Photoshop without the higher price. Corel R.A.V.E. allows the user to create custom animation and graphics. Corel Trace is a digital tracing utility. Corel Capture is an easy-to-use utility that captures the content of any computer screen the user chooses. CorelDRAW Graphics Suite is a good value for someone who needs to create graphics destined for any medium, including the Internet.

### Adobe Creative Suite (Mac/Windows)

http://www.adobe.com/products/creativesuite/main.html

Adobe Creative Suite is a comprehensive software suite that gives the user a complete and seamless design environment for producing content suitable for print as well as the Internet. This software suite includes all of Adobe's graphics programs. These include Adobe Photoshop, Adobe Illustrator, Adobe InDesign®, Adobe GoLive, and Adobe Acrobat Professional. This software suite is geared toward the intermediate to advanced user and is a good fit for the Internet enabled real estate agent who has some desktop publishing experience.

### Greenstreet® Publishing Studio 4 (Windows)

**http://www.greenstreetsoftware.co.uk/product/details/
071442.htm**

Greenstreet Publishing Studio 4 is a high-value, easy-to-use software suite. It combines page layout, drawing, image editing, and text art software modules to comprise a software suite suitable for the production of all sorts of marketing content. It is relatively inexpensive yet fully featured. All of the modules are tightly integrated with one another so the user can work seamlessly between them. It is a high-quality graphic design software suite for the beginner to intermediate project design coordinator.

## *Desktop Publishing*

### Adobe InDesign (Mac/Windows)

**http://www.adobe.com/products/indesign/main.html**

Adobe InDesign is the preeminent desktop publishing page layout software package. It is extremely powerful yet easy to use. It has seamless integration with the other Adobe applications, allowing for easy information sharing and multimedia support. This is the best package for all-around desktop publishing needs. It can be used to create business flyers, open house notices, newsletters—almost anything you can think of. It handles text as well as graphical images with ease.

### RagTime (Mac/Windows)

**http://www.ragtime-online.com/index.html**

RagTime is billed as a professional business publishing solution. It is useful for blending written text, tables, drawings, graphs, and pictures into a comprehensive layout that can then be published on a variety of media. It supports both Macintosh OS X and Windows. Embedded in the software is a powerful word processor on par with Microsoft Word. Also embedded in the software is a powerful spreadsheet program comparable to Microsoft Excel. The output of both of these submodules can be used to generate professional-looking content within RagTime. This is a nice alternative to Adobe's InDesign.

### Serif PagePlus (Windows)

**http://www.serif.com**

PagePlus is an affordable yet powerful desktop publishing software program. It can be used as a stand-alone product or as part of a comprehensive suite of individual software modules from Serif. It is easy to use and well suited for the creation of all kinds of marketing and sales materials.

### Ready,Set,Go! (Mac/Windows)

**http://www.diwan.com/ready/prsg.htm**

Ready,Set,Go! is a classic software package that has been available for many years. It is feature-rich and allows a user to create all sorts of sales and marketing content. Within the software is a powerful word processing package that can be used to output content into the page layout portion of the program. Ready,Set,Go! is an intuitive program that is easy to master.

### Greenstreet Publisher (Windows)

**http://www.greenstreetsoftware.co.uk/index.htm**

Greenstreet Publisher is one of the simplest desktop publishing programs on the market today. The program integrates photo editing, drawing, and page layout so the user can create high-impact sales and marketing documents within a simple-to-use software environment. This is a highly efficient and affordable desktop publishing software package.

## *Creative Printing Software*

### The Print Shop® (Mac/Windows)

**http://www.broderbund.com/ProductGroup.asp?CID=117**

The Print Shop is a desktop publishing software staple in the software industry. The Print Shop makes it easy to create visually stunning projects that lend themselves to marketing and sales. It is easy to enhance an existing newsletter or flyer with The Print Shop. The software allows you to incorporate high-end design elements such as artwork, photos, fancy stylized fonts, art-altered text, and stylized headlines. The Print Shop can make the casual desktop publisher look great. The latest version includes over 300,000 images that are royalty-free and can be used in enhancing a desktop publishing project. This software is a must-have for anyone creating high-impact marketing and sales literature.

### PrintMaster® (Windows)

**http://www.broderbund.com/ProductGroup.asp?CID=116**

PrintMaster allows the user to incorporate high-end print and online creative design elements into newsletters, stationery, brochures, and other marketing materials. PrintMaster allows for total artistic control and imaginative expression for desktop publishing novices. It is a great solution for those wanting to inject a lot of creativity into otherwise mundane graphics projects.

### Print Artist® (Windows)

**http://www.sierra.com/product.do?gamePlatformId=50**

Sierra's Print Artist is a project-enhancement software package that allows the desktop publishing novice to become more creative with graphic design projects. It is similar to PrintMaster, by Broderbund. Print Artist features over 4,000 layouts, clip art, and other software tools that can be combined to create numerous projects and project enhancements.

## *Drawing/Illustration/Diagramming*

### Adobe Illustrator (Mac/Windows)

**http://www.adobe.com/products/illustrator/main.html**

Adobe Illustrator is a professional-level digital drawing program. It allows a user to create object-oriented drawings for use in print or on the Web. It integrates seamlessly with other Adobe applications, such as Adobe Photoshop. It is suited to users with some desktop publishing and image editing experience who want to create semiprofessional- and/or professional-level design projects. This program is an industry standard in the creation of marketing and sales literature.

### SmartDraw® (Windows)

**http://www.smartdraw.com/index.htm**

SmartDraw is an easy-to-use yet powerful business diagramming and drawing software package. It is an excellent tool for use in a sales and marketing environment. It can be used to create standard business organizational charts and procedure diagrams. Where the application shines is in its ability to import hundreds of ready-made application-specific drawing templates that make preparing subject-specific charts, diagrams, and presentations easy. New drawing templates, which can be downloaded off the Internet, are applicable to many different subject matters. SmartDraw exports its files to Microsoft PowerPoint; therefore, it is easy to use SmartDraw to create Microsoft PowerPoint slides. This is another must-have application for people in sales and marketing.

### Macromedia FreeHand MX (Mac/Windows)

**http://www.macromedia.com/software/freehand**

Macromedia FreeHand is a design staple in the software industry. It is an illustration package in which the user can create simple to elaborate designs. FreeHand is best used to create illustrations for use on and export to the Internet. Macromedia FreeHand is an excellent complement to Macromedia Dreamweaver in the creation of graphics and drawings. FreeHand is an intuitive and powerful application that is easy to learn.

## Web Development

### IBM WebSphere Homepage Builder (Linux)

**http://www-306.ibm.com/software/awdtools/hpbuilder/linux**

For designing web pages in the Linux computing environment, IBM has a web design package called WebSphere. WebSphere makes web site creation a snap with easy-to-use tools. If you use Linux as your operating system and you are designing web pages, you might want to consider WebSphere.

### Apache WebServer Software (Linux/Windows)

**http://www.apache.org**

Apache web server is an industry standard for serving web site content over the Internet. If you are planning to host your own site on your own web server, you should consider Apache web server. This software is designed for the person who is experienced at web design as well as computer networking. This package is so popular that a majority of web sites on the Internet are being served by Apache web server software. If you are an Internet empowered real estate agent with an extensive computer background and would like to host your own web site, consider this software package.

### Macromedia Dreamweaver MX 2004 (Mac/Windows)

**http://www.macromedia.com/software/dreamweaver**

Macromedia Dreamweaver is a full-featured web design software package. Although it is suitable for basic web site design, it shines when used in creating database-driven Internet applications such as shopping cart software and e-commerce web sites. The design components within Dreamweaver are top-notch. If you are a person with prior web development experience and would like high-end design tools to create a web site, this is the package for you. A more middle-of-the-road package suitable for most people is Adobe GoLive.

### Adobe GoLive (Mac/Windows)

**http://www.adobe.com/products/golive/main.html**

Adobe GoLive is an industry-standard web site content creation package. It is used by sales professionals, marketing communications professionals, and web content developers in all types of businesses. If you need to output content to the Internet via a web site, Adobe GoLive should be on your short list of products to consider. It has all of the tools you need to create visually dynamic yet informative web content.

### HomePage (Mac)

**http://www.mac.com/1/iTour/tour_homepage.html**

This is a great web site development package for anyone who uses a Macintosh computer. HomePage takes care of all of the background details in terms of writing HTML code while you concentrate on selecting and placing design elements on the page. HomePage also comes with a theme selector and a large array of web site templates from which the user can select. Once the content is in place, all the user does is press the publish button; the result is a finished web site.

## Image/Photo Editing

### Adobe Photoshop (Mac/Windows)

**http://www.adobe.com/products/photoshop/main.html**

Adobe Photoshop is the industry standard in image editing and desktop digital imaging. It is suitable for all ability levels, but some computer novices may find it overwhelming. This package is the best digital imaging editor in the software industry. It can do almost anything in terms of processing digital photos for print or the Internet. The software is not inexpensive, but it is worth the price. In the past, full versions of Adobe Photoshop were bundled with high-end color computer scanners. Here is a money-saving tip: You might shop for a high-end premium computer scanner and look for a complementary version of Adobe Photoshop bundled with it.

### Adobe Photoshop Elements (Mac/Windows)

**http://www.adobe.com/products/photoshopel**

Adobe Photoshop Elements is an excellent image-editing software package. It combines the power and flexibility of Adobe Photoshop with a simpler user interface. The average person who needs to edit and enhance digital photos can use the program to produce spectacular results with minimal effort. The program produces outstanding digital images and incorporates a wide variety of options from which to choose. Unless you are an industry professional or high-end Photoshop user, Adobe Photoshop Elements is a good choice for your image-editing needs.

## Jasc Paint Shop™ Pro® (Windows)

### http://www.jasc.com/products/paintshoppro/?

Another excellent image-editing program is Paint Shop Pro. Paint Shop Pro gives the user Adobe Photoshop power with a lower price. Paint Shop Pro is an easy-to-use, powerful piece of software that produces professional results. The online integrated learning tutorials help the user get up to speed quickly. If you would like to go beyond Adobe Photoshop Elements but don't want to spend the money for the full Adobe Photoshop package, this is an excellent solution.

## Gimp (Linux)

### http://www.gimp.org

Gimp is an image-editing software package that has several of the same features and options as Adobe Photoshop but with a lower price. It is designed for the Linux computing platform. If you use Linux and need to do complex digital image editing, you might consider this program.

## iPhoto (Mac)

### http://www.apple.com/ilife/iphoto

iPhoto is an intuitive, easy-to-use digital image organization center. It allows you to classify, arrange, and organize all of your digital images according to the criteria you specify. iPhoto makes it easy to share digital image via print, e-mail, or the Web,. This is a must-have application for anyone using a Macintosh computer.

## Adobe Photoshop Album (Windows)

### http://www.adobe.com/products/photoshopalbum/main.html

Adobe Photoshop Album is a digital image organizational tool. This software helps anyone who works with digital images to organize, classify, and find them. Adobe Photoshop Album seamlessly integrates with Adobe Photoshop Elements and the full package of Adobe Photoshop.

### ACDSee™ (Windows)

**http://www.acdsystems.com/English/Products/ACDSee/index.htm**

ACDSee is a full-featured digital image organizing software package. It is used by millions of people around the world as the standard in digital image organization. It has many features, including batch photo file renaming and batch automated exposure adjusting of photos. This program is widely used in graphic arts and web development companies. It is affordable and powerful and is suitable for novices and experts alike.

## *Digital Video/DVD Editing*

### iMovie (Mac)

**http://www.apple.com/ilife/imovie**

iMovie is an easy-to-use nonlinear editing program for producing digital video. It is the best digital video editing package available for computers running Mac OS X. It is easy to integrate still photos as well as audio soundtracks in conjunction with raw video footage to create a final digital video file.

### iDVD (Mac)

**http://www.apple.com/ilife/idvd**

iDVD is a DVD authoring program. It allows the user to assemble a professional- looking DVD, complete with chapter points and menu selections. iDVD contains tremendous functionality, including the ability to render video, automatically create submenus from chapter markers, and quickly burn video files onto blank DVD media. This is a great tool for people in sales and marketing, such as real estate sales agents. It allows sales agents to showcase properties by transferring video footage and photographic still shots to DVDs and then distributing them to clients.

### Soundtrack (Mac)

**http://www.apple.com/soundtrack**

Soundtrack is an easy-to-use music production software package that allows the user to create custom music scores for DVDs. The user can incorporate music by using public domain loop sample sounds or by recording instrumentation on to soundtracks, which the user then mixes to make up the final musical score. This is an easy and fun way to add musical tracks to DVDs slated for distribution to clients or business associates.

### Final Cut Express (Mac)

**http://www.apple.com/finalcutexpress**

Final Cut Express is an advanced nonlinear editing package designed for editing digital video files. The product requires the use of intricate and complex editing techniques to produce professional-grade digital video files ready for recording onto DVD. For most sales and marketing professionals, iMovie is probably sufficient.

### Adobe Premiere Pro 1.5 (Mac/Windows)

**http://www.adobe.com/products/premiere/main.html**

Adobe Premiere Pro is the flagship digital video editing product from Adobe. It is extremely powerful yet easy to master. It gives the user exacting control over every aspect of video production. It is suitable for those who are new to digital video production as well as advanced videographers. It integrates seamlessly with other Adobe digital video applications. It is suitable for producing professional-grade sales and marketing video files on DVD.

### Pinnacle Studio (Windows)

**http://www.pinnaclesys.com/ProductPage_n.asp?Product_ID=1501&Langue_ID=7**

Pinnacle Studio is an excellent digital video-editing program. It is not expensive, and it is easy to master. It is an excellent choice for the real estate professional who wants to include DVD video content as part of his or her marketing mix. The software is functional and flexible, producing professional DVD results. Pinnacle Studio allows the user to add titles, music, special effects, and narration. The user can output video not only to DVD, but also to videotape and the Internet.

### Pinnacle Instant CD/DVD (Windows)

http://www.pinnaclesys.com/ProductPage_n.asp?Product_
ID=1431&Langue_ID=7&division_id=

Pinnacle Instant CD/DVD allows duplication of CD and DVD media. Once a CD or DVD master has been burned and is ready for distribution, using this software, the user can make multiple copies to distribute to clients or other recipients. Pinnacle Instant CD/DVD makes copies of DVD movie files and allows for transfer of content from DVD originals to video CDs. It also allows for the building of digital slide shows that can be encoded onto a DVD and played on any DVD player. This last feature can be used to showcase properties to potential clients.

## Digital Media Suites

### Apple iLife (Mac)

http://www.apple.com/ilife

Apple Computer's iLife is a digital media suite made up of five digital media applications: iTunes, iPhoto, iDVD, iMovie, and GarageBand. The interface between these five applications is seamless. All of them have been designed so the user can utilize all five applications simultaneously to create a single project. This is an excellent one-stop-shopping approach for anyone with an Apple Macintosh computer who wants to create digital media content for distribution via DVD or the Web.

### Adobe Video Collection (Mac/Windows)

http://www.adobe.com/products/dvcoll/main.html

Adobe Video Collection is another digital media suite that encompasses five digital media applications. These include Adobe Premiere® Pro, Adobe After Effects®, Adobe Audition™, Adobe Encore™ DVD, and Adobe Photoshop. All of the programs are designed to work seamlessly with one another. This program is aimed more toward the intermediate and advanced user, as compared to the Apple digital media suite, which is aimed at more of a mainstream user. Any Internet empowered real estate agent who is using a Windows-based computing platform and who has a good working knowledge of graphic design and/or video production should consider the Adobe Video Collection for producing digital media content for DVD or the Web.

# E-mail Software

## *Nisus Email (Mac)*

### http://www.nisus.com/NisusEmail

Nisus Email has been finely tuned for the Macintosh computing platform that runs OS X. Nisus Email has a three-click send procedure that makes sending e-mail messages a snap. It integrates itself with other applications on the computer, such as the word processor. For instance, instead of composing e-mail messages within the e-mail program, you can do it within the word processor. One of the unique features of this product is that any Macintosh application that supports drag-and-drop or file saving can be used as an e-mail program although you never have to leave the resident application in which you are working. This is an excellent alternative to Apple's Mail application.

## Mail (Mac)

### http://www.mac.com/1/iTour/index.html

Mail for Macintosh is an advanced e-mail program specifically for the Mac OS X platform. It features an address book that is synchronized with Mac OS X. It also offers online storage capabilities for messages and files. You can retrieve e-mail messages over the Internet on any Windows or Macintosh computer using the program's online features.

## Eudora Email (Mac/Windows)

### http://www.eudora.com

Eudora is a classic e-mail client with polish and professionalism. The programmers anticipated virtually every e-mail software problem imaginable and created a solution. Eudora is easy to use and feature-rich. It has a special filtering system targeted at filtering out spam. It is highly regarded and widely used in corporations and educational institutions internationally. It is a realistic alternative to Microsoft Outlook and several other Macintosh based e-mail programs.

## Pegasus Mail (Windows)

**http://www.pmail.com/index.htm**

Pegasus Mail is a mature, powerful, and feature-filled e-mail program for Microsoft Windows. It delivers enormous power in a relatively simple interface. Pegasus Mail has an extremely robust yet flexible filtering system for incoming e-mail, as well as an e-mail template layout system used in composing e-mail messages. It handles encrypted and secured e-mail messages with its built-in encryption and decoding algorithm. It is an excellent program if you need to use a mailing list to send out an e-mail blast to several recipients at once. Pegasus Mail is an excellent choice for anyone in sales and marketing who wants to take advantage of e-mail as a marketing tool. This software package does not advocate or help in the delivery of spam e-mail, but does help in the delivery of targeted opt-in marketing e-mail messages sent to a list of willing recipients. An Internet empowered real estate agent can benefit greatly by using Pegasus Mail as his or her e-mail client.

## Popcorn 1.69 (Windows)

**http://www.ultrafunk.com**

Popcorn is an easy-to-use e-mail program. It is a small program, which means it can fit on floppy disk. Popcorn does one thing and does it very well. Popcorn is best utilized for accessing POP (Post Office Protocol)-based e-mail accounts. Most Internet service providers (ISPs) provide e-mail accounts designed to use a program that accesses POP-based e-mail. (Accessing an e-mail account via a web browser window is considered web-based e-mail and doesn't require the use of a program such as Popcorn.) Because of its small file size, Popcorn is a portable program, one of its biggest advantages. Its ability to fit on a floppy disk means you can bring the disk with you and check your POP-based e-mail anywhere you have access to a computer. Popcorn also allows you to import and export messages to and from other e-mail programs. If you travel a lot, use different computers, and need to access POP-based e-mail, this product is a must-have.

### Mozilla/Thunderbird (Mac/Linux/Windows)

**http://www.mozilla.org/products/thunderbird**

Thunderbird is a next-generation e-mail client. It features advanced implementation of software to filter out spam, spell-checking software, and one of the best user interfaces in an e-mail client in the software industry today. Thunderbird is cross platform and works on Macintosh-, Linux-, and Windows-based computers.

### Yahoo! Messenger (Mac/Linux/Windows)

**http://messenger.yahoo.com**

Yahoo! Messenger is one of the most popular instant messaging programs on the Internet. Yahoo provides this software in three versions: one for Macintosh, one for Linux, and one for Windows computing platforms.

### Pine (Linux/Windows)

**http://www.washington.edu/pine**

Pine was one of the first e-mail client programs to appear on the Internet. Besides being an e-mail client, it also provides functionality as a USENET newsgroup reader. It is free and works on both Windows and Linux computing platforms. It is simple and straightforward, not offering too many features, but still provides the basics of sending and receiving e-mail. This is a classic and mature program that provides reliability and stability with regard to e-mail management.

## *Web Browsing Software*

### Netscape (Mac/Linux/Windows)

**http://channels.netscape.com/ns/browsers/default.jsp**

Netscape Navigator is the original web browsing program for the Internet, and it spawned a host of imitators. Even Microsoft copied Netscape Navigator, calling its copy Internet Explorer. Netscape Navigator is still one of the premier web browsing programs available. It runs on Windows, Macintosh, and Linux computing platforms. It has built-in pop-up advertising-killing software. It also intelligently loads web pages into a tabbed interface that allows a user to casually browse numerous web pages.

## Opera (Mac/Linux/Windows)

### http://www.opera.com

Opera is a highly advanced and highly customizable web browser. Opera is available on a variety of computer platforms, including Microsoft Windows, Apple Macintosh, and Linux. Opera pioneered the use of a tabbed window interface for multiple open browser windows. It also uses a unique and proprietary software algorithm that enables web pages to load extremely fast. In fact, Opera has the fastest web page loading time of any Internet browser on the market today. For high-speed surfing, Opera is a must-have.

## OmniWeb Browser (Mac)

### http://www.omnigroup.com/applications/omniweb

OmniWeb is a newer web browsing program designed specifically for Macintosh computers running OS X. The program utilizes the same core software routines as Apple to ensure stability and compatibility. It has a number of specialized features that make it a particularly good web surfing application for the Macintosh. It features ad blocking, keyword history searching, built-in Google searching, web site change notifications, spell checking, and the ability to create new web windows behind the one the user is currently viewing so browsing is not interrupted. This is a first-rate product that showcases a lot of the amenities Mac OS X has to offer.

## Safari (Mac)

### http://www.apple.com/safari

Safari is the latest web browser designed and marketed by Apple Computer for Apple Macintosh computers running Mac OS X. Safari loads web pages faster than most comparable web programs. Being an Apple product, Safari takes advantage of every strength the Mac OS X platform has to offer. Safari integrates well with the Macintosh OS X operating system and interface. It is feature-rich, requiring a short learning curve. If you own a Mac and it is running Mac OS X, you might consider Safari.

## Mozilla (Mac/Linux/Windows)

### http://www.mozilla.org/products/mozilla1.x

Mozilla is a technologically sophisticated web browser utilizing high-tech code. Mozilla is an open-source program, it is free to use, and it runs on multiple computing platforms. It has a useful pop-up ad blocker, an intelligent cookie and password management system, and an onboard Internet relay chat client as well as a USENET newsgroup reader. It also features a tabbed interface for multiple open web windows. This last feature allows the user to surf multiple sites with ease, eliminating screen congestion.

# PDA Computing

The personal digital assistant (PDA) is a necessity for the Internet empowered real estate agent. He or she should consider productivity enhancements that automate the sales process and improve the relationship between agent and client. PDAs are a necessary component in reaching this goal. PDAs allow the Internet empowered real estate agent to gather, process, and retrieve pertinent information that relates to the buying and selling of properties. PDAs allow the Internet empowered real estate agent access to MLS property data; e-mail; word processing and office applications; databases of information on properties, clients, and communities; the Internet; and in-car navigation and GPS. PDAs also provide integration with electronic property lockboxes from national companies such as Supra (now part of General Electric). A PDA is necessary for an Internet empowered real estate agent doing business in "Internet time."

PDAs allow the ultimate in data portability. Laptops are great, but they can't fit in a pocket, they weigh several pounds, and they require a few minutes to boot up. PDAs allow the agent to carry his or her computer in a pocket or purse, providing convenient access to client information at the push of a button. And although PDAs are portable, the Internet empowered real estate agent still doesn't sacrifice information synchronization and data connectivity.

All PDAs have the ability to synchronize information with the host PC so that information entered and processed in the sales field is updated on the host PC back at the office. Likewise, any information that has been entered and processed on the main PC and needs to be taken into the field is updated on the PDA. The synchronization process is simple, usually requiring the push of a button while the PDA is connected to a USB computer port of the host computer. One of the nice things about PDA-to-PC synchronization is that the host PC contains backups of files that are stored on the PDA. This is an excellent security precaution in the event the PDA is lost or stolen. There are also several dedicated software packages for backing up PDA data to a memory card. Most professionals working with critical data rely on both methods to keep their data secure.

Palm OS-based PDAs as well as Pocket PC-based PDAs are suitable for use in the sales field by the Internet empowered real estate agent.

When deciding which platform to use, the agent's main criteria should be determining compatibility with the hardware and software of the PDA.

Thousands of software applications are available for both Palm and Pocket PC PDAs. Palm and Microsoft have software databases and directories on their web sites (PalmOne: http://software.palmone.com/PlatformSoftware.jsp?siteId=291&platformId=1; Microsoft Pocket PC: http://www.microsoft.com/windowsmobile/pocketpc/ppc/default.mspx). These are great places to start looking for PDA software to help make your business more productive.

Loyal Palm PDA users may want to check out PalmGear at http://www.palmgear.com when looking for Palm PDA software. PalmGear has one of the largest and oldest databases of Palm PDA software. The software descriptions combined with user reviews and comments make this site an indispensable resource in comparing different software titles.

Pocket PC fans will want to make PocketGear at http://www.pocketgear.com one of their first stops in shopping for Pocket PC-based software. PocketGear has a large collection of software, complete with full descriptions, user reviews, and the latest happenings within the Pocket PC world.

Other web sites that deserve mention are Handango™ at http://www.handango.com, PDAStreet at http://www.pdastreet.com, and Mobile Planet® at http://www.mobileplanet.com. These sites are devoted to software based on Palm and Pocket PC operating systems. By visiting these sites, you can gain a broad understanding of the different types of applications available on both PDA platforms.

A lot of PDA software titles are developed by small independent companies who, in a lot of cases, have limited funding for research and development. Therefore, you should look at the popularity of a specific software application as well as user comments and reviews, which will tell you about people's experiences with specific applications. By researching applications you are considering, you can make a more informed choice and will probably end up more satisfied with the software you do purchase.

The next two sections provide a more detailed overview of the Palm-based PDA and the Pocket PC-based PDA.

## *Palm*

One of the most useful digital tools that the Internet empowered real estate agent can own is a personal digital assistant. The Palm PDA is one of the most successful handheld computing devices in the history of computing. The original Palm Pilot PDA ignited the current trend of professional people moving their day-to-day organizational activities from paper format to the electronic realm.

Palm Inc. began in 1992 with initial designs of the first mass-market PDA. In 1995, U.S. Robotics acquired Palm just as the first Palm Pilot PDA was reaching critical mass acceptance and use in the marketplace. A few years later in 1997, 3Com, a networking company, acquired U.S. Robotics and the Palm computing subsidiary. Today Palm Computing is once again its own company under the name of Palm Source, Inc. PalmOne Inc. is the hardware division that actually makes the Palm PDAs. The name *Pilot* was used for a long time as a brand name of Palm's PDAs. A few years ago the name was dropped as a result of naming infringement rights brought upon Palm Computing by another company.

Palm enjoys a healthy share of the PDA market worldwide. It manufactures the Palm OS software that runs the handheld computers. It manufactures Palm handheld computers. Palm also licenses the Palm OS software to different manufacturers, such as Sony, who build their own Palm-compatible handheld computers. Palm and its licensees manufacture a variety of Palm OS-compatible handheld computers. Each Palm handheld device runs the same Palm OS-compatible applications so that any Palm handheld is compatible with any other Palm handheld.

PDAs are becoming a necessity for the Internet enabled real estate agent, helping with such duties as contact management, time management, and task management. PDAs allow the Internet enabled real estate agent to focus on daily business without worrying about the day-to-day repetitive tasks a professional salesperson needs to do to be successful.

As of this writing, there were more than 20,000 add-on applications available for PDAs running the Palm OS operating system. These applications include the freeware, shareware, and commercial applications.

Every Palm OS-based PDA comes with standard computing applications that create the foundation of day-to-day task management for the Internet enabled real estate agent. Following are the built-in software applications included in each Palm OS-based PDA.

- The Address Book. This application is basically an electronic Rolodex. The user enters client contact information, such as first and last names, address, phone numbers, fax numbers, e-mail address, and notes. The user can sort this data in a variety of ways and place the information into user-definable categories.

- The Calculator. This application is what it says it is—a calculator. It has standard calculator functions, including percent and memory.

- Datebook. This application is an electronic scheduling application. You might think of it as an electronic version of a DayTimer or Week-at-a-Glance or Month-at-a-Glance. The user can set appointment times for daily, weekly, and monthly schedules. The user can set alarms for specific events occurring in the future. Essentially, the user can use the Datebook as a real-time, ever-changing, live appointment book that references the companion Address Book application with its client information. Everything is updated in real time as appointments and events and client information change.

- To-Do List. With this application, the user can prioritize and remind himself or herself of important things to do. The user can group to-do items into specific categories and attach notes to them.

- Notepad. Using the Notepad, the user can create simple drawings and text. Notepad is best thought of as an electronic scratch pad.

- MemoPad. This application allows a user to input short memos of up to approximately 4,000 characters. The user can sort memos into user-defined categories and arrange them alphabetically and manually. This application is suited more for text, not drawings.

- Expense. This application allows the user to input and keep track of business expenses. The full functionality of this application is utilized when the PDA is synchronized with the host computer and the expense data is downloaded into a spreadsheet application such as Microsoft Excel. The Palm PDA does not do expense calculations within itself. An outside spreadsheet such as Excel must be used.

The Palm PDA has been a huge success. Estimates are that more than 1 million Palm PDAs have been sold since Palm started manufacturing them. As was stated earlier, thousands of software applications can be found in stores and on the Internet. The handwriting recognition input method of the Palm PDA has been a huge success as well, making the PDA intuitive and easy to use.

# Pocket PC

Another useful digital appliance tool is the Pocket PC personal digital assistant (PDA), which is based on Microsoft's Windows CE/Pocket PC OS. The Pocket PC emulates the capabilities of the Palm PDA, yet in a Microsoft Windows format.

In 1996, Microsoft decided to pursue the development of an operating system for forthcoming digital appliances such as PDAs, enhanced wireless smart phones, and computing applications in the automotive industry. The wizards at Microsoft decided to create this new operating system as a scaled-down modular version of their corporate flagship operating system called Windows NT. The result was an operating system called Windows CE. (*CE* stands for compact edition.) Pocket PCs run a derivative of Microsoft's Windows CE operating system. This derivative has certain specifications in terms of operating system extensions, graphical user interface modifications, and software applications specific to a PDA device. As of this writing, the latest version of Pocket PC was Pocket PC 2003.

Because the Pocket PC runs a Microsoft operating system, thousands of applications have been written and continue to be written for the Pocket PC platform. Pocket PCs come in a wide assortment, and many hardware add-ons are available that allow the PC to perform functions such as that of a GPS receiver. Pocket PCs are manufactured by a variety of computer hardware vendors. Microsoft has stated for it licensees that in order to sell PDAs that include the Pocket PC operating system, the Pocket PC must include several standard features. These include a version of the Pocket PC operating system, a preselected set of software applications that reside in the Pocket PC read-only memory (ROM), a display that is capable of touch-based input, a hardware directional pad and application buttons, and a resident CPU that is based on an Intel "StrongARM" chip design (also known as XScale). (XScale is Intel's brand name for the StrongARM chip.)

Pocket PC PDAs have gained tremendous market share in the corporate environment due to its interoperability with Microsoft Windows operating systems and Microsoft office applications. The Palm OS is currently the market leader by a small margin due to its more user-friendly and crash-resistant operating system. In the corporate environment, however, the Pocket PC is the leader due to the heritage it shares with Microsoft operating systems and applications such as Microsoft Outlook, Internet Explorer, Word, Excel, and Windows Media® Player.

Pocket PC is attracting attention in a very unlikely place; namely, the Macintosh computer user population. There is a small company in La Jolla, California, called PocketMac. (Its web address is http://www.pocketmac.net.) The company is marketing several software packages, one of which allows a Macintosh computer to be synchronized to a Microsoft-based Pocket PC PDA. This software is called PocketMacPro. PocketMac Pro helps to synchronize Contacts, Calendar, Tasks, E-mail, Word and Excel Docs, iTunes, and iPhoto files between the Pocket PC and Mac Entourage, Calendar, Address Book, Tasks and Mail, and Microsoft Word and Excel on Macintosh OS X. PocketMac Backup is another of PocketMac's products. It is used to back up Pocket PC PDA files to a Macintosh computer. This type of cross-platform ingenuity is happening a lot in the PDA market. An Internet enabled real estate professional should watch for emerging cross-platform software technologies that allow him or her to work more synergistically between different computing environments.

The Pocket PC has been a huge catalyst in acquiring Microsoft market share and in gaining awareness in the minds of professionals and in the PDA marketplace. The Pocket PC has been a big success for Microsoft, especially in the corporate computing environment. The ability of the Pocket PC to integrate easily with other Microsoft applications and operating systems has been its number one advantage over other PDA devices. Pocket PC and its growing number of software titles have eroded the commanding lead that Palm PDAs once enjoyed.

# ANSWERS TO SELF-ASSESSMENT QUESTIONS

# CHAPTER 1 SELF-ASSESSMENT

To determine the extent of knowledge you acquired in this chapter, choose the correct answer for each of the following.

1. E-commerce:
   a. Is a multibillion-dollar operation
   b. Has dramatically changed the world of business
   c. Has an excellent future for growth
   d. All of the above*

2. When did the e-world emerge?
   a. In the early 1990s
   b. In late 1995*
   c. In the early 2000s
   d. It has not emerged yet.

3. Who introduced the term *Internet Empowered Consumer?*
   a. Mike Russer*
   b. Stephan Swanepoel
   c. Bradley Inman
   d. Saul Klein

4. Which of the following is a professional designation sponsored by the National Association of REALTORS®?
   a. New Real Estate Professional*
   b. e-PRO
   c. Real Estate Cyber Specialist
   d. Cyber professional

5. All of the following are characteristic of the Internet Empowered Consumer except:
   a. Spends less time with an agent in locating a property to purchase
   b. Likes having control and anonymity
   c. Prefers the use of electronic means for communicating
   d. Earns less money than the traditional buyer*

6. Which one of the following is *not* a characteristic of the traditional buyer?
   a. Has less education than Internet buyer
   b. Earns more money than Internet buyer*
   c. Spends more time in the buying process
   d. Pays less money on a purchase

7. What is a typical software program used in the property management profession?
   a. The Marketing Library
   b. Rolodex®
   c. EDI
   d. YARDI*

8. The typical e-buyer utilizes which method when searching for a
   home?
   a. Search engine
   b. Virtual tour
   c. E-mail
   d. All of the above*

9. Characteristics of the New Real Estate Professional include all of
   the following except:
   a. Utilizes e-mail and has a web site
   b. Has an individual domain name
   c. Uses mobile devices such as a laptop and cell phone
   d. Uses only a cell phone and fax*

10. The typical e-agent uses all of the following equipment except:
    a. Digital camera
    b. Desktop or laptop computer
    c. Real estate software
    d. Could use all of the above*

11. The wired C-P is capable of conducting business:
    a. Between 8 a.m. and 5 p.m.*
    b. 24/7/365
    c. Anytime, anywhere
    d. Both b and c

12. Examples of digital innovators are:
    a. Russer and Inman*
    b. Canale and Murphy
    c. Peckham and Klein
    d. None of the above

13. To become an e-PRO, one must:
    a. Complete a specific course of study
    b. Be a member of NAR
    c. Pay a fee
    d. All of the above*

14. Characteristics of the cyber professional include which of the following?
    a. Utilizes traditional real estate techniques
    b. Utilizes contemporary computer tools
    c. Continuously learns new approaches in the practice of real estate
    d. All of the above*

15. The emerging e-agent is best described as an agent who:
    a. Is open to learning technology
    b. Has not had the time to learn about technology
    c. Did not get the opportunity to learn about technology
    d. All of the above*

# CHAPTER 2 SELF-ASSESSMENT

To determine the extent of knowledge you acquired in this chapter, choose the correct answer for each of the following.

1. A common brand name for a CPU is:
   a. Celeron
   b. Athlon
   c. Pentium*
   d. All of the above

2. The clock speed for a computer would most likely be related to:
   a. Gigahertz*
   b. Megabytes
   c. Nanosecond
   d. Mbps

3. Which storage device holds the most information?
   a. Floppy disk
   b. CD-ROM
   c. Zip drive
   d. DVD*

4. All of the following are different types of printers except:
   a. Dot matrix
   b. Modem*
   c. Ink jet
   d. Laser jet

5. Cache refers to:
   a. Keyboard
   b. Mouse
   c. Memory*
   d. Software

6. A mouse can be any of the following types except:
   a. Trackball
   b. Rollerball
   c. Eraser head
   d. Zip*

7. RAM would most likely be measured in:
   a. Hertz
   b. Ppm
   c. Bytes*
   d. Kps

8. Pixels are related to:
   a. Sharper images*
   b. ROM
   c. RAM
   d. Keyboards

9. Input is to keyboard as output is to:
   a. Mouse
   b. Printer
   c. Monitor
   d. Both b and c*

10. Companies that manufacture processors include:
    a. Intel and AMD*
    b. Dell and Gateway
    c. Apple and Microsoft
    d. Toshiba and Sony

11. In the development of the computer, which event occurred first?
    a. Supercomputer
    b. Microcomputer
    c. Telephone
    d. Abacus*

12. Which term is used in connection with a monitor?
    a. Output device
    b. CRT/LCD
    c. TFT
    d. All of the above*

13. Use of which of the following may result in repetitive stress injury?
    a. Keyboard/Mouse*
    b. Printer/Monitor
    c. CD-ROM/DVD-ROM
    d. RAM/ROM

14. What is the most important component of a computer?
    a. Monitor
    b. Keyboard
    c. Processor*
    d. Mouse

15. Examples of real estate computer software include:
    a. TOP PRODUCER
    b. Agent Office
    c. The Marketing Library
    d. All of the above*

# CHAPTER 3 SELF-ASSESSMENT

To determine the extent of knowledge you acquired in this chapter, choose the correct answer for each of the following.

1. An example of a computer manufacturer includes:
   a. Dell
   b. IBM
   c. Hewlett-Packard
   d. All of the above*

2. What is the major advantage of a laptop over a desktop?
   a. Portability*
   b. Large size
   c. Large keyboard
   d. More hard drive capacity

3. The decision to buy a Mac over a PC may be related to:
   a. Durability
   b. Users' needs*
   c. Emotional needs
   d. Cost

4. Which of the following is an operating system?
   a. WordPerfect
   b. Windows
   c. DVD
   d. All of the above*

5. A refurbished computer would most likely:
   a. Cost more
   b. Cost less*
   c. Not have an extended warranty
   d. Be easy to find and purchase

6. What is the criterion for choosing a computer manufacturer?
   a. Performance
   b. Repetition
   c. Reliability
   d. All of the above*

7. A customized computer would:
   a. Be made to order*
   b. Cost less
   c. Have unnecessary hardware
   d. Have unnecessary software

8. What is a major consideration when buying a computer package?
   a. Technical support
   b. Warranty
   c. Service
   d. All of the above*

9. The term *bundled* refers to:
   a. A single computer by itself
   b. A total computer package*
   c. A computer missing major parts
   d. A computer without any software

10. What is the device that is used to connect to the Internet?
    a. Modem
    b. DSL
    c. Cable
    d. All of the above*

11. A typical word processor is:
    a. Windows
    b. OS X
    c. QWERTY
    d. Microsoft Word*

12. What is a common type of software for the cyber professional?
    a. TOP PRODUCER
    b. Agent Office
    c. The Marketing Library
    d. All of the above*

13. Which of the following is a commonly used Internet browser?
    a. Netscape*
    b. MSN
    c. AOL
    d. Earthlink

14. What is an advantage of building your own computer?
    a. No need for technical skill
    b. Ease of assembly
    c. Speed of assembly
    d. None of these*

15. A major decision when selecting a computer includes:
    a. PC or Mac
    b. Desktop or laptop
    c. Manufacturer
    d. All of the above*

# CHAPTER 4 SELF-ASSESSMENT

To determine the extent of knowledge you acquired in this chapter, choose the correct answer for each of the following.

1. The turning point for efficient computer operation was the development of:
   a. GUI*
   b. DOS commands
   c. Browser
   d. Internet

2. Key devices used to work with an operating system are:
   a. Modem/Cable
   b. Mouse/Keyboard*
   c. Monitor/Printer
   d. Internet Explorer/Netscape

3. A pointer:
   a. Looks like an I-beam
   b. Is controlled by the mouse
   c. Can be controlled to move around the screen
   d. All of the above*

4. The keyboard command to print is:
   a. CTRL + V
   b. CTRL + B
   c. CTRL + P*
   d. CTRL + I

5. The Windows desktop taskbar is found where?
   a. Right side of the screen
   b. Left side of the screen
   c. Top of the screen*
   d. Bottom of the screen

6. All of the following can be found on the Start button except:
   a. GUI*
   b. My Documents
   c. My Computer
   d. Programs

7. Settings that can be changed for the mouse include:
   a. Speed
   b. Pointer
   c. Single/double click
   d. All of the above*

8. The taskbar contains:
   a. Start button
   b. Notification area
   c. Open programs
   d. All of the above*

9. Which of the following is referred to as "gooey"?
   a. Disk operating system
   b. Graphical user interface*
   c. Control keys
   d. Voice recognition software

10. Which Windows version came first?
    a. Windows XP
    b. Windows 95
    c. Windows Me
    d. Windows 3.1*

11. Which of the following is an operating system?
    a. Linux
    b. Windows
    c. Mac OS
    d. All of the above*

12. What is a special key features of Windows XP?
    a. More user-friendly
    b. Enhanced digital features
    c. Ability to establish a home network
    d. All of the above*

13. To place an icon on the Windows desktop, you use which command?
    a. Create Shortcut*
    b. Taskbar
    c. Control Panel
    d. Start button

14. What does the term interface mean?
    a. To log on
    b. To delete
    c. To communicate*
    d. To save to My Documents

15. One way to avoid repetitive stress injury is to use:
    a. The mouse only
    b. The keyboard only
    c. Voice recognition software*
    d. Handwriting recognition software

# CHAPTER 5 SELF-ASSESSMENT

To determine the extent of knowledge you acquired in this chapter, choose the correct answer for each of the following.

1. A word processor available in the marketplace is:
   a. Apple
   b. Linux
   c. Microsoft Word
   d. All of the above*

2. A word processing program can be found in:
   a. Internet Explorer
   b. Netscape
   c. Microsoft Windows*
   d. My Documents

3. A word processor can be used for which of the following activities?
   a. Prospecting
   b. Marketing
   c. Communicating
   d. All of the above*

4. A Word document can be saved in:
   a. Control Panel
   b. Accessories
   c. My Documents*
   d. Title bar

5. To execute a command in Microsoft Word, the cyber professional:
   a. Uses the mouse
   b. Uses the keyboard
   c. Uses voice recognition
   d. All of the above*

6. All of the following are fonts except:
   a. Times New Roman
   b. New American*
   c. Tahoma
   d. Verdana

7. What feature should the cyber professional use when he or she has a question about how to work with Microsoft Word?
   a. Search
   b. Find
   c. Help*
   d. None of these

8. To make sure a business letter or memo looks professional, the cyber professionalcan:
   a. Call tech support
   b. Run a virus check
   c. Run a spell check*
   d. Add the date and time to the document

9. What should the cyber professional do if My Documents becomes too cluttered with necessary documents?
   a. Delete the documents
   b. Send the documents to the Recycle Bin
   c. Create a folder in My Documents*
   d. Do nothing

10. Some of the commands that can be used in Microsoft Word include:
    a. Cut, Copy, Paste
    b. Bold, Italic, Underline
    c. Align right, left, center
    d. All of the above*

11. All of the following can be found on the menu bar except:
    a. File
    b. Help
    c. Control Panel*
    d. Tools

12. The first step in changing how text looks is to:
    a. Print it
    b. Select/Highlight it*
    c. Delete it
    d. Copy it

13. The Minimize button:
    a. Appears on the File menu
    b. Appears on Control Panel
    c. Appears with the Maximize, Restore, and Close buttons*
    d. Opens a document

14. What does a software suite imply?
    a. Several programs bundled in one package*
    b. Only one feature in the package
    c. Available only to businesses
    d. Available only to cyber professionals

15. The menu bar contains all of the following except:
    a. View
    b. Format
    c. Windows*
    d. WordArt

# CHAPTER 6 SELF-ASSESSMENT

To determine the extent of knowledge you acquired in this chapter, choose the correct answer for each of the following.

1. What was the impetus behind the development of the Internet?
   a. The stock market
   b. Consumer needs
   c. E-commerce
   d. National defense*

2. When did the World Wide Web become a reality?
   a. 1989*
   b. Early 1990s
   c. 2000
   d. 1972

3. Who was the person responsible for the invention of the World Wide Web?
   a. Ray Tomlinson
   b. Tim Berners-Lee*
   c. President Eisenhower
   d. J. C. R. Licklider

4. Which of the following is an example of an ISP?
   a. MSN
   b. EarthLink
   c. America Online
   d. All of the above*

5. An example of a search engines is:
   a. AltaVista
   b. Ask Jeeves
   c. Google
   d. All of the above*

6. Which words are included in a Boolean search?
   a. AND, OR, NOT*
   b. And, or, not
   c. ALL, BOTH, NONE
   d. None of these

7. The concept of spiders and crawlers refers to:
   a. Microsoft Windows
   b. Microsoft Word
   c. The Internet
   d. Search engines*

8. Methods of connecting to the Internet include:
   a. Cable modem
   b. DSL
   c. Dial-up
   d. All of the above*

9. Which of the following suggests a faster speed for an Internet connection?
   a. 10 bps
   b. 10 Kbps
   c. 10 Mbps
   d. 10 Gbps*

10. To set up an Internet connection on a computer, the user goes to:
    a. Toolbar
    b. Status bar
    c. Control Panel*
    d. Menu bar

11. In terms of an Internet service provider, what does DSL stand for?
    a. Designated Subscriber Lines*
    b. Digital Subscriber Lines
    c. Double Speed Lines
    d. None of these

12. Where is a URL entered?
    a. Address Bar*
    b. Menu bar
    c. Taskbar
    d. Control bar

13. Which of the following statements about spam is true?
    a. There is no way to prevent it.
    b. It is solicited e-mail.
    c. Many ISPs protect against it.
    d. The government has not become involved in the issue.*

14. Examples of browsers include all of the following except:
    a. Netscape
    b. Opera
    c. Internet Explorer
    d. Windows*

15. An important consideration for choosing an ISP includes all of the following except?
    a. Cost
    b. Business needs
    c. Brand of computer*
    d. Technical support

# CHAPTER 7 SELF-ASSESSMENT

To determine the extent of knowledge you acquired in this chapter, choose the correct answer for each of the following.

1. One of the most popular browsers for interfacing with the World Wide Web is:
   a. Opera
   b. Safari
   c. Internet Explorer*
   d. Internet Windows

2. What type of program is necessary to interact with the World Wide Web?
   a. Windows
   b. Word processor
   c. Browser*
   d. Search engine

3. Why would a new version of a browser be introduced?
   a. To take advantage of advances in technology
   b. To correct past problems
   c. To increase the efficiency of the browser
   d. All of the above*

4. All of the following can be found on the menu bar except:
   a. View
   b. Edit
   c. File
   d. Search*

5. The File menu contains which of the following:
   a. Cut
   b. Paste
   c. Select All
   d. None of these*

6. The primary function of Favorites is to:
   a. Access frequently used web sites*
   b. List the top ten web sites on the Internet
   c. Use as a search engine
   d. Troubleshoot computer problems

7. You may see all of the following in the Address Bar except:
   a. Home page web address
   b. E-mail address*
   c. Favorites web address
   d. URL

8. The Explorer bar contains which of the following?
   a. Search
   b. History
   c. Media
   d. All of the above*

9. Frequently used web sites are found in:
   a. Search
   b. Help
   c. Favorites*
   d. View

10. Save As is found in what menu?
    a. File*
    b. Edit
    c. View
    d. Favorites

11. When a cyber professional wants to print a document, he or she goes to:
    a. Edit
    b. Status bar
    c. Address Bar
    d. File*

12. To change the start page, the cyber professional goes to:
    a. Start
    b. Title bar
    c. Tools*
    d. Status bar

13. Which of the following is a navigation tool?
    a. Back
    b. Forward
    c. Stop
    d. All of the above*

14. To save an often-used URL, the cyber professional goes to:
    a. Favorites*
    b. Search
    c. Help
    d. None of these

15. Why might the cyber professional use Internet Explorer?
    a. To search real estate web sites
    b. To access the Multiple Listing Service
    c. To obtain information about real estate topics
    d. All of the above*

# CHAPTER 8 SELF-ASSESSMENT

To determine the extent of knowledge you acquired in this chapter, choose the correct answer for each of the following.

1. Why is encryption software used?
   a. To prevent the intended recipient from reading a sensitive e-mail message
   b. To promote data security in Internet business transactions
   c. To prevent unauthorized parties from reading or changing data.
   d. Both b and c*

2. Which two protocols are necessary for e-mail to be processed?
   a. SMTP/POP3*
   b. TIA
   c. URL/WWW
   d. None of these

3. What is a common web-based e-mail program?
   a. Yahoo
   b. Hotmail
   c. Eudora
   d. Both a and b*

4. If the cyber professional wants to send a message to a group of clients without others knowing about it, he or she uses:
   a. To
   b. From
   c. Cc
   d. Bcc*

5. To compose a new message, the cyber professional clicks on which feature?
   a. Reply
   b. Forward
   c. New*
   d. In-box

6. To receive and read a message, the cyber professional uses which feature?
   a. In-box*
   b. Compose
   c. New
   d. Delete

7. When sending a message, the cyber professional should always include which of the following:
   a. Signature
   b. Subject*
   c. Autoresponder
   d. Attachment

8. What is a primary advantage of Hotmail and Yahoo e-mail accounts?
   a. They are free.
   b. They are easy to learn and to use.
   c. They can be used anywhere there is Internet access.
   d. All of the above*

9. What is a major disadvantage of a free e-mail account?
   a. It is vulnerable to spam.
   b. It has limits on how much data it can store.
   c. It has limits on how many activities can be conducted in a 24-hour period.
   d. All of the above*

10. For the cyber professional to set up an e-mail account, he or she must have:
    a. Encryption software
    b. An autoresponder
    c. A password*
    d. Emoticons

11. To get information on how to work with e-mail, the cyber professional goes to:
    a. Search
    b. Help*
    c. Find
    d. Compose

12. Junk mail is the same as:
    a. Acronyms
    b. Spam*
    c. Netiquette
    d. Emoticons

13. Which of the following is an e-mail address?
    a. http://www.realtor.com
    b. eagent at realtor.com
    c. eagent@realtor.com*
    d. None of these

14. What is an example of an acronym that might be used in the body of an e-mail message?
    a. POP3
    b. SMTP
    c. @
    d. LOL*

15. The main section of an e-mail message is found where?
    a. To
    b. Subject
    c. Body*
    d. Signature

# CHAPTER 9 SELF-ASSESSMENT

To determine the extent of knowledge you acquired in this chapter, choose the correct answer for each of the following.

1. The Outlook Today window includes all of the following except?
   a. Calendar
   b. Contacts
   c. Autoresponder*
   d. Tasks

2. To compose a new message, the cyber professional clicks:
   a. Reply
   b. Forward
   c. New*
   d. Send/Receive

3. What feature is accessed to set up a signature?
   a. File
   b. Edit
   c. View
   d. Tools*

4. To find out if there are any messages in the Inbox, the cyber professional clicks on:
   a. Favorites
   b. Receive*
   c. New
   d. Help

5. What does the cyber professional do to send a saved document to a recipient?
   a. Create a folder
   b. Send an attachment*
   c. Create a signature
   d. Access Outlook Express

6. Why might the cyber professional want to include an attachment to an e-mail message?
   a. To send digital photos to clients
   b. To send a database to a fellow colleague
   c. Both a and b*
   d. None of these

7. Besides allowing the cyber professional to send and receive messages, Outlook also provides:
   a. A calendar
   b. A contact list
   c. A tasks list
   d. All of the above*

8. What feature does the cyber professional use to send a message that he or she received to other recipients?
   a. Reply
   b. Reply to All
   c. Forward*
   d. Recycle Bin

9. The main function of Outlook Express is to allow the cyber professional to :
   a. Receive an e-mail message quickly
   b. Send an e-mail message quickly
   c. Both a and b*
   d. None of the above

10. Which of the following statements is true about Outlook's Notes feature?
    a. Notes cannot be printed out.
    b. Notes cannot be saved.
    c. Notes serve as electronic sticky notes.*
    d. None of these

11. Which of the following does not appear on Outlook's menu bar?
    a. View
    b. Tools
    c. Help
    d. Send*

12. What does the cyber professional click to reply to an e-mail message?
    a. Reply to All
    b. Reply
    c. Both a and c*
    d. None of these

13. An e-mail header includes all of the following except:
    a. To
    b. Message body*
    c. Cc
    d. Bcc

14. What does the cyber professional use to organize related e-mail messages?
    a. Address Book
    b. Folder*
    c. Attachment
    d. Autoresponder

15. What does the cyber professional use to set up a system to send mass e-mail communications?
    a. Distribution List*
    b. Address Book
    c. Return Receipt
    d. Autoresponder

# CHAPTER 10 SELF-ASSESSMENT

To determine the extent of knowledge you acquired in this chapter, choose the correct answer for each of the following.

1. What is the purpose of the Outlook Today window?
   a. To show an overview of all Outlook Activities*
   b. To show a list of contacts in the Outlook program
   c. To show appointments only for the day
   d. To show tasks only for the day

2. What is the main difference between Outlook and Outlook Express?
   a. Outlook Express is more complicated and harder to use.
   b. Outlook Express has more bells and whistles.
   c. Outlook Express is a condensed version of Outlook.*
   d. There is no difference between Outlook and Outlook Express.

3. When the cyber professional wants to e-mail information to a select group, what does he or she use?
   a. Address Book
   b. Distribution list*
   c. Contacts
   d. Appointments

4. When using the Calendar feature, what can the cyber professional see?
   a. Daily activities
   b. Weekly activities
   c. Monthly activities
   d. All of the above*

5. What can the cyber professional use to organize his or her e-mail messages?
   a. Address Book
   b. Distribution list
   c. Folder*
   d. Favorites List

6. What feature of Outlook does the cyber professional use to insert information about clients?
   a. Contacts*
   b. Notes
   c. Journal
   d. None of these

7. What does the cyber professional click to add a prospect to the Address Book?
   a. New appointment
   b. New contact*
   c. New event
   d. New reminder

8. The best way to locate a contact in Outlook is to access the:
   a. Help feature
   b. Delete feature
   c. Find feature*
   d. Sent feature

9. Where are new e-mail messages found?
   a. Outbox
   b. Inbox*
   c. Recycle Bin
   d. Draft file

10. What can the cyber professional do to have Microsoft Outlook on his or her computer?
    a. Download the program from the Internet
    b. Purchase and install it
    c. Buy a computer with it already preinstalled
    d. All of the above*

11. Which of the following is a feature of Outlook?
    a. Calendar
    b. Tasks/Notes
    c. Journal
    d. All of the above*

12. What feature does the cyber professional use to keep an ongoing account of conversations and activities?
    a. Calendar
    b. Journal*
    c. Reminders
    d. Tasks

13. What feature can the cyber professional use to set up an event that needs to be accomplished at a certain time?
    a. Notes
    b. Calendar
    c. Tasks
    d. All of the above*

14. What feature does the cyber professional use to set up an electronic paper trail for a seller or buyer?
    a. Journal
    b. Notes
    c. None of these
    d. Both a and b*

15. In addition to Outlook, what is another contact and time management system?
    a. GoldMine
    b. ACT!
    c. Both a and b*
    d. None of these

# CHAPTER 11 SELF-ASSESSMENT

To determine the extent of knowledge you acquired in this chapter, choose the correct answer for each of the following.

1. The cyber professional can produce real estate flyers using which program?
   a. Microsoft Windows
   b. Microsoft Word
   c. Microsoft Publisher
   d. Both b and c*

2. What special tool in Microsoft Word can the cyber professional use to create real estate flyers?
   a. AutoShapes
   b. WordArt
   c. Hyperlinks
   d. All of the above*

3. Which of the following statements about WordArt is true?
   a. It is used to create text with special shapes and designs.*
   b. It is used to insert predrawn shapes into a document.
   c. It is a feature of Publisher.
   d. None of these

4. Examples of AutoShapes include all of the following except:
   a. Rectangle
   b. Oval
   c. Lines
   d. Hyperlinks*

5. Which of the following statements about a table is not true?
   a. The cyber professional can decide on the number of rows and columns.
   b. A table can be used to organize information in a document.
   c. Tables can be created using the Wizard in Publisher.*
   d. Both a and c

6. What is an advantage of adding a hyperlink to a document?
   a. It allows the recipient to go directly to a web site.
   b. It allows the cyber professional to insert photos in documents.
   c. It offers convenience for the recipient.
   d. Both a and c*

7. To insert a hyperlink, what does the cyber professional access?:
   a. File
   b. Insert*
   c. View
   d. Edit

8. Which program is best for creating real estate flyers?
   a. Microsoft Word
   b. Internet Explorer
   c. Microsoft Publisher*
   d. Microsoft Windows

9. Which of the following statements about clip art is not true?
   a. It is available on the Internet.
   b. It is text on a page that a person clicks to go to another page.*
   c. It is a collection of images that can be inserted into documents.
   d. It is available in Word.

10. All of the following are options for a brochure except:
    a. Informational
    b. Event
    c. Fundraiser
    d. Announcement*

11. The main function of the wizard in Publisher is to:
    a. Serve as a guide
    b. Make the task of creating a publication easier
    c. Save time
    d. All of the above*

12. All of the following colors are offered in Publisher's Color Schemes except:
    a. Burgundy
    b. Mist
    c. Black Forest*
    d. Bluebird

13. Which of the following statements about Microsoft Publisher is not true?
    a. It comes preinstalled on all computers.*
    b. It can be purchased as part of Microsoft Office Small Business Edition 2003.
    c. It can be purchased as part of Microsoft Office Professional Edition 2003.
    d. It can be purchased as a stand-alone software program.

14. Using Microsoft Publisher, the cyber professional can create all of the following except:
    a. Catalogs
    b. Business cards
    c. Postcards
    d. Spreadsheets*

15. By learning how to use Microsoft Word and Publisher, the cyber professional:
    a. Can promote his or her real estate business
    b. Doesn't have to pay a graphic designer to create real estate documents
    c. Create his or her own real estate documents
    d. All of the above*

# CHAPTER 12 SELF-ASSESSMENT

To determine the extent of knowledge you acquired in this chapter, choose the correct answer for each of the following.

1. PowerPoint can be used to:
   a. Create presentations for real estate seminars
   b. Create presentations that can be duplicated onto CDs
   c. Create web presentations
   d. All of the above*

2. To start PowerPoint, the cyber professional:
   a. Clicks Start, then Programs*
   b. Clicks File, then Open
   c. Clicks File, then New
   d. None of these

3. PowerPoint may be purchased:
   a. As a stand-alone product
   b. As part of all Microsoft Office Editions 2003
   c. Both a and b*
   d. None of these

4. With which program does PowerPoint have things in common?
   a. Word
   b. Windows
   c. Publisher
   d. All of the above*

5. To create a new slide show, the cyber professional clicks:
   a. Edit
   b. File*
   c. View
   d. Insert

6. All of the following features can be incorporated into a Power-Point presentation except?
   a. WordArt
   b. AutoShapes
   c. Office Assistant*
   d. Hyperlinks

7. Choices for different types of Slide Layouts include:
   a. Text Layouts
   b. Content Layouts
   c. Text and Content Layouts
   d. All of the above*

8. What is involved with changing a slide design?
   a. Each slide must be changed individually.
   b. The slides cannot be changed once the program is begun.
   c. All slides change automatically.*
   d. None of these

9. To start a slide show, the cyber professional:
   a. Clicks File, then New
   b. Clicks Insert, then Picture
   c. Clicks Slide Show on the menu bar*
   d. Clicks Start, then Programs

10. Which of the following features can be inserted into a slide?
    a. Table
    b. Picture
    c. Organization Chart
    d. All of the above*

11. What is the purpose of including animation in a PowerPoint presentation?
    a. To add excitement to the program*
    b. To distract the audience
    c. So the presenter can impress the audience with his her PowerPoint skills
    d. Animation serves no useful purpose.

12. Which of the following views is not available in PowerPoint?
    a. Slider Sorter view
    b. Normal view
    c. Continuous view*
    d. Slide Show view

13. Why is a hyperlink included in a PowerPoint presentation?
    a. To allow viewers to access a web site*
    b. To add color
    c. To distract the audience
    d. To impress the audience

14. What should the cyber professional do after he or she has created a presentation?
    a. Delete it
    b. Save it*
    c. Store it in the Recycle Bin
    d. Send it to a client

15. What is an advanced feature and function of PowerPoint?
    a. Record Narration
    b. Package for CD
    c. Meeting Minder
    d. All of the above*

# CHAPTER 13 SELF-ASSESSMENT

To determine the extent of knowledge you acquired in this chapter, choose the correct answer for each of the following.

1. To have a presence on the Internet, the cyber professional must have:
   a. An ISP
   b. A web host
   c. A webmaster
   d. Both a and b*

2. A web site gives the cyber professional:
   a. 24/7/365 accessibility
   b. The ability to compete with larger organizations
   c. A web presence
   d. All of the above*

3. What is the main difference between a web site and a web page?
   a. There is no difference.
   b. A web site is part of a web page.
   c. A web page is part of a web site.*
   d. A web site costs more than a web page.

4. What is the first page that usually appears on a web site?
   a. Home page*
   b. Web page
   c. Secondary page
   d. Portal

5. A top-level domain name includes all of the following except?
   a. edu
   b. mil
   c. gov
   d. con*

6. What is a commercial web development software?
   a. Dreamweaver
   b. FrontPage
   c. GoLive
   d. All of the above*

7. What is a major advantage of commercial web development software?
   a. No need for programming knowledge
   b. Ease of construction
   c. Use of predesigned templates
   d. All of the above*

8. When choosing a host company, the cyber professional should consider:
   a. Service fees
   b. Technical support
   c. Reputation
   d. All of the above*

9. A web site can be established by:
   a. Developing your own
   b. Hiring a web site developer
   c. Using web development software
   d. All of the above*

10. Which of the following is a design layout for a web page?
    a. Hierarchical*
    b. Diagonal
    c. Bottom-up
    d. Top-to-bottom

11. Who is responsible for maintaining a web site?
    a. Graphic artist
    b. Programmer
    c. Webmaster*
    d. Systems analyst

12. What is the most important consideration for designing a web site?
    a. Cost
    b. Target audience*
    c. Ease of access
    d. Speed of access

13. Which of the following should not be a consideration for a web site?
    a. Ease of access
    b. Speed of access
    c. Ease of navigation
    d. All of these should be considered*

14. What is an important part of domain name selection?
    a. Cost
    b. Type of extension
    c. Use of capital letters
    d. Simple and descriptive name*

15. What is a major design flaw for a web site?
    a. Too complicated
    b. Too much content
    c. No white space
    d. All of the above*

# CHAPTER 14 SELF-ASSESSMENT

To determine the extent of knowledge you acquired in this chapter, choose the correct answer for each of the following.

1. A major disadvantage of a free web site is that it is:
   a. Easy to construct
   b. Less expensive
   c. Has a long and complicated URL*
   d. Has limited exposure

2. A major advantage of a commercial web site is that it:
   a. Costs less
   b. Allows the cyber professional to use his or her own domain name*
   c. Has a long URL
   d. Is difficult to construct

3. All of the following are free web site development systems except?
   a. GeoCities
   b. Angelfire
   c. Advanced Access*
   d. Tripod

4. Which of the following is a commercial web site?
   a. Advanced Access
   b. Homes.com
   c. REALTOR.com
   d. All of the above*

5. What is the first tag usually used in an HTML file?
   a. <Body>
   b. <Head>
   c. <Title>
   d. <HTML>*

6. Which of the following is not a tag used in an HTML file?
   a. <TITLE>
   b. <PARAGRAPH>*
   c. <BODY>
   d. <HR>

7. Which symbol indicates the end of an HTML tag?
   a. (<)
   b. (>)
   c. (</)*
   d. (/>)

8. Which program can be used to construct a web site without the use of HTML?
   a. Composer*
   b. Messenger
   c. Windows
   d. Internet Explorer

9. Which of the following programs offers a free web site with hosting?
   a. Angelfire
   b. Tripod
   c. GeoCities
   d. All of the above*

10. Which of the following is an example of an add-on to a web page for GeoCities?
    a. Guestbook
    b. Links
    c. News and Weather
    d. All of the above*

11. What is the main objective of a hitometer?
    a. To track how many users viewed the site
    b. To track who visited the site
    c. To track when users visited the site
    d. All of the above*

12. What does the cyber professional use to connect to another web site from the home page?
    a. Hyperlink*
    b. Template
    c. Hitometer
    d. Guestbook

13. The toolbar in GeoCities includes all of the following features except?
    a. Textbox
    b. Background
    c. Template*
    d. Hyperlinks

14. To promote a user domain name, the cyber professional submits the name to a:
    a. Search Engine*
    b. Webmaster
    c. Programmer
    d. Guestbook

15. Once constructed, a web site must be
    a. Promoted
    b. Monitored
    c. Evaluated
    d. All of the above*

## CHAPTER 15 SELF-ASSESSMENT

To determine the extent of knowledge you acquired in this chapter, choose the correct answer for each of the following.

1. What is the device most often used by real estate professionals today?
   a. Scanner
   b. Webcam
   c. PDA*
   d. Camcorder

2. A PDA is best described as a/an?
   a. Miniature computer
   b. Organizer
   c. Personal Digital Assistant
   d. All of the above*

3. What is the major advantage of a handheld over a laptop?
   a. Size
   b. Capability
   c. Weight
   d. Both a and c*

4. Handhelds have more capacity and capability than a:
   a. Desktop
   b. Laptop
   c. Notebook
   d. None of these*

5. The Pocket PC is based on what platform?
   a. Windows CE*
   b. OSX
   c. Linux
   d. Opera

6. What is a major benefit of the handheld?
   a. Has many of the same features and functions as a PC*
   b. Is faster that a desktop
   c. Is faster than a laptop
   d. None of these

7. What is the main advantages of the Palm OS over the Pocket PC?
   a. More available software*
   b. More memory
   c. A faster processor
   d. More storage

8. Who is a manufacturer of Tablet PCs?
   a. Acer
   b. Toshiba
   c. Fujitsu
   d. All of the above*

9. What is the major advantage of a digital camera over a 35 mm camera?
   a. Costs less
   b. Is lighter
   c. Takes better pictures
   d. None of these*

10. What can digital photos be used for?
    a. To create real estate flyers
    b. To create brochures
    c. To post on a web site
    d. All of the above*

11. What does an all-in-one device refer to?
    a. A scanner and a printer
    b. A copier and a scanner
    c. A printer and a fax machine
    d. A scanner, a copier, a fax machine, and a printer*

12. What is an advantage of a home network?
    a. Requires more equipment
    b. Requires less equipment
    c. Can be done wirelessly
    d. Both b and c*

13. Specialty phones often include features that are similar to
    a. A handheld*
    b. A laptop
    c. A desktop
    d. None of these

14. What is the idea behind the Virtual Assistant?
    a.  It is "technology for hire."
    b.  It was developed by Michael Russer.
    c.  Real estate professionals prefer doing their own technical work.
    d.  Both a and b*

15. What is a result of technology and information overload?
    a.  Depression
    b.  Anxiety
    c.  Sleep disturbance
    d.  All of the above*

# GLOSSARY OF KEY TERMS

## -A-

**ACT!:** a commercial contact and time management system

**Address Bar:** located under the navigation bar in Internet Explorer; used to enter the address of a web site

**Address Book:** an area in Microsoft Outlook for storing e-mail addresses

**animation:** moving graphics; in Microsoft PowerPoint, the user can use animation to create a livelier presentation.

**attachment:** a file that is sent along with an e-mail message

**autoresponder:** a program used to notify e-mail senders when the receiver is not available to respond.

**AutoShapes:** a Word feature used to insert predrawn shapes into a document

# -B-

**Back:** a button on the navigation bar of Internet Explorer that allows the user to go back to the previous web page

**blind carbon copy (bcc):** used to send a copy of a message to someone without the receiver knowing the other recipients

**body:** the main section of an e-mail message

**bold:** a character format that can be applied to text

**bundled:** refers to a computer purchase that includes multiple components from the same vendor

**byte:** a unit of measure of computer memory

# -C-

**cache:** computer memory with very short access time used for storing frequently or recently used data or instructions

**Calendar:** a feature of Microsoft Outlook for keeping track of meetings, appointments, and other obligations

**camcorder:** a combination camera/VCR that allows the user to film live images

**carbon copy:** Cc; gives the sender the option of sending the same e-mail message to other recipients

**carpal tunnel syndrome:** a condition caused by compression of a nerve where it passes through the wrist into the hand

**CD-ROM:** compact disc read-only memory; a storage medium that can hold up to 650 MB of data, which is equal to 20 floppy disks

**clip art:** a collection of images that can be inserted into documents

**clock speed:** the speed at which a processor executes instructions

**close:** a button to the right of the title bar used to close a window, thereby closing the program and removing the corresponding item from the taskbar

**Composer:** an HTML web document-authoring tool

**contact management:** a system used to save and organize personal and business contacts for future reference.

**Control Panel:** a Windows configuration utility that allows the user to personalize the computer

**Copy:** an option on the Edit menu used to copy text or items from a document and store them for later insertion using Paste

**crawlers:** software programs that visit web sites to create indexes for search engines

**CRT:** cathode-ray tube; the major component of a computer monitor, one that closely resembles a television screen

**Cut:** an option on the Edit menu used to remove text or an image from a document and store it for later insertion using Paste

**cyber professional (C-P):** one who is striving to find out more about technology and how to apply it to the real estate profession

# -D-

**desktop:** refers to a nonportable computer

**digital cameras:** cameras that record images as digital objects that are then downloaded to a computer system

**directory:** a list of categories or subjects that link to more information on a given topic

**distribution list:** a group of e-mail addresses that can be used to send a message to all members of the group

**domain name:** the unique name that identifies an Internet site

**DVD-ROM:** digital versatile disc read-only memory; capable of holding about 5GB of data

# -E-

**e-agent:** a real estate agent who uses computer technology

**e-buyer:** one who is very sophisticated in applying technology to the housing-hunting process

**e-commerce:** the marketing and selling of products, tangible and intangible, over the Internet

**e-consumer:** a group that is well versed in technology and that uses the Internet to the fullest extent in meeting real estate goals

**electronic data interchange (EDI):** an electronic system for transferring data over the Internet.

**emoticons:** a combination of keyboard characters sometimes used in e-mail messages to convey a particular emotion, much like tone of voice is used in spoken communications

**encryption:** the transformation of data that prevents any unauthorized party from reading or changing data

**e-PRO:** a well-recognized designation sanctioned by the National Association of REALTORS® (NAR) and operated by the Internet Crusade (an Internet company that promotes technology for real estate professionals)

**e-real estate:** encompasses the ways in which computer technology can be applied to the real estate profession

**ergonomics:** the science of designing workplace equipment so people can use them safely and efficiently

**e-seller:** one who is as equally knowledgeable as an e-buyer about how to maximize the value of the Internet

**Explorer bar:** located below the address bar in Internet Explorer

# -F-

**F key:** a function key labeled F1 through F12 on the keyboard; used to execute commands

**farming:** a systematic method used to solicit business

**Favorites:** a feature of Internet Explorer that allows the user to return to a web site without having to remember or retype the address

**File:** a menu on the Windows menu bar

**floppy disk:** a portable magnetic disk used to store data and programs

**Forward:** a button on the navigation bar of Internet Explorer that allows the user to return to the page he or she just came from

# -G-

**GoldMine:** a commercial contact and time management system

**graphical user interface (GUI):** a program that allows users to interact with a computer system by clicking and dragging objects with a mouse instead of entering text at a command line

**guestbook:** an electronic means for keeping track of visitors who access a web site.

# -H-

**handheld:** a small portable computer that offers many of the same features and functions of a desktop computer but is limited in terms of capacity

**handout:** print-out of a PowerPoint presentation.

**Help:** a feature of Internet Explorer (and other Microsoft software programs) that allows the user to get answers to specific questions

**Help and Support:** a Windows feature that combines Search, Index, and Favorites with current online content

**hertz:** a unit of frequency, or how many times an action repeats per second; abbreviated Hz

**hierarchical:** a web site style that starts with the most important page and then diverts to supplemental pages

**hitometer:** device that counts the number of visitors to a web site.

**hits:** instances of people connecting to a web site

**home page:** the web page a browser is set to display when it starts up

**hosting:** the process of a company providing a place on their servers for housing, servicing, and maintaining a web site

**Hotmail:** a free web-based e-mail program provided by Microsoft

**hyperlinks:** elements of an electronic document that link to another place in the same document or to an entirely different document

**Hypertext Markup Language (HTML):** the language used to create documents on the World Wide Web

# -I-

**icons:** small graphics used to represent objects on a computer; can be manipulated by the user

**ink jet:** a printer that sprays ink onto paper to form characters

**Internet:** a global network of millions of computers

**Internet Empowered Consumer (IEC):** a new type of consumer who likes to be in control of the home-buying process

**Internet Explorer:** Microsoft's web browser

**Internet service providers (ISPs):** companies that provide access to the Internet, thereby allowing the user to take advantage of the World Wide Web

**italic:** a character format that can be applied to text

# -J-

**Journal:** a feature of Outlook that can be used as an electronic paper trail for ongoing conversations and actions that have taken place with a contact

# -L-

**laptop:** a computer small enough to sit on the user's lap

**laser jet:** a printer that uses a laser to form images that are transferred to paper electrostatically

**LCD:** liquid crystal display; a display technology common in portable computers

**lead capture:** method used to acquire email addresses of potential clients

**lead generation:** method used to acquire a list of potential clients

**Linux:** an alternative operating system

# -M-

**Maximize:** a button to the right of the title bar in Windows used to expand a window to fill the entire screen

**memory:** the capacity for storing information

**menu bar:** appears below the title bar in Windows; has several categories of actions, called menus

**meta tags:** text in the coding of the HTML structure of a web page; used by search engines and directories as one method of indexing or finding web sites

**Minimize:** a button near the right end of the title bar in Windows used to remove a window from the desktop; the program is still running and is represented by a button on the taskbar

**modem:** a device that allows a computer to connect with the Internet over telephone lines

**My Computer:** displays a computer's drives and folders in Windows

**My Documents:** a folder in Windows that contains all saved documents

# -N-

**navigation bar:** located below the menu bar in Internet Explorer

**netiquette:** an informal set of guidelines that dictates the proper way to communicate on the Internet

**New Real Estate Professional (NREP):** a new type of real estate professional that has evolved to address the needs of a computer-savvy real estate consumer

**Notes:** a feature of Outlook for writing down thoughts, ideas, or follow-up tasks

# -O-

**Open:** an option on the File menu used to call up and reuse an existing file

**operating system (os):** preinstalled software that allows a computer to function

**outline:** outline that appears in the left-hand pane of a PowerPoint Slide Show

**Outlook Express:** Shortcut to accessing email without having to go through Microsoft Outlook

**Outlook Today:** represents an overview of Outlook's entire e-mail system

# -P-

**Paste:** an option on the Edit menu used to transfer a copy of text or an image to a document; used in combination with Cut and Copy

**PC:** personal computer; often used to refer to a particular type of desktop computer

**personal digital assistant (PDA):** any small handheld wireless device that provides computing and data storage capabilities

**Pocket PC:** a PDA that runs the Windows operating system

**portal:** a web site that is intended to be the first place people see when using the web

**protection plan:** an option available when purchasing electronics where the retailer or manufacturer guarantees to replace/repair a defective product; should be considered as a factor when purchasing computer-related equipment

# -Q-

**QWERTY:** the standard computer keyboard layout; refers to the first six letters on the upper alphabet row

# -R-

**RAM:** random-access memory; temporary memory that is the main working memory of a computer

**Real Estate Cyber Specialist (RECS):** a special designation offered through the Real Estate Cyber Society

**Recycle Bin:**  a temporary storage place in Windows for deleted files

**Refresh:** a button on the navigation bar of Internet Explorer that allows the user to update the currently displayed web page

**Restore:** a button to the right of the title bar in Windows used to restore a window to its original size; available only when the window is maximized or minimized

**ROM:** read-only memory; memory that cannot be changed; stores startup instructions used by the computer

# -S-

**Save:** a button on the standard toolbar in Windows used to preserve a document so it can be used again

**Save As:** a button on the standard toolbar in Windows used to save a document using a particular name

**scanner:** a device that reads and translates regular photos and documents into a form the computer can use

**scroll bar:** a bar the user moves to change his or her position within a window

**Search:** a button on the Explorer bar of Internet Explorer that opens a search engine

**search engine:** a computer program used to locate and retrieve information from the World Wide Web

**secondary pages:** all of the pages beyond the splash page or home page of a web site

**Select All:** an option on the Edit menu used to select the entire text of an open document

**signature:** information automatically included at the end of an e-mail message that identifies the sender

**Slide Design:** a feature of PowerPoint that allows the user to choose a design template already created by the software

**Slide Layout:** different options in PowerPoint for displaying information on the slides: Text Layout, Content Layout, Text and Content Layout, and Other Layouts

**Slide Show:** sequence of slides in a PowerPoint file

**spam:** unsolicited "junk" e-mail sent to large numbers of people to promote products or services

**spiders:** software programs that regularly search the Internet, indexing text from web pages

**splash page:** an opening page that a user must click on to enter a web site

**stand-alone:** refers to a computer purchase where the CPU, but no peripherals, is purchased

**Start button:** located at the left end of the taskbar in Windows; used to open the Start menu

**sticky:** a term used to imply that a user will *stick* with a web site to get the information he or she wants easily and quickly

**Stop:** a button on the navigation bar of Internet Explorer that stops the browser from loading the current page

**Subject:** states what an e-mail message is about

**synchronization:** a process that copies files between two folders on a host and a remote computer to make the folders identical to one another

# -T-

**tables:** used to organize information in a Word document

**Tablet PC:** a computer much like a laptop, but with many features that make it unique

**tags:** special codes used in HTML coding

**taskbar:** the bar that contains the Start button and that appears by default at the bottom of the Windows desktop

**Tasks:** a feature in Outlook for recording personal and work-related errands and tracking them through completion

**tech support:** a service offered by computer and software manufacturers in which they provide a phone number that users can call for advice and trouble-shooting

**time management:** a system for keeping track of appointments and tasks to be accomplished.

**title bar:** the bar located at the top of the Windows screen that displays the name of the application and the name of the active document

**toolbars:** display buttons in Windows that provide access to common commands

**traffic report:** an electronic report that details all the visitors to a given web site and when they visited.

**Transition Effects:** vary the way one slide replaces another in PowerPoint presentations

# -U-

**underline:** a character format that can be applied to text

**Uniform Resource Locator (URL):** the technical name for a web site address

# -V-

**viral:** a term used to describe a web site whose aim is to get a user hooked on the site so he or she returns time after time

**Virtual Assistant (VA):** a concept developed by Michael Russer that implies that many real estate professionals would rather hire someone else to do the technical work than take the time to learn or do the work themselves

**virus protection:** software that periodically checks a computer system for the best-known types of viruses

**voice e-mail:** software that allows a user to send and listen to e-mail messages, although both parties must have the software

**vortal:** a specialized portal that serves a particular organization or interest group

# -W-

**warranty:** a company guarantee against product failure; should be considered as a factor when purchasing computer-related equipment

**webcam:** a device that allows a user to view objects and individuals live on the Internet

**webmaster:** a person responsible for the overall operation of a web site

**web pages:** documents that can be accessed on the World Wide Web

**web site:** a collection of web pages that collectively represents a company or an individual on the World Wide Web

**WordArt:** a Word feature used to create text with special shapes and designs

**World Wide Web:** a collection of electronic documents, or pages, that can be viewed on a computer using a web browser

**WYSIWYG:** acronym for "what you see is what you get"

# -Y-

**Yahoo:** a free web-based e-mail program provided by yahoo.com

# INDEX

cut  78, 423

cyber professional (C-P)  18-19, 423

## D

Desktop  45, 423

dial-up  97

digital cameras  316-319, 423

digital subscriber lines (DSL)  98

directory  100-101, 423

discussion group  322

display  34-35

distribution list  183, 424

DNS (Domain Name System)  258

domain name  257, 260-264, 424

dot pitch  35

double data rate random-access memory (DDR-RAM)  31

Dragon NaturallySpeakingTM  61

Dreamweaver  271

DVD-ROM  32, 424

## E

e-agent  4, 10, 14, 424

e-buyer  8-9, 424

e-commerce  2, 424

e-consumer  5, 424

Electronic Data Interchange (EDI)  5, 424

e-loans  18

emoticons  145, 424

encryption  145, 424

e-PRO  11, 424

e-real estate  10, 424

Ergonomics  33, 425

e-seller  9-10, 425

Explorer bar  115, 425

## F

favorites  114, 425

F key  79, 425

file  80, 425

floppy disk  31, 425

forward  114, 425

FrontPage  271

## G

GeoCities  287, 291-293

gigahertz (GHz)  28-29

Global Positioning System (GPS)  320-321

GoldMine  179-180, 425

GoLive  272

graphical user interface (GUI)  58-59, 425

guestbook  288, 425

## H

handheld  306-308, 426

help  114, 426

help and support  65, 426

hertz (Hz)  28-29, 426

hibernate  67

hierarchical  266, 426

High Tech, High Touch  12-13

hitometer  299, 426

home page  114, 258, 426

Homes.com  286

Homestead  287